# Remaking Chicago

The Political Origins of
Urban Industrial Change

# Remaking Chicago

# Joel Rast

Northern

Illinois

University

Press

DeKalb

1999

© 1999 by Northern Illinois University Press

Published by the Northern Illinois University Press,

DeKalb, Illinois  60115

Manufactured in the United States using acid-free paper

Deisgn by Julia Fauci

Library of Congress Cataloging-in-Publication Data

Rast, Joel, 1956–

Remaking Chicago : the political origins of urban

industrial change / Joel Rast.

     p.     cm.

Includes bibliographical references and index.

ISBN 0-87580-248-6 (cloth) — ISBN 0-87580-593-0 (paper)

1. Chicago (Ill.)—Economic conditions. 2. Chicago (Ill.)

—Politics and government—1951. 3. Manufacturing

industries—Illinois—Chicago—History—20th

century. 4. Urban economics—Case studies.  I. Title.

HC108.C4  R37  1999

338.9773'11—dc21

98-33177

CIP

*To my parents*

Susanna and Walter Rast

# Contents

# List of Tables and Maps

# Preface

This book began its life as my doctoral thesis in political science at the University of Oregon. During the summer of 1994, having just completed comprehensive examinations, I was in the position of many new ABDs: euphoria at finally having all exams and course work behind me was quickly giving way to anxiety over the need to identify a suitable dissertation topic. While poring through the urban politics literature that summer, I stumbled across an article on land-use conflicts in Chicago between centrally located manufacturers and real estate developers seeking to rehabilitate near-downtown industrial loft buildings for new commercial and residential uses during the administration of progressive mayor Harold Washington (1983–1987). At the time the article was written, the administration was considering a number of policy options to protect manufacturers from redevelopment pressures, thereby preserving well-paying blue-collar jobs for Chicago residents. These policies were being challenged by a powerful coalition of business interests eager to see land use in the outlying portions of Chicago's downtown area give way to activities that more directly complemented the retail and corporate functions that dominate the city's downtown business core.

I had lived in Chicago for several years of Washington's tenure as mayor, working as a legal assistant in a large downtown law firm (an experience that soon had me furiously typing applications for graduate school). However, most of my information on Chicago politics during those years came from local media sources, which tended to cover redevelopment issues concerning the central area of the city largely from the perspective of real estate developers and their allies within the downtown business community. Like most Chicagoans at the time, I believed that the decline of city manufacturing was due largely to changes in locational preferences and decreasing competitiveness on the part of industries themselves. The possibility that, in truth, viable industrial firms were being uprooted from the downtown area was intriguing enough that I decided to investigate the issue further. Within several months, I was convinced I had discovered a worthy subject for my dissertation.

In my efforts to come to grips theoretically with what I was observing in Chicago, I was drawn to recent scholarship in the field of urban political economy, particularly the work of Clarence Stone and Stephen Elkin on urban regimes. By emphasizing the role of urban governing coalitions rather than broad structural factors in the formulation of public policy, regime theorists have sought to introduce a wider appreciation for political choice and agency within the urban political economy paradigm. The focus on coalition building could seemingly help account for the neighborhood-oriented policies of progressive mayors such as Harold Washington in Chicago, Raymond Flynn in Boston, and Art Agnos in San Francisco during the 1970s and 1980s, despite powerful structural pressures favoring greater responsiveness to the interests of property developers and other downtown business elites.

Yet the more I learned about downtown redevelopment in postwar Chicago, the less convinced I became that existing urban political economy provided a satisfactory explanatory framework. The problem was this: Despite the emphasis on political variables in much contemporary urban theory, scholars today continue to privilege the role of economic structure in city politics. The market, it is generally understood, operates according to its own logic (a logic of efficiency), which city officials are largely powerless to influence. The role of city government is to redistribute and regulate wealth. If economic forces have determined that cities be refashioned into producers of advanced corporate services instead of manufactured goods, there is little that even progressive administrations can do besides taking steps to ensure that low- and moderate-income neighborhoods receive a share of the benefits of economic growth.

At a time when basic redevelopment patterns in cities are attributed largely to the activities of private investors in the market, this book seeks explanations for urban economic change in an unlikely place: local politics. The argument of this study is that two equally efficient possibilities for the redevelopment of Chicago's central area presented themselves following World War II. Although a corporate-center strategy favoring commercial and residential growth proved to be temporarily victorious, it has been successfully contested more recently by proponents of a viable alternative development strategy built around locally rooted forms of industrial development. Local politics have played a decisive role, not simply in redistributing the rewards of economic growth or regulating the activities of private investors but also in establishing the very trajectory of redevelopment itself.

·   ·   ·

In writing this book and the dissertation upon which it is based, I received valuable support from a variety of sources. First and foremost, I owe a tremendous debt to my dissertation committee members: Gerald Berk, Dick Kraus, Dan Goldrich, and Quintard Taylor. My advisor Gerald Berk's own work in American political development and his collaborations with Todd Swanstrom in urban political economy provided the key inspiration for the questions posed in this study. Although we were not always in complete agreement, his thoughtful criticisms of my dissertation chapters forced me to sharpen and, at times, rethink my arguments. In addition, Todd Swanstrom and Paul Kleppner both read the entire manuscript and provided constructive feedback and detailed suggestions for revision. If significant errors remain, it is only because I was too stubborn to heed the good advice I received.

The University of Oregon provided generous financial support for this effort through a university Doctoral Research Fellowship, allowing me to devote the entire 1995–1996 academic year to full-time research and writing. My employer, the Center for Neighborhood Technology, graciously agreed to a leave of absence during the summer of 1998, providing me with the time I needed to complete revisions to the manuscript necessary for its transformation into a book. My brothers, Tim and Pete, came to the rescue with last-minute technical support, straightening out a computer glitch that threatened to send one of my chapters into oblivion. All maps were prepared by Tom Willcockson of Mapcraft in Woodstock, Illinois.

Various individuals with firsthand knowledge of events or issues discussed in the book gave graciously of their time, sitting for interviews or otherwise sharing key information. I am especially grateful to Margie Gonwa and Michael Holzer from the Local Employment and Economic Development (LEED) Council; Donna Ducharme and Greg Longhini from the City of Chicago; Wim Wiewel, David Ranney, and Lauri Alpern from the University of Illinois at Chicago; Jody Kretzmann from Northwestern University; Paul Ginger from the Chicago Association of Neighborhood Development Organizations (CANDO); James Lemonides from Greater North Pulaski Development Corporation; Ken Govas from the Industrial Council of Northwest Chicago; Michael Buccitelli from Jane Addams Resource Corporation; Vickie Shea from Greater Southwest Development Corporation; Maureen Hellwig from Erie Neighborhood House; Dorothy Fuller from the Chicago Apparel Center; Carl Liametz from Chicago Manufacturing Center; Joseph Costigan from UNITE; James Niesen from the Printing Industry of Illinois and Indiana Association; and James Maar.

A number of friends and family members provided lodging and valuable companionship during lengthy stays in Chicago. My uncle and aunt, Lawrence and Elaine Rast, went above and beyond the call of duty, making their condominium on Aldine Street available to me for several extended research trips. I also spent a number of months at the home of my parents, Susanna and Walter Rast. Their enthusiasm for this project and good company helped the time spent away from my partner in California pass far more quickly than it otherwise would have. Scholarship sometimes yields unanticipated benefits, and the opportunity to return home once again for more than a short visit was certainly one of them.

Last, but by no means least, I thank my partner, Cliona. Her intellectual and emotional support, sense of humor, and unwavering confidence in my abilities kept me going during sometimes trying weeks and months. For that and much more, I am fortunate beyond words.

# List of Abbreviations

| | |
|---|---|
| CAD | computer-aided design |
| CANDO | Chicago Association of Neighborhood Development Organizations |
| CAP | Citizens Action Program |
| CCAC | Chicago Central Area Committee |
| CDBG | Community Development Block Grant |
| CDC | Community development corporation |
| CHA | Chicago Housing Authority |
| CMC | Chicago Milwaukee Corporation |
| CTA | Chicago Transit Authority |
| CUED | Center for Urban Economic Development |
| CWED | Community Workshop on Economic Development |
| DED | Department of Economic Development |
| GNPDC | Greater North Pulaski Development Corporation |
| HUD | U.S. Department of Housing and Urban Development |
| ICNC | Industrial Council of Northwest Chicago |
| IRB | Industrial Revenue Bond |
| JARC | Jane Addams Resource Corporation |
| LEED | Local Employment and Economic Development |
| LIRI | Local Industrial Retention Initiative |
| MCMEA | Mayor's Council of Manpower and Economic Advisors |
| NCBG | Neighborhood Capital Budget Group |
| NORBIC | North Business and Industrial Council |
| OEM | original equipment manufacturer |
| PMD | Planned Manufacturing District (prior to 1988 known as Protected Manufacturing District) |
| RERC | Real Estate Research Corporation |
| TIF | tax increment financing |
| UDAG | Urban Development Action Grant |

# Remaking Chicago

*Chapter One*

# The Politics of
# Urban Economic Development

A merican cities have long been symbols of our greatest potential and deepest failings as a society. Cities like Chicago, New York, Boston, and New Haven play hosts to prestigious universities where the nation's rich and powerful send their children to be educated, yet inner-city elementary schools are often ill-equipped to teach even basic reading and writing skills. Fifth Avenue apartments in New York City's Trump Tower sell for over $10 million, while sixty thousand to seventy thousand homeless city residents struggle to survive on the streets below. In Chicago, the notorious Cabrini-Green public-housing development stands little more than a stone's throw from the luxury high-rises and town houses overlooking Lake Michigan along the city's Gold Coast. White, Latino, and African-American office workers in the Loop, Chicago's central business district, interact today with a degree of mutual respect unimaginable thirty years ago, yet at the end of the day they still ride separate trains home. The juxtaposition of wealth and poverty, tolerance and intolerance, hope and despair, has bedazzled observers of American cities since the nineteenth century.

In the decades following World War II, the failings of cities seemed to grow especially pronounced. During the 1950s, middle-class whites began what would become a massive exodus from central cities to newly developing suburban communities, helping to trigger an urban fiscal crisis and causing a major decline in downtown retailing. Alarmed city officials responded with the bulldozers of urban renewal, clearing vast tracts of near-downtown land occupied at the time by small businesses and low- and moderate-income residents. The hope was that private developers would build new commercial and middle- to upper-income housing developments in centrally located areas, helping to stabilize downtown property values and creating new markets for downtown retail establishments. Redevelopment, however, was slow to come. Meanwhile, central area residents displaced by urban renewal projects were herded into high-rise public-housing projects that became glaring symbols of a failed urban policy.

During the early 1980s, widespread disillusionment with the future prospects of American cities gave way in some circles to guarded optimism. Evidence of a "back-to-the-cities movement" led by middle- and upper-class young professionals began to receive growing attention in the mass media (Cicin-Sain 1980). New downtown developments such as Boston's Quincy Market and Baltimore's Harborplace were hailed as signs of an "urban renaissance" (Rosenthal 1980, 9). City officials soon grew mesmerized with the tourist and convention trades, promoting hotel construction, building convention centers, and competing in cutthroat fashion for professional sports franchises. Strong corporate demand for centrally located office space fueled a downtown construction boom that lasted for much of the 1980s.

Yet many observers soon began to see a downside to the new urban renaissance. Despite successful efforts to resuscitate decaying central business districts in cities like Boston, Philadelphia, Chicago, and Baltimore, poor inner-city neighborhoods continued to deteriorate (Abravanel and Mancini 1980; Levine 1989; Bartelt 1989). The growing preoccupation of city officials with the glittering trophies produced by downtown revitalization efforts was creating "divided cities" in which professional workers from gentrified neighborhoods shared space uncomfortably with low-income and homeless city residents holding few meaningful economic opportunities (Fainstein, Gordon, and Harloe 1992). The success of Harborplace notwithstanding, poverty rates increased in 90 percent of Baltimore's predominantly black neighborhoods during the 1970s (Levine 1989, 25). As Mayor Kurt Schmoke remarked in 1987, "If you were revisiting Baltimore today after a twenty-year absence, you would find us much prettier and much poorer" (Judd and Swanstrom 1994, 349).

The roots of the problem, most agreed, lay in the changing structure of postwar urban economies. Shortly after the close of World War II, manufacturers began moving out of central cities, taking well-paying blue-collar jobs with them. During the following decades, cities increasingly became producers of services rather than goods. Although job growth in the downtown service sectors of many cities helped offset the decline of manufacturing employment, the kinds of new jobs being created tended to be either high-paying or low-paying, fostering a two-tiered distribution of income with a relatively small middle class (Stanback and Noyelle 1982, 140–142). For many unemployed factory workers with limited formal education, unskilled positions opening up at the bottom end of the expanding service sector represented the only real prospects for reentry into the workforce.

Urban economic restructuring seemed to pose a dilemma for city officials.

With opportunities for meaningful employment rapidly diminishing in many inner-city neighborhoods, the pursuit of economic growth was proving less and less effective as a panacea for the social problems of cities. Yet the alternative—to divert policies and programs from accumulation in favor of efforts to improve conditions in low- and moderate-income neighborhoods—threatened to result in a withdrawal of private investment and a loss of resources for redistribution. Studies of development politics in postwar cities began to uncover a similar pattern: in most cases, city officials formed close partnerships with business leaders focused around downtown redevelopment efforts of one form or another, while residents of low- and moderate-income neighborhoods fought with varying degrees of success for a share of the benefits (Squires 1989; Cummings 1988; Frieden and Sagalyn 1989). By most accounts, urban economic restructuring seemed destined to produce an increasingly adversarial politics of growth versus redistribution, forcing policymakers to straddle a growing divide between downtown business elites and less privileged neighborhood residents (see Berk and Swanstrom 1994).

This book examines urban redevelopment in Chicago from 1955 to 1997, focusing in particular on the redevelopment of Chicago's central area. The subject matter has been treated elsewhere (see, for example, Bennett 1989; Squires et al. 1987; Weiss and Metzger 1989; Ferman 1991; Greer 1983), but the line of argument pursued here differs from most other accounts in at least one key respect. Studies of downtown redevelopment in Chicago and other central cities typically begin with a discussion of the underlying economic context, namely, the transformation of the urban economic base from manufacturing to services following World War II. In general, this process is understood to be driven by forces outside the control of city officials, such as corporate restructuring efforts and regional variations in land and labor costs. Urban economic development policy, by most accounts, is highly constrained by the market. Officials can tax or regulate investment, but they cannot easily influence the form or trajectory it takes. Because the market has determined that cities have become efficient locations for service sector growth, but not for industrial development, city officials must focus economic policies on the central business district or face the political consequences of economic decline.

There is much at stake in such efforts to come to grips theoretically with the key structural features of the urban political economy. If it is indeed true that structural economic change places well-defined limits on the range of viable urban economic development strategies, then the policy choices open to public officials are likely to be similarly constrained. Under such circumstances, perhaps the best that residents of low- and moderate-income city neighborhoods can hope for are urban regimes committed to some form of reallocation of the economic rewards generated downtown in their favor. Suppose, however, that theorists have generally misinterpreted the role of private investment activity in the process of postwar urban economic restructuring, and that public policy has had a significant impact on the *trajectory* of economic growth, as well as on the distribution of benefits. If so, then we need to reexamine the course of postwar urban redevelopment to determine why certain growth strategies were chosen over others, who they favored, and what the consequences were.

This study represents such an undertaking. Put briefly, I will show that Chicago's central area emerged as the focus of a heated political conflict over the direction of urban economic growth in the postwar era. Within the context of global economic change, two coherent economic development alternatives presented themselves, each favoring very different segments of the urban community. On the first model, the chief beneficiaries would be downtown property developers, landowners, and other groups with a stake in the commercial and residential redevelopment of Chicago's downtown area. On the second model, those standing to gain were a select group of manufacturers, workers, and residents from working-class communities with an interest in preserving the city's blue-collar jobs base. Both models presented coherent opportunities for economic growth. Neither one could be put into practice without aggressive support from city government. Contrary to much popular thinking on the subject of urban economic development, the choice between them would be made, to a great extent, through politics.

## Urban Economic Restructuring and the Corporate-Center Strategy

Contemporary urban scholarship is grounded in a shared narrative of postwar urban redevelopment, which portrays key characteristics of the contemporary urban political economy as the outcome of a far-reaching process of urban economic restructuring. During the late nineteenth and early twentieth centuries, the argument goes, the economic fortunes of cities were determined largely by the strength of their manufacturing industries, which tended to cluster in downtown locations, close to centrally located transportation nodes. By the end of World War II, however, central city manufacturing showed signs of growing stagnation, while new industrial development began to locate increasingly in outlying portions of metropolitan areas (Vernon 1959, 49). By most accounts, the development of the interstate highway system and growth of the trucking industry fueled the exodus of manufacturing from central cities during the 1950s and the 1960s by making the inexpensive land and nonunion labor on the urban periphery accessible to industrial firms (Kain 1968; Moses and Williamson 1967; Hoover and Vernon 1959).

During the following several decades, as innovations in transportation and communications technologies continued to grow by leaps and bounds, urban economic restructuring began to assume a global dimension as well (Castells 1985; Froebel, Heinrichs, and Kreye 1977). By the 1970s, a growing number of U.S. corporations had relocated their production facilities in Third

World countries, where wages were a fraction of those earned by American workers and organizing efforts on the part of labor were typically well contained (Bluestone and Harrison 1982; Harvey 1986; Beauregard 1989). With land and labor costs well in excess of those elsewhere, American central cities were said to be increasingly obsolete as sites for industrial production (Fainstein and Fainstein 1989, 25; Peet 1987; Massey 1987).

Urban scholars were quick to point out, however, that the decline of manufacturing jobs within postwar American cities was to some degree offset by the rapid growth in service sector employment during the same time period. Corporations shifting their production facilities to the urban periphery and beyond frequently concentrated decision-making and administrative capacity within the downtown areas of central cities. Faced with increasingly complex business environments following World War II, corporate managers came to rely on a range of advanced corporate services too costly and inconvenient to develop in-house but found in ample supply within the central business districts of large cities (Cohen 1979). Downtowns ultimately became magnets for legal, financial, accounting, and advertising firms, which grew in proportion to the rise in corporate headquarters' activities (Mollenkopf 1983; Noyelle and Stanback 1983; Stanback and Noyelle 1982).

According to most contemporary urban theorists, structural economic change, occurring exogenously to municipal politics, left city officials with relatively few economic development policy options. Most have employed what sociologist Richard Child Hill has termed the "corporate-center strategy" for downtown redevelopment (Hill 1983). Recognizing that the heyday of manufacturing-led urban economic growth is over, development officials have instead focused their attention on efforts to transform aging industrial cities into modern corporate service centers. Typically, this involves the promotion of office building and hotel construction downtown, the development of convention centers and large sports complexes, the fostering of cultural and entertainment activities in the central business district to promote tourism and keep downtown streets lively during after-business hours, and the replacement of industrial and lower-income residential districts in the near-downtown area with middle- and upper-income housing for downtown office workers.

The concentration of economic resources on the downtown area and the disruptive effects of land-use changes have frequently jeopardized public support for the corporate-center strategy. Responding to critics, proponents of downtown commercial and residential redevelopment insist that their plans represent the "highest and best use" for central area property, creating job opportunities, enhancing the city's tax base, and easing the tax burden for middle-class homeowners and other city residents. City government, they argue, can see to it that the benefits of the corporate-center strategy are truly widespread by redistributing tax revenues generated downtown in favor of low- and moderate-income city neighborhoods and ensuring that city residents win a fair share of the jobs and contracts produced by downtown revitalization efforts.

## Urban Political Economy

The narrative of postwar urban economic restructuring provides the key historical underpinning for the paradigm of urban political economy, which emerged during the 1970s and the 1980s to unseat pluralism as the model of choice for studying community power structures. Pluralists had argued that the most effective way of gauging the true distribution of power within a given municipality was to determine who prevailed in community decision-making, independently of economic structure (Polsby 1963, 4). Case studies of community power in New Haven, Chicago, and other cities utilizing the pluralist framework generally found political power to be widely dispersed among relatively small interest groups, consisting most often of temporary coalitions formed around particular issues (Dahl 1961; Polsby 1963; Banfield 1961). Pluralists viewed elections as a key mechanism for holding politicians accountable to their constituents. Because of widespread indifference among voters on many issues, even small groups could wield considerable power in a given situation (Dahl 1961, 191).

Pluralists assumed that the government and the economy represented two distinct, nonoverlapping spheres of activity. As Nelson Polsby wrote, "If a man's major life work is banking, the pluralist presumes he will spend his time at the bank and not in manipulating community decisions" (Polsby 1963, 117). Economic power was of interest to pluralists only to the extent that it influenced the outcomes of electoral contests. The possibility that business interests could exercise power in less observable ways, such as implicit threats to withhold investment, was left unaddressed in pluralist studies of community power.

With the postwar economic prosperity of the 1950s and the 1960s serving as a backdrop for the pluralist model of community power, the latter assumption seemed more plausible than it would during the following decades. By the 1970s, nationwide economic stagnation and the continuing exodus of manufacturing firms from older central cities left many urban communities bending under the weight of impending economic and fiscal collapse. Increasingly, city officials undertook austerity measures, diverting funds from redistributive social programs into efforts designed to leverage private investment and enhance the local tax base. The space for interest group bargaining seemed to narrow, while businesses profited from a wide array of economic development incentives, including tax abatements, tax increment financing, and Urban Development Action Grants (Swanstrom 1985). By the late 1970s, even former pluralists such as Charles Lindblom began to speak of a "privileged position" for business among interest groups (Lindblom 1977).

The urban political economy literature contains a wide range of perspectives, held together by the shared assumption that political power in cities cannot be understood in isolation from underlying economic structure. In a fundamental break from pluralism, urban political economists increasingly emphasized ways in which public officials were systemically predisposed to favor the concerns of business over other interest groups (Stone 1980; Crenson 1971; Lukes 1974). Interest in coalition-building waned as theorists sought to explain how economic constraints shaped public policy in ways favorable to business, oftentimes with little prodding from business leaders themselves (Peterson 1981; Goodman 1979; Kantor 1987). According to structural Marxists, fiscal and economic pressures alone were enough to explain the active and enthusiastic participation of city officials in downtown redevelopment, urban renewal, and gentrification schemes, all of which allocated costs and benefits among different segments of the community in a highly inequitable fashion (Beauregard 1984; Gordon 1978; Smith 1982; Hill 1978).

For structural urban theorists, the key feature of the contemporary urban political economy responsible for the privileged position of business was the dramatic increase in capital mobility beginning in the 1960s. Innovations in transportation and communications technologies increasingly freed producers from the need to locate in close proximity to customers and suppliers (Bluestone and Harrison 1982; Peet 1987). No longer tied to dense urban agglomerations with high land and labor costs, capitalist firms became free to roam the globe in search of the least expensive production sites (Fainstein and Fainstein 1989; Castells 1985). According to structural theorists, the consequences of capital mobility for cities have been far-reaching: interurban competition generates intensive pressure for more permissive work and environmental regulations (Goodman 1979); the presence of a "reserve army of places" allows firms to extract costly concessions from workers and communities that may exceed the employment and fiscal benefits provided by investment (Glickman 1987; Jones and Bachelor 1984; Blair, Fichtenbaum, and Swaney 1984); internationalization imposes a "global logic" on urban development policy reflecting the interests of powerful multinational corporations, forcing even progressive urban regimes to fall in line (Castells 1985; Kantor 1987); redistributive policies disappear from the public agenda as the space for genuine political debate shrinks to a narrow range of nondevelopmental issues that do not affect the local business climate one way or the other (Peterson 1981; Kantor 1987; Gottdiener 1987).

Most urban theorists eventually recognized the efforts of urban political economists to integrate economic structure into studies of community power as a healthy corrective to the one-dimensional pluralist framework. At the same time, however, the structural bent of much of the new literature

produced a wave of studies remarkably devoid of human content and incapable of accounting for important differences in the way cities responded to
fiscal and economic pressures. Dissatisfaction with the high level of abstrac-
tion at which many structural urban theories were being pitched led to two
new theoretical strains within the urban political economy approach, both of
which emphasized the role of business-led coalitions as determinants of political power in cities.

The first of these perspectives, introduced by sociologists John Logan and
Harvey Molotch, holds that community power structures are dominated by
coalitions of land-based interests that stand to profit from the growth of the
municipalities in which they are based (Molotch 1976; Whitt 1982; Feagin
1983; Molotch and Logan 1984; Logan and Molotch 1987). "Growth coalitions" are spearheaded by local property owners (rentiers) who seek to enhance the value of their individual holdings through efforts to intensify land
use. Other coalition partners typically include developers, financiers, utility
companies, the local media, and sympathetic public officials anxious to reap
the increasing tax revenues produced by economic growth. According to Logan and Molotch, this coalition has been the driving force behind urban redevelopment schemes in cities across the nation since World War II. As a
consequence, cities have been rendered "growth machines" (Molotch 1976;
Logan and Molotch 1987).

Growth machine theorists do not view economic growth as a universal
good. To the contrary, conflict over economic development policy is said to
form the central political cleavage in contemporary cities, pitting progrowth
activists against community residents who bear the costs of economic growth
in rising rents, displacement, and environmental degradation. In their semi-
nal work *Urban Fortunes,* Logan and Molotch (1987) describe this as a conflict between use values and exchange values. Communities struggle to maintain social ties and stability, while the proponents of economic growth seek to
maximize profits and develop property for its highest and best use. Community challenges to the growth machine in the form of growth control movements have been a popular subject of investigation within the literature on
growth machines (see Molotch and Logan 1984; Vogel and Swanson 1989;
Warner and Molotch 1995; Schneider 1992; Shlay and Giloth 1987; Green
and Schreuder 1991; Tulloss 1995; Calavita 1992; Folz et al. 1993).

A relatively new body of literature focusing on urban regimes represents a
second wave of theorizing emphasizing the role of coalition-building in city
politics within a political economy approach (see Elkin 1985, 1987a; Stone
1989, 1993; Stone and Sanders 1987; Stone, Orr, and Imbroscio 1991).
Regime theorists stress that political power within liberal democratic societies
is divided into two spheres of influence, where economic decision-making remains largely within the purview of private investors and control of public
policy in the hands of popularly elected government officials. The division of

labor between state and market means that city officials can accomplish relatively little through their powers of command. Power is exercised instead largely through informal partnerships between public officials and private citizens who control resources necessary for governing. Regimes represent the informal arrangements through which public and private actors collaborate in order to produce governing decisions (Stone 1989, 6). Structural constraints, including the need to generate satisfactory levels of economic activity, mean that business is almost certain to be well represented in such partnerships (Elkin 1985; Stone 1987b).

A typical urban regime is a growth coalition, featuring the alliance between public officials and place-bound rentiers that serves as the focus of the growth machine literature. However, other possibilities also exist. In the words of regime theorist Clarence Stone, "a regime represents an accommodation between the potentially conflicting principles of the popular control of government and the private ownership of business enterprises" (Stone 1987b, 269). The need to reconcile these two principles limits the range of viable regime types. A regime that responded only to the imperative of capital accumulation would be no more successful than one that responded exclusively to the demands of the electorate. Nevertheless, the tension between popular control and economic productivity can be accommodated in more ways than one. In addition to the growth machine model, regime theorists have uncovered a variety of regime types, encompassing a range of social, political, and economic concerns and objectives (see Elkin 1985; Fainstein, Fainstein, and Armistead 1983; Stone 1993; Body-Gendrot 1987; Clavel 1986; DeLeon 1992; Orr and Stoker 1994; Nickel 1995; Robinson 1995; Imbroscio 1995).

Regime theory goes further than any other variant of the urban political economy literature in asserting the relative autonomy of the political sphere from structural economic constraints. Yet even regime theorists concede that progrowth governing coalitions centered around downtown commercial revitalization largely dominate the contemporary urban landscape. According to Stephen Elkin, "The battlefield of city politics is not flat but is tilted toward an alliance of public officials and land interests" (Elkin 1987a, 100). In most contemporary cities, downtown redevelopment is the order of the day.

In his study of community power in postwar Atlanta, Clarence Stone (1989) explains the privileged position of Atlanta's business elite by pointing to the unequal distribution of resources among potential governing coalition partners. The downtown redevelopment efforts advanced by Atlanta's progrowth coalition produced visible signs of progress for which city officials could claim partial responsibility. They also generated selective incentives such as jobs, contracts, and retainer fees that could be used as side payments to boost support for the regime. The unified outlook and extensive associational networks among the downtown business leadership minimized the difficulty of coordinating extensive redevelopment efforts involving a wide range of actors. According to Stone, attempts to form a progressive, neighborhood-based regime with minimal business participation failed in Atlanta precisely because the neighborhoods lacked such economic and associational resources. For progressive mayor Maynard Jackson, such a regime was not an empowering one, leading him "inevitably toward accommodation" with the downtown business community (Stone 1989, 95).

## Summing Up

Despite important differences among the various perspectives within the urban political economy literature, there is widespread agreement on a number of crucial points. First, it is widely assumed that the division of labor between state and market within liberal democratic societies places most private investment decisions outside the control of city officials. Fundamental economic changes such as the transformation of urban economies from manufacturing to services are seen as occurring prior to, and outside the sphere of, municipal politics. Such developments set limits on the range of policy choices available to city officials. They provide the underlying economic context for political conflict over redistributive and regulatory questions. Thus, while contemporary urban theorists disagree over the possibilities for reconciling capitalism and democracy within the context of global economic restructuring, they generally concur that city officials are largely powerless to intervene in the process of restructuring itself.

In addition, urban political economists typically subscribe to a model of firm locational behavior borrowed from neoclassical economics. Under this view, firms choose production sites through a purely instrumental logic based on estimates of future production costs in various alternative locations. Recent technological innovations have helped minimize the "stickiness" caused by transportation- and communications-related constraints on firm mobility. As a result, capital today is more footloose than ever, a situation that places cities in increasingly subservient relationships with mobile investors and increasingly competitive relationships with one another. As regime theorist Alan DiGaetano observes,

> American cities, as tax-dependent creatures, are forced to compete for footloose capital in order to sustain themselves fiscally. Competition for capital investment within the American system of cities means that cities with the ability to attract and retain mobile capital will grow, while cities that fail to do so will sink into economic decline. In short, the unevenness of economic development, a byproduct of capital mobility, creates a hierarchy of cities. (DiGaetano 1989, 264)

The mobility of capital and the division of labor between state and market, in turn, set limits on the range of viable urban economic development strategies. For many industrial firms, the price of land and labor figures prominently in locational decisions. The relatively high cost of urban factory workers and production space places cities at a disadvantage vis-à-vis suburban, rural, and Third World locations in the competition for mobile industrial investment. However, because many high-level corporate services find it necessary to locate within the central business districts of certain cities, some municipalities may successfully weather the disruptive effects of capital mobility through efforts to build on the agglomeration economies provided by their downtown areas (Hill 1983; Mollenkopf 1983; Cohen 1979; Noyelle and Stanback 1983). Under this strategy, the importance of redistributive policies becomes paramount, as the replacement of well-paying manufacturing jobs with low-level service sector occupations increases disparities in the social and spatial distribution of wealth and income. Redevelopment efforts may also clash with residential use values, causing displacement of lower-income residents in near-downtown locations (Molotch 1976; Logan and Molotch 1987).

Downtown redevelopment and urban economic restructuring thus tend to magnify the tension between capital and community, which urban political economists today widely recognize as the central political cleavage in contemporary cities (O'Connor 1973; Mollenkopf 1981; Logan and Molotch 1987; Stone 1987a). On one side are progrowth coalitions dominated by downtown business elites; on the other side are neighborhood representatives battling the disruptive effects of accumulation strategies emanating increasingly from the central business district, imposing substantial costs while providing little in the way of benefits to neighborhood workers and residents. Caught in the middle of this divide are city officials, who must find a way to reconcile the tension between accumulation and legitimation if the governing arrangements over which they preside are to be successful. Given the division of labor between state and market and the mobility of capital, however, their options for doing so are normally seen as quite limited.

## Overview of the Narrative

To a certain point, the redevelopment of Chicago's central area following World War II seems consistent with the prevailing narrative of urban economic restructuring. When Richard J. Daley became mayor of Chicago in 1955, the city's economy was in decline. Under pressure to act, Daley soon forged an alliance with key representatives from the downtown business community focused around rearranging land use in central Chicago in accordance with the corporate-center strategy for downtown redevelopment. In 1958, the administration announced plans for a major restructuring of the central area, featuring a new university campus, a convention center, several new government office buildings, and a network of expressways designed to link the central business district with outlying portions of the metropolitan area (Department of City Planning 1958). During the next several decades, the city would use its powers over land use, infrastructure provision, the distribution of federal urban development funds, and other policy tools to help make these plans a reality.

By most accounts, the Daley administration's downtown redevelopment efforts were enormously successful, reversing a thirty-year decline in downtown property values and fueling the construction of thirty-two million square feet of new office space in the Loop between 1962 and 1977 (Weiss and Metzgar 1989, 135). Yet downtown revitalization also involved certain less visible economic development trade-offs. When city officials began to implement their development plans for the central area of Chicago in the late 1950s, the Loop was surrounded by a ring of industrial districts that provided nearly 25 percent of Chicago's manufacturing jobs at the time. By the 1970s, the economic turnaround of the Loop had begun to make turn-of-the-century industrial loft buildings in near-downtown manufacturing districts such as Printing House Row and River North desirable properties for alternative uses, as living space for downtown office workers and back office space for downtown businesses. Both uses commanded rents considerably higher than manufacturing, luring real estate developers and land speculators to the area. By the mid-1980s, rising rents, property tax increases, and complaints from new loft-dwelling "urban pioneers" had driven all but a few industrial firms from this section of the city. Missing from most accounts of downtown redevelopment in Chicago is the story of industrial decline that accompanied the dramatic resurgence of the central business district following World War II.

The prevailing narrative of urban economic restructuring suggests that the decline of these near-downtown industrial districts was a foregone conclusion once transportation improvements and technological innovations made it possible for central city manufacturers to abandon the high-density environment of the near-downtown area. However, the lure of cheaper land and labor costs on the urban periphery proved sufficient to attract only certain types of central area industrial establishments to new suburban and rural locations. In general, such firms tended to be relatively large, vertically integrated, and producing for national or international markets. By contrast, another class of near-downtown manufacturers—typically small-to-medium in size, engaged in contracting or subcontracting activities, and producing for local or regional markets—showed little interest in vacating their existing central area locations. As Chapters 2 and 3 will illustrate, the Daley administration's corporate-center strategy for downtown commercial and residential redevelopment would prove disastrous for the latter group of manufacturers.

## Industrial Districts and Regional Development

The notion that some manufacturing firms might actually prefer central city production sites over suburban, rural, or Third World locations is difficult to accept within the dominant paradigm of capital mobility and industrial decentralization. Increasingly, however, empirical research on firm behavior within certain industrial regions of Europe, North America, and Japan has begun to call aspects of this paradigm into question. Since the late 1970s, researchers have identified a growing number of industrial districts in such areas as the Emilia-Romagna province of Northern Italy, Baden-Württemberg in Germany, West Jutland in Denmark, the Silicon Valley in California, and the Route 128 Corridor near Boston, all of which feature spatially rooted agglomerations of manufacturing firms bound to one another through extensive subcontracting and networking relationships (Brusco 1982; Pyke, Becattini and Sengenberger 1990; Pyke and Sengenberger 1992; Hirst and Zeitlin 1989; Saxenian 1994). Industrial districts such as these have become the object of considerable scholarly attention in recent years because the regions within which they are concentrated have, in many instances, experienced superior economic performance.

The economic success of the new industrial districts comes less from low-cost factors of production such as cheap land or labor than from the organizational structures of the districts themselves (Sengenberger and Pyke 1992). Typically, individual firms specialize in one or several phases of a total production process. Subcontracting and specialization among firms foster economies of scope, making small-batch production economically feasible and facilitating rapid response to the quickly changing consumer demands characteristic of today's markets.[1] In addition, producers can easily increase or curtail output simply by adding or reducing the number of subcontractors they employ, relieving them of the risk and expense involved in adding to their own productive capacities. The most successful districts feature a combination of competition and cooperation among subcontractors, who may share tools, information, and workers with one another while at the same time competing intensely for each new job opportunity (Harrison 1992; Sengenberger and Pyke 1992). Local and regional governments oftentimes play supportive roles, providing infrastructure, technical support, and other business services.

According to much of the contemporary literature on industrial districts, the cement that binds firms in the districts together and accounts for much of the dynamism of the districts as a whole is *trust* (Sabel 1989; Lorenz 1989; Zeitlin 1992; Harrison 1992). Subcontractors are willing to pass along design ideas and share information on new production technologies with one another because they know, based on past experience, that their neighbors will reciprocate (Sengenberger and Pyke 1992). Each firm owner is acutely aware that his or her individual success is tied to that of the entire district, encouraging a collective outlook among district-member firms. The line between business and community tends to blur. In contrast to the rational, self-interested behavior attributed to capitalist firms within the neoclassical model of interfirm relations, economic relations within the industrial districts are socially embedded (Zeitlin 1992; Lorenz 1989; Granovetter 1985). Producers and subcontractors will not relocate at the drop of a hat because they know that these relationships, built through years of repetitive, face-to-face interactions, cannot be easily reproduced elsewhere.

The new literature on industrial districts is of interest to the story of downtown redevelopment in Chicago because several of the near-downtown area's largest industrial sectors following World War II, namely, printing and apparel, were organized along lines similar to this. Beginning in the early twentieth century, manufacturers from both of these sectors clustered in well-defined printing and garment districts in the Loop area, where they maintained close ties with important downtown customers and contracted and subcontracted extensively with one another. During the postwar years, even as many larger, vertically integrated producers abandoned the districts for lower-cost locations elsewhere, a solid core of small- to medium-sized printers and apparel manufacturers remained well-rooted in the near-downtown area. As Chapter 3 illustrates, these manufacturers ultimately fell victim less to structural economic change than to the Daley administration's corporate-center strategy for downtown commercial and residential redevelopment.

## The Local-Producer Strategy for Neighborhood Revitalization

During the 1960s and 1970s, proponents of the corporate-center strategy encountered little resistance either from central area manufacturers experiencing displacement pressures or from the nearby residential communities from which industrial firms drew their employees. In part, this is undoubtedly because, to the untutored eye, downtown redevelopment seemed to be driven largely by market forces. What manufacturers saw were property developers and land speculators seemingly exercising legitimate property rights by converting industrial loft buildings to higher-rent commercial and residential space, or otherwise rearranging land use. What they failed to see, however, were the land-use plans, zoning decisions, capital improvements programs, building-code revisions, and other public policy initiatives that attracted property developers and real estate speculators to the central area in the first place. Convinced that their problems originated in the market rather than in politics, many central area manufacturers were initially discouraged from seeking political solutions.

Reinforcing the quiescence of manufacturers were the crippling effects of Chicago's well-entrenched political machine on neighborhood political mobilization during the postwar years. The overwhelming concentration of public resources on the downtown area that accompanied the corporate-center strategy was politically feasible, largely because of the well-defined separation between electoral politics and public policy that characterized Chicago politics at the time. Machine leaders used patronage appointments and selective incentives to assemble winning coalitions of voters from the city's working-class neighborhoods, keeping electoral politics on an individual and largely issueless basis. With potential neighborhood opposition largely diffused, policy benefits could be channeled into the hands of downtown property developers and other business elites with little fear of voter repercussions. Under these circumstances, central area manufacturers seeking protection from displacement pressures would have found it difficult to identify ready allies.

Nevertheless, by the mid-to-late 1970s this set of conditions was clearly beginning to change. To begin with, cracks in the machine's stronghold on political power in Chicago were becoming visible on the horizon. A federal court decision declaring the patronage system of political firing unconstitutional and a reduction of federal funds for urban development and social welfare programs both jeopardized the machine's control over key resources it had long used to reward its supporters in the neighborhoods. In addition, Chicago's already well-developed neighborhood movement was becoming increasingly vocal and united in its outlook by this time, demanding collective benefits from city officials who nevertheless continued to respond to their low- and moderate-income constituents as individuals.

The mobilization of lower-income and working-class communities was soon accompanied by a strategic shift within certain factions of the neighborhood movement, away from its consumer-based, social-protest origins toward a new focus on neighborhood economic development. Prompted by the precipitous decline of Chicago's manufacturing base during the 1970s, a growing number of community-based organizations began to experiment with various methods of assisting neighborhood manufacturers—establishing business incubators to nurture small, start-up firms, helping to foster inter-firm linkages among local manufacturers, and providing technical assistance and other business services to industrial companies. As the policy implications of these new experiments became apparent, new coalitions of neighborhood economic development organizations, manufacturers, workers, and working-class residents became forceful advocates of city government support for neighborhood industrial retention.

Within this context of regime change and neighborhood political mobilization, proponents of neighborhood economic revitalization began to articulate the features of a coherent economic development alternative to the corporate-center strategy. This alternative, which I call the "local-producer strategy" for neighborhood redevelopment, rested above all on the argument that preserving Chicago's base of locally and regionally owned manufacturing firms was a necessary counterpart to downtown area commercial and residential growth. Its proponents rejected the widely shared belief that manufacturing in Chicago was either dying or dead, ultimately setting forth a detailed range of policy proposals that they insisted could help revitalize the city's industrial base. These proposals included the targeting of public investments to industrial areas of the city, the promotion of worker training programs appropriate for the needs of local manufacturers, greater community involvement in the planning of economic development programs, and policies designed to make credit available to locally owned businesses. Rejecting the argument by downtown business leaders that economic development was synonymous with real estate development, proponents of the local-producer strategy urged city officials to make the creation and preservation of well-paying jobs the centerpiece of economic development policy.

Appropriately enough, advocates of the local-producer and corporate-center strategies clashed first over competing visions of the future of Chicago's central area, the section of the city where the two strategies confronted one another most directly. Clearly, the real estate community's postindustrial vision of a ring of affluent residential and commercial neighborhoods surrounding the Loop could not become a reality as long as manufacturers continued to occupy significant portions of the central area's loft space. The struggle between the two groups broke out into the open first around the issue of zoning policy. A coalition of groups allied with centrally located manufacturers on Chicago's Near North Side argued that the piecemeal rezoning of central area industrial districts to permit new residential and commercial uses was forcing otherwise viable manufacturers from the area. Criticizing city government for its culpability in Chicago's industrial decline, the coalition called for legislation to set aside certain portions of the central area as protected manufacturing districts where further zoning changes to nonindustrial land uses would be prohibited.

Proponents of the local-producer strategy found key sympathizers within the administration of progressive mayor Harold Washington, who served as Chicago's first nonmachine mayor in the post-Daley era from 1983 to 1987. When community leaders first questioned the city's zoning policies in the central area, Washington officials helped place the issue squarely on the public agenda, ensuring it would receive a full public airing. The ensuing conflict helped generate a new dialogue over Chicago's economic future. As people discovered that certain manufacturers were leaving Chicago only under duress, they increasingly questioned the necessity or the desirability of the postindustrial vision of Chicago that downtown business leaders seemed to embrace. Proponents of the corporate-center strategy were put on the defensive, no longer able to defend their land-use preferences through simple ideo-logical pronouncements such as "highest and best use." City government's role in downtown redevelopment was unmasked and increasingly called into question. Ultimately, legislation to protect central area industries from fur-ther encroachment by incompatible land uses was passed. Since then, city manufacturers and their allies have won the reluctant support of an adminis-tration led by the late Mayor Daley's eldest son, who, despite strong down-town business ties, has taken a number of significant steps toward the imple-mentation of a citywide industrial policy.

## Revisiting Urban Political Economy

As we saw earlier, the political economy approach to the study of urban politics provided the important insight over pluralism that public officials cannot take economic activity for granted, a condition that in turn shapes the balance of power within cities. Politicians need votes, as pluralists empha-sized. However, public confidence in city government depends in no small part on the extent to which healthy levels of economic activity can be sus-tained. Jobs and tax revenues are contingent upon it. Politicians thus need more than just votes. To be viable over the long term, a regime must include a strategy for economic development and coalition partners who control the resources necessary to implement such a strategy. Business *is* therefore privi-leged. It is not simply one among many private-sector interest groups.

Still, the critique of pluralism offered by urban political economy remains a partial one. Recall that pluralists conceived of politics and markets as dis-creet, nonoverlapping spheres of activity. By showing how social and eco-nomic factors such as capital mobility, fiscal crisis, and class struggle permeate and shape the political arena, urban political economists convincingly put to rest the notion of a self-contained political sphere driven largely by the give and take of pluralist interest-group bargaining. Political decision-making could only be understood, they argued, by taking into account the complex web of social and economic relations within which politics are embedded. To do any less would simply invite pluralist conclusions.

By the same token, however, urban political economy has largely failed to extend the same insight into its portrayal of economic relations. Instead, the market is typically conceptualized as a largely autonomous sphere of activity, driven in this case by the rational, self-interested behavior of profit-maximiz-ing capitalist firms. As a result, developments in the marketplace take on an almost organic appearance. The economy becomes part of the "natural" ex-ternal environment with which political decision makers must learn to cope. Urban regimes are portrayed as intervening or dependent variables, respond-ing to events in the marketplace such as global economic restructuring with little to no capacity to affect basic economic outcomes.

This view of the economy can support only certain kinds of development politics. By most accounts, the instrumental behavior of mobile, profit-maximizing private investors has signaled that cities are becoming efficient loca tions for only a limited range of economic activities, primarily those that cater to the needs of corporations and financial institutions located in the central business district. Current scholarly analysis tends to use the corporate-center strategy as its point of departure, focusing empirical investigation on struggles over the allocation of costs and benefits associated with downtown redevelopment. The axis of political conflict is typically drawn to pit progrowth coalitions dominated by downtown business elites against neighborhood residents seeking protection from gentrification pressures and demanding a greater share of the jobs, contracts, and other side payments that downtown redevelopment makes available. City officials, meanwhile, straddle the divide between accumulation and legitimation, carefully weighing redistributive policies against the dampening effects they are likely to have on investment, since overburdensome taxes and regulations will prompt mobile corporations to take their investment dollars to some other city where the business climate is perceived as friendlier.

The above model captures certain characteristics of postwar urban politics that are beyond dispute. Without question, struggles between growth coalitions and neighborhood residents over downtown revitalization efforts have been a defining feature of city politics since the 1950s. Nevertheless, the pitfalls of viewing urban politics exclusively in these terms become apparent if we place this model alongside the narrative of postwar redevelopment in Chicago outlined in the previous section. For example, what if certain industrial producers representing significant numbers of manufacturing jobs are not the footloose, atomistic competitors of the urban political economy literature but instead rely heavily on extensive networking relationships that root them firmly in central city industrial districts? And what if public policy, along with market forces, plays a significant role in determining which kinds of economic activities will survive in such areas of the city? And, finally, what if manufacturers threatened by displacement pressures caused in part by unsupportive public policies should join with neighborhood residents and workers to demand an alternative set of policies and programs?

To understand the full range of conflicts, development opportunities, and political possibilities that presented themselves in connection with the redevelopment of Chicago's central area following World War II, it is necessary to extend the critique of pluralism offered by urban political economy to its logical conclusion. The insight that economic and social factors affect political outcomes in significant ways, while important, is only part of the story. To complete the picture, we must also take into account the *equally* significant external influences that shape outcomes in the economic sphere, leading profit-seeking investors to behave in sometimes unexpected ways and presenting opportunities for local actors to shape basic economic developments such as urban economic restructuring. Put briefly, we need to move beyond investigation of the economics of political relations in order to examine the politics of economic relations as well.[2]

Contemporary urban political economy, with its emphasis on the economics of political relations, invites a particular set of questions. For example, can mobile investors be compelled to pay their fair share of the city tax burden? Or, under what circumstances, if any, can low- and moderate-income city neighborhoods become beneficiaries of economic growth led by downtown commercial redevelopment? Or, finally, are urban regimes that pursue community services over economic growth viable within liberal democratic societies? These are not unimportant questions, but they are also not the only ones worth asking. A model that takes into account the politics of economic relations generates an additional set of questions. For instance, how can networking relationships among local producers be fostered to root businesses more firmly in the community? Or, what types of growth strategies appear to hold the greatest direct benefits for lower-income and working-class neighborhoods? Or, finally, what kinds of power structures do urban regimes pursuing alternatives to the corporate-center strategy tend to encounter?

The latter questions are the kind that this study principally seeks to address. Unlike contemporary urban political economy, this study does not assume that capital and community are on opposite sides of a deep divide that city officials can hope to bridge only imperfectly. By looking seriously at the politics of economic relations in postwar Chicago, I intend to show how various groups competed to impose their own distinct visions of redevelopment on the central area of the city. According to one vision, downtown commercial and residential redevelopment would generate a large share of the wealth necessary to provide city services and material rewards to lower-income and working-class neighborhood residents. According to another vision, efforts to protect and revitalize near-downtown industrial districts would help rebuild neighborhood productive capacities, reducing the need for a redistribution of benefits produced by downtown commercial and residential growth. Both strategies would require strong support by city government. Both presented opportunities for the formation of viable urban regimes. However, seen through the lens of contemporary urban theory, only one would be clearly visible.

# Chapter Two

# Downtown Redevelopment and the Chicago Political Machine

To the casual observer, downtown Chicago today may well seem to epitomize the triumphant postindustrial American city. The Loop, surrounded just forty years ago by a semicircle of residential slums and industrial loft buildings threatening the value of downtown real estate, now appears vibrant and self-assured. The acres of nearby slum dwellings have, for the most part, long since been cleared away, and many of the old multistory loft buildings once home to small- and medium-sized manufacturing establishments just north, south, and west of the central business district have now been converted to upscale residences for downtown office workers or back office space for downtown corporations.

Studies of the deindustrialization of American cities have often focused on the job losses associated with the closure of large plants in major sectors such as the steel or automotive industries (Bluestone and Harrison 1982). The Gary-Hammond-East Chicago area, for years the center of a thriving steel industry anchored by the Inland and U.S. Steel mills along the lakefront, lost twenty thousand steelworker jobs in 1979 alone due largely to global overcapacity in steel production and the failure of multinational conglomerates such as USX (formerly U.S. Steel) to reinvest profits in their Chicago area steel-making facilities (Squires et al. 1987, 30–31).

In fact, the loss of manufacturing jobs like these is only part of the story of Chicago's industrial decline since the second World War. At roughly the same time that hundreds of steelworkers were receiving their pink slips on Chicago's far South Side, the long-term viability of another set of industries located in the city's central area was increasingly being called into question as well. These were the printers, garment makers, metalworkers, and other manufacturers who occupied the small, affordable spaces provided by Chicago's turn-of-the-century industrial loft buildings, the majority of which are concentrated in the

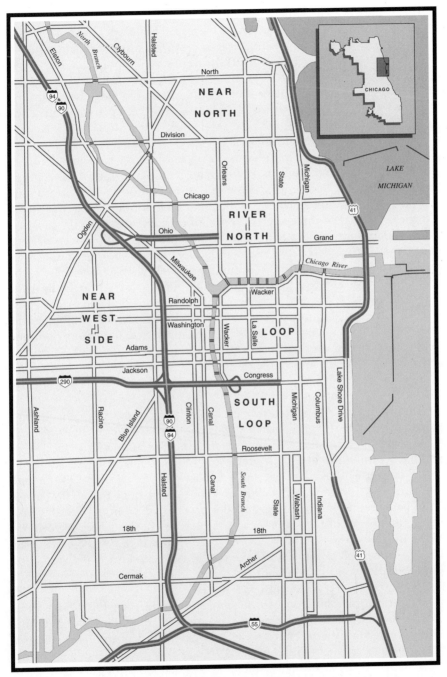

Map 1. Chicago Central Area

near-downtown area of the city. With yearly rents as low as fifty cents per square foot and strategic downtown locations, loft buildings provided low-cost production space and convenient access to centrally located customers, suppliers, and support services (Real Estate Research Corporation 1970, 19; Ducharme, Giloth, and McCormick 1986). Although much smaller and less visible than the smokestack industries of the far Southeast Side, these firms still provided 115,000 jobs for Chicago residents in 1970, 23 percent of the city's total manufacturing jobs at the time (McDonald 1984, 25; Mayor's Council of Manpower and Economic Advisors 1974).

Chicago's central area includes the Loop and roughly ten square miles of additional land.[1] As recently as 1970, manufacturing accounted for approximately 25 percent of overall land use in this portion of the city (Real Estate Research Corporation 1970, 2). In the decades following World War II, industries clustered in three distinct areas immediately north, south, and west of the Loop, forming a rough semicircle around the central business district. The South Loop and Near South Side were home to large numbers of graphic communications firms. Within this area lies Printing House Row, the city's historical center of printing and publishing. As of 1970, the district's twelve late-nineteenth- and early-twentieth-century loft buildings still housed a total of ninety-six printing establishments (Pruska-Carroll 1987). On the Near West Side, food processing was the leading sector, followed by printing and apparel manufacturing. Just north of the Loop, in the River North and Near North Side portions of the central area, the printing and publishing industry was dominant, followed closely by food processing and apparel (Real Estate Research Corporation 1970, 10).

During the twenty-eight-year reign of Chicago's postwar machine mayors Richard J. Daley, Michael Bilandic, and Jane Byrne, large portions of these three areas were transformed from centers of manufacturing into upscale residential communities and back office space for downtown corporations. In many cases, this took place without a fundamental restructuring of the built environment. Industrial loft buildings were refitted from the inside out for new, higher-rent uses—as living space for new "urban pioneers" seeking relief from the tedium of the suburbs, and as office space for service-sector firms requiring downtown locations but unwilling or unable to pay the more costly rents commanded in the heart of the central business district. Between 1963 and 1981 alone, manufacturing employment in the central area experienced a 36 percent decline (McDonald 1984, 8–12).

Analysts commonly point to a combination of market forces and transportation improvements to explain this transformation. The cost of central area manufacturing space, already high vis-à-vis suburban and rural industrial sites, grew increasingly so during the 1960s and 1970s as real estate speculators and commercial and residential property developers bid up the price of near-downtown industrial land (McDonald 1984; Ducharme, Giloth, and

McCormick 1986). With growing use of truck transportation following World War II freeing manufacturers from their dependence on centrally located freight terminals, many chose to relocate in suburban and rural locations to escape the congestion and high land costs of the central area (Mayor's Committee for Economic and Cultural Development 1966, 8; Stone 1974, 7). Cheaper land outside the central city enabled firms to build sprawling new one-story production facilities, more efficient for rationalized, assembly-line production techniques than the multistory loft buildings of the near-downtown area. In addition, the absence of traffic congestion in rural locations reduced delivery times and difficulties loading and unloading trucks (Center for Urban Studies 1966, 51–53; Department of City Planning 1964, 58; Greer 1983, 115–116).

The new commercial and residential development in the central area was ultimately linked to a changing international division of labor, incorporating cities like New York, London, and Chicago as centers of command and control for global corporations (Noyelle and Stanback 1983). As industrial firms gravitated increasingly to the urban periphery and beyond, Chicago's Loop continued to attract a range of corporate and financial activities requiring downtown locations. Rapidly escalating property values in the central business district eventually led corporations to seek back office space nearby for less important functions, while the explosion of downtown office workers during the 1960s and 1970s helped create a market for near-downtown residential space (Bennett 1989). By most accounts, the transformation of central area industrial districts to new commercial and residential areas was a logical by-product of Chicago's metamorphosis from an industrial into a postindustrial city (Greer 1983, 115–116; Real Estate Research Corporation 1970).

Few would question the significance of decision-making by actors in the marketplace in the shaping of urban land-use patterns. Yet private investment activity in any particular city takes place according to a set of publicly determined rules and incentives in which municipal policy decisions figure prominently. For example, land-use plans prepared by city officials inform developers what types of investment activity city government will support within a given area of the metropolis. Public support for private investment assumes various guises, such as financial incentives, the placement of capital improvements, zoning decisions, and the like. Regulations and incentives such as these help determine whether private investment will be forthcoming, where it will occur, and what form it will assume. Property zoned exclusively for manufacturing can be redeveloped for commercial or residential purposes only if city officials agree to furnish the requisite zoning variances. Industrial loft buildings may become viable for higher-rent alternative uses only to the extent that public subsidies are available for building conversions, to name just two examples.

Local rules and incentives governing private investment do not simply respond to structural economic changes in the marketplace. Rather, they are actively shaped by the composition of a city's governing coalition. As the following section will show, postwar Chicago was governed by a progrowth regime consisting of a well-insulated, exclusive alliance between downtown business leaders and city officials. The key objective of the alliance was the revitalization of the central business district, which planners believed could not occur without a fundamental restructuring of near-downtown land use. According to planning officials, centrally located industrial districts were a principal cause of an unhealthy relationship that existed between the Loop and surrounding areas, threatening property values and investment activity in the central business district. Downtown redevelopment ultimately required that industry and lower-income residents be relocated outside the central area so that near-downtown property could be reused for new commercial and middle- to upper-income housing developments that would reinforce the growth of corporate and financial activities in the Loop.

Whether Chicago's central area remained a viable location for manufacturing following World War II is a question we will take up in the following chapter. For the time being, however, it is enough to show that public policy was not an intermediate or otherwise derivative force in the redevelopment of the city's downtown area during the postwar period. To the contrary, land-use plans, capital improvements, financial incentives, and zoning- and building-code regulations were all used aggressively to impose a particular trajectory of redevelopment on Chicago's central area. A governing coalition dominated by downtown corporations, financial institutions, retailers, property developers, and other land-based interests produced a redevelopment strategy that responded overwhelmingly to the narrow interests of its own membership. The following section examines the nature of this coalition and the political and economic strategies that sustained it for nearly thirty years.

## Central Area Planning Under the Richard J. Daley Administration

When Richard J. Daley began his first term as mayor of Chicago in 1955, the city's manufacturing and service sectors were both in decline. Following a wartime boom in manufacturing employment, there were already signs that industry was being lost to the suburbs. Between 1947 and 1954, the city lost 53,209 manufacturing jobs, while manufacturing employment in the rest of Cook County rose by over 30,000 jobs (McDonald 1984, 10). The central business district, meanwhile, was suffering falling property values and declining retail sales. Between 1930 and 1955, construction of new office buildings in the Loop came to a virtual standstill (Berry et al. 1976, 76). Stagnation of downtown employment, white flight to the suburbs, and the growing physical decay of the residential communities surrounding the Loop all contributed to a decrease in downtown pedestrian traffic following World War II. Retail sales in the central business district fell steadily from 1948 to 1963 (Berry et al. 1976, 73). In 1962, the net profits of the five main Loop department stores stood at only 30 percent of their 1948 levels (Berry et al. 1976, 75).

Responding to these dire economic circumstances, Daley quickly set out to forge an alliance with key segments of the downtown business community. Business leadership had been newly consolidated within the Chicago Central Area Committee (CCAC), established in 1956 to provide the business community with a collective voice to address the problems of the downtown area. Formed by Holman Pettibone, chairman of the Chicago Title and Trust Company, the CCAC included representatives from the city's leading corporate, real estate, and financial sectors.[2]

Business leaders initially kept the new mayor at arm's length, and understandably so. Daley hailed from the working-class neighborhood of Bridgeport on Chicago's South Side, a world miles apart from the exclusive North Shore communities where many of the city's top business executives resided. He was a loyal machine politician, having risen dutifully through the ranks of the Democratic party from precinct captain to chairman of the Cook County Democratic Central Committee, the party's top position. Such accomplishments meant nothing to business leaders. In their eyes Daley was a ward heeler, whose tenure as mayor would likely be marked by the same corruption, fiscal irresponsibility, and lack of vision for which previous machine mayors had won well-deserved reputations (Greer 1983, 121).

However, Daley soon proved he was no party hack. He filled cabinet positions and department directorships with respected professionals lacking political ties to the machine, prompting the *New York Times* to praise the new mayor as a "reformer at heart" (Biles 1995, 45). Daley quickly made downtown revitalization the economic development priority of his administration, establishing a new Department of City Planning in 1957 to coordinate and oversee his new building program. By 1964, the department's budget had ballooned from $149,500 to $914,500, while staffing increased from twenty-four to eighty-four employees (Biles 1995, 47). Several new downtown office buildings, the first to be constructed in over twenty years, were completed barely two years into Daley's fledgling mayoralty, followed soon by many others. These actions rapidly earned Daley the loyalty and respect of the downtown business elite, allowing him to cement a progrowth alliance. By paying top wages to city workers and providing thousands of jobs for the construction trades, Daley also incorporated organized labor as a junior partner in the coalition. As a result, Chicago experienced little of the labor unrest that crippled many other cities during the 1960s and 1970s.

Mayor Daley accomplished his planning and development objectives as successfully as he did due in large part to his skillful use of the machine. By holding the offices of mayor of Chicago and chairman of the Cook County

Democratic Central Committee simultaneously, Daley amassed an unprece-
dented degree of power, quickly whipping an undisciplined city council into
line.[3] As mayor and party chair, Daley himself controlled roughly thirty
thousand patronage jobs and had a key voice in the slating of Democratic
candidates for office (Rakove 1975, 112). Rebellious council members lost
patronage employees and were not slated for reelection by the party. With
the city's formal and informal political authority concentrated in the
Mayor's Office, favored redevelopment projects sailed through the city bureaucracy. In some cases, a brief visit by a developer to the mayor accomplished what under previous administrations would have required months or
even years of painstaking navigation through various layers of city government (O'Connor 1975, 137). Under Daley's leadership, Chicago earned its
reputation as "the city that works."

More problematic was Daley's electoral coalition, consisting of middle-
class white ethnic voters from the city's Northwest and Southwest Sides and
lower-income black voters from the South and West Sides. Throughout Daley's twenty-one-year reign as mayor of Chicago, two key sources of tension
threatening the integrity of this coalition had to be carefully held in check.
The first was caused by the administration's overwhelming policy emphasis
on redevelopment activities in the central business district. In general, the
residents of Chicago's lower-income and working-class neighborhoods stood
to gain little from Mayor Daley's downtown redevelopment efforts. Some, in
fact, had much to lose, particularly those located near the downtown area,
since the city's plans to surround the Loop with a ring of middle- and upper-
income neighborhoods could not be realized until the homes and industries
occupying these areas were removed.

The second cause of tension stemmed from divisions between the black
and white factions of the machine's electoral coalition itself. Following World
War II, much of Chicago's rapidly growing African-American population was
squeezed into a six-square-mile Black Belt on the city's Near South Side.
Overcrowding caused living conditions in the black ghetto to deteriorate
rapidly during the 1950s and 1960s, creating tremendous pressure for access
by African Americans to housing markets in the surrounding white ethnic
communities (Kleppner 1985, 40–41). Whites, however, motivated by racism
and fear of declining property values, resisted efforts on the part of blacks to
purchase or rent housing in their neighborhoods. School integration, another
point of contention by the early 1960s, was also opposed by many whites
(Biles 1995, 97–101). As racial tensions continued to mount during the
1960s, it became clear that the machine's biracial coalition could be preserved only to the extent that divisive racial issues could be kept out of the
municipal policy arena (Kleppner 1985, 71).

In managing these two potential threats to his electoral coalition, Mayor
Daley's skillful handling of the machine once again served him well. Soon af-

ter taking office, Daley undertook significant steps to increase the ranks of his patronage army of city employees, hiring an additional 2,500 policemen, 800 firemen, and 500 sanitation workers (Biles 1995, 46). By emphasizing patronage jobs, improved city services, and other discretionary favors and rewards in his dealings with the neighborhoods, Daley discouraged group mobilization around collective demands. Electoral politics became a politics of the individual, structured around patronage and selective incentives (Ferman 1991). Low-income blacks, with few opportunities for material gain outside the machine, became Daley's strongest supporters even though he steadfastly ignored calls for racial fairness (Kleppner 1985, 71). Likewise, voters from both white ethnic and African-American neighborhoods were strong machine supporters despite Daley's one-dimensional policy emphasis on downtown redevelopment (Ferman 1991).

## Redevelopment Phase One: The 1958 Development Plan

Mayor Daley's downtown redevelopment goals were set in motion with the help of several key land-use plans for the central area. The first was the *Development Plan for the Central Area of Chicago* issued by the Department of City Planning in 1958, which proposed to anchor the Loop's corporate and retail sectors with a series of public and private improvements in the downtown and greater downtown areas of the city (Department of City Planning 1958). Under the plan, 130 acres of underutilized railyards south of the Loop were to be cleared to make room for a new University of Illinois campus on the Near South Side. New government buildings were to be constructed on both the north and south ends of the Loop as additional barriers to surrounding blight. To improve access to the downtown area, the plan contained proposals for a network of expressways linking the central business district with outlying portions of the metropolitan area, along with new parking facilities on the periphery of the Loop. Finally, planners recommended construction of middle-income housing for up to 50,000 families in areas immediately north and south of the Loop. Housing was to be privately developed on land assembled and cleared by the city under powers of the 1949 U.S. Housing and Redevelopment Act.

There was little mention of central area manufacturers in the 1958 Development Plan. Several square miles west of the central business district from Halsted Street to Ashland Avenue were set aside under the plan for light industrial and commercial uses. However, virtually all central area industrial land south of the Loop, including Printing House Row, was designated for "residential re-use" and the future University of Illinois campus. Likewise, the plan's long-range projections for extensive residential development north of the Chicago River did not bode well for the occupants of industrial loft buildings concentrated in the River North area.

The postindustrial thrust of the 1958 Development Plan comes as no real surprise, given the close working relationship that was evolving between the downtown business community (as represented by the CCAC) and Mayor Daley's planning and development staff.[4] A series of reports issued by the Mayor's Council of Manpower and Economic Advisors and the Department of Development and Planning during the 1960s and 1970s contain a similar theme, remarkably consistent with the economic development preferences of downtown business leaders (see Department of Development and Planning 1967; Mayor's Council of Manpower and Economic Advisors 1974, 1977; Greer 1983, 106). According to these reports, national economic trends were encouraging the flight of industry from cities like Chicago. The decline of manufacturing was inevitable, but Chicago's economic vitality could be restored if appropriate steps were taken to encourage the growth of high-level professional, technical, and financial services. For city planning officials and their allies in the downtown business community, citywide economic development would, in future, necessarily emanate more exhaustively from the city's downtown commercial core. Basic economic trends made it increasingly unnecessary and futile for city government to make painful choices between support for industrial or commercial growth. Manufacturing was dying or dead; economic development would have to become increasingly synonymous with downtown commercial growth.

The coalition forged between the Daley administration and the CCAC was largely successful in reversing the long decline in downtown real estate activity. Between 1962 and 1977, 32 million square feet of new office space were added to the central business district, servicing a growing demand for centrally located corporate administrative facilities and professional service firms (Weiss and Metzgar 1989, 135). A new University of Illinois campus was built just west of the site proposed in the 1958 Development Plan, despite protests by Near West Side residents and business owners located in the construction path (Rosen 1980). By 1964, in addition, the first major effort to open up the downtown area for large-scale middle- and upper-income residential development was in place. Marina City's two 60-story towers along the north bank of the Chicago River contained 896 residential units, along with shopping facilities, restaurants, and a movie theater.

## Redevelopment Phase Two: The Chicago 21 Plan

Despite the magnitude and expediency of the Daley administration's early redevelopment efforts, by the late 1960s it was becoming painfully clear to members of Chicago's growth coalition that their long-term revitalization plans for the central area were being threatened by a number of unanticipated new developments. For one thing, demolition and rising real estate assessments were beginning to put pressure on the small retail shops and places of entertainment that helped keep downtown streets alive, particularly after business hours. Between 1968 and 1972, the central business district lost 13 percent of its small retailers, 15 percent of its entertainment spots, and 8 percent of its restaurants (Berry et al. 1976, 75). For another, the rapidly changing demographic balance in the Chicago metropolitan area—suburbanization of whites accompanied by a growing inner-city African-American population—was leading to an increase in the ratio of black to white pedestrian traffic downtown. Business leaders typically assumed there was a "tipping point," well below 50 percent black, after which whites would begin staying away altogether (Gapp 1973). As one prominent real estate developer put it at the time, "I'll tell you what's wrong with the Loop. It's people's conception of it. And the conception they have about it is one word: Black. B-L-A-C-K. Black" (Greer 1983, 140).

These concerns ultimately prompted a sequence of closed monthly meetings between Daley administration planning officials and key representatives of the CCAC (Greer 1983, 133). Informing these discussions were a series of commercial, residential, and industrial land-use studies for the central area undertaken by two private consulting firms, the Real Estate Research Corporation (RERC) and Barton-Aschman Associates, under contract with the City of Chicago (Real Estate Research Corporation 1970; Barton-Aschman Associates 1970). According to these reports, the current problems of the downtown area stemmed largely from the "unsound" relationship that existed between the central business district and its immediate surroundings. Land given over to low-income housing and industrial uses in neighborhoods bordering the Loop did nothing to enhance the development of corporate and retail activity in the central business district and in some cases actively undermined it. The viability of the downtown commercial core could be best protected by surrounding the area with middle- and upper-income residential communities, providing downtown corporations with a nearby pool of workers to draw from and downtown retail establishments, restaurants, and places of entertainment with ready markets. This had been an important, though largely unrealized, goal of the 1958 Development Plan. It was now time to reposition it to the center of the city's planning agenda for the central area.[5]

Fortunately, according to the RERC and Barton-Aschman plans, the costs associated with such a transformation would be minimal, because land use in much of the greater downtown area was already in flux. Industry, in particular, was said to be in decline due to economic forces largely "exogenous to the central communities and the city of Chicago" (Real Estate Research Corporation 1970, 14). Echoing similar arguments by the Mayor's Council of Manpower and Economic Advisors and the city's Department of Development and Planning, RERC warned officials against "futile and wasteful efforts" to retain industries in the central communities. Policies should be designed instead to "prepare the city of Chicago and the central communities for their eventual relocation" (Real Estate Research Corporation 1970, 21).

The monthly meetings between administration planning officials and CCAC representatives continued for several years, culminating in the 1973 publication of *Chicago 21: A Plan for the Central Area Communities.* Though published by the CCAC itself, the plan credited twelve City of Chicago agencies with consulting roles and opened with an introduction by Mayor Daley, symbolizing the well-integrated public-private partnership that the Daley administration had fostered around downtown redevelopment. The findings and recommendations of the Chicago 21 Plan were generally consistent with the views expressed in the Barton-Aschman and RERC land-use studies: the upgrading of the central business district was to be the linchpin of citywide economic development, and the physical deterioration and "economic obsolescence" of industrial and residential areas surrounding the Loop were the major obstacles to be overcome. Once again, emphasis was placed on calls for a ring of stable residential communities to surround the city's downtown business core.

The centerpiece of the Chicago 21 Plan was a proposal for a "new town in town" called Dearborn Park that would eventually house up to 120,000 middle-income residents on a 600-acre site south of the central business district. The southern boundary of the Loop had long been a sore spot for city planners and business leaders alike, due mainly to its proximity to Chicago's Near South Side black ghetto. The 1958 Development Plan originally proposed to anchor this site with the city's new University of Illinois campus, but difficulties with land assembly prompted planning officials to choose a Near West Side location for the university instead, leaving the southern end of the Loop unprotected. The new South Loop residential development would, it was hoped, serve two purposes by creating an effective barrier between the central business district and low-income communities on the Near South Side and spurring further transformation of near-downtown areas to middle- and upper-income residential communities (Emmons 1977; Suttles 1990, 180–186).

Construction of the first phase of the new Dearborn Park housing development began in 1978. Land assembly was financed and promoted by Chicago 21, a limited dividend corporation whose board members included some of the city's most prominent business leaders.[6] Investor profits were capped at a 6.5 percent annual return to keep the cost of Dearborn Park homes within reach of the middle-income families seen as the backbone of the new community (Emmons 1977, 15). In spite of the low returns, however, the Chicago 21 Corporation had no trouble lining up investors within the downtown business community. The reason for this, according to a study of the development undertaken by the Citizens Information Service of Illinois, is straightforward:

The appeal is not to profits as such but institutional self-interest. For large firms headquartered in the Loop with substantial investments in land and buildings, [Dearborn Park] offers a source of nearby housing for its employees, retail buyers for its stores, and frequenters for its restaurants and theaters. It assures the presence of whites at a time when blacks are increasingly users of the Loop. It offers a stimulus to redevelopment of the Loop's deteriorated southern fringe. And it provides what the developers term "a more secure environment to all of the Loop." (Emmons 1977, 16)

Although the size of the project was eventually pared down considerably, Dearborn Park was probably the strongest affirmation yet of the viability of the downtown area for middle-income residential development. Within one year after the first phase of the project was completed in 1979, 128 of the development's 144 town houses were occupied (Enstad 1980). By 1986, the complex had 1,500 housing units, with few vacancies, and plans to launch a second phase to include another 1,300 to 1,700 units immediately south of the existing development site were underway (Suttles 1990, 175).

Following closely on the heels of Dearborn Park were several additional large-scale downtown residential developments. River City, located several blocks west of Dearborn Park along the Chicago River, added 2,500 more dwelling units to the South Loop. In the West Loop, the construction of Presidential Towers on two square blocks assembled and cleared by the Chicago Land Clearance Commission created 2,460 additional units of middle- and upper-income living space, ready for occupancy by 1985. Conversion of the industrial loft space south and west of the Loop to residential and commercial uses closely tracks these three residential developments. By one estimate, 99 percent of South Loop loft dwellers moved in only after Dearborn Park broke ground (Suttles 1990, 175). Of the twenty-six loft conversions undertaken in the West Loop between 1979 and 1990, only two were carried out before groundbreaking for Presidential Towers began in August 1983 (Ludgin and Masotti 1985, 1986; Ludgin 1989).

Much of this development took place after Daley's death in 1976, but it was the framework created by his administration's planning efforts that ultimately made it possible. City planning under the Daley administration was focused overwhelmingly around one goal—economic growth. It was economic growth that cemented the alliance between the administration and the CCAC, making it unsurprising that administration officials came to share the view of business elites that the downtown commercial center should serve as the primary engine of citywide economic development. Once it became clear to Daley's planning staff that the vitality of the downtown business core required middle- and upper-income families and office workers to occupy areas being utilized at the time by small- and medium-sized industries, they were unwavering in their support for commercial and residential redevelopment. Indeed, they saw little conflict in this. For them, the choice was not between two viable trajectories of growth but between growth and stagnation.

## Capital Improvomcnts and Business Subsidies

Chicago's postwar downtown revitalization plans were put into practice in large part through a combination of carefully placed capital improvements and business subsidies designed to facilitate private commercial and residential redevelopment activity in the downtown area. Capital improvements are public investments in the basic infrastructure of a municipality for projects such as street and expressway construction and repairs, bridge and viaduct improvements, mass transit, and water and sewer systems. They also include public buildings like hospitals, universities, and courthouses. Such projects can leverage private investment by increasing the value of nearby land parcels, making such properties more attractive to developers. The reverse, however, also holds—areas suffering from public disinvestment are likely to experience private disinvestment as well.[7]

The Daley administration's early planning efforts were organized around an extensive set of public improvements designed to help rekindle private investment activity in the city's downtown commercial core. In the administration's five-year capital improvements budget for 1959–1963, 20 percent of citywide capital investments were targeted for a handful of projects identified in the 1958 *Development Plan for the Central Area of Chicago* (Department of City Planning 1959). These included the completion of a network of expressways linking the central business district with outlying suburban communities and the national interstate highway system ($148 million); the construction of a civil courts building and a new city-county office building in the Loop ($65 million); a new exposition center, McCormick Place, along the lakefront just south of the central business district ($33 million); land acquisition and construction of the initial stage of the Chicago campus of the University of Illinois ($54 million); and the clearance of 744 acres of land designated as "blighted" by the Chicago Land Clearance Commission ($79 million).[8]

The downtown emphasis of public capital investments continued for the duration of Daley's tenure as mayor of Chicago, culminating in the city's 1977–1981 capital budget, which committed nearly $1.1 billion to the downtown area alone for such projects as the new State Street mall, the conversion of Navy Pier to a new recreational and shopping area, and the upgrading of the city's lakefront museums (Department of Planning 1978).[9] The budget designated the new Dearborn Park residential development in the South Loop as one of thirty-nine "community improvement project areas" to receive an average of $2.3 million each for street and sidewalk repairs, landscaping, and other improvements. Between 1979 and 1990, public capital investments in Dearborn Park and Printing House Row combined would ultimately rise to nearly $50 million, leveraging some $700 million in private investment funds (Ludgin 1989, 17).

Aside from their beneficial effects on downtown development, capital improvements also have a major impact on the viability of central city industrial districts, where manufacturers are dependent upon city government to provide, to maintain, and to upgrade basic infrastructure. For example, low overpasses and viaducts may, in some instances, force large trucks to take time-consuming detours in order to reach local industries, delaying shipments and increasing freight transportation costs. Restrictive load limits for bridges and streets present similar difficulties. Narrow inner-city streets create loading and unloading problems, while traffic congestion increases delivery times. In some cases, sewer and water lines may be in need of repair. The extent to which a municipality undertakes basic infrastructure improvements in industrial areas of the city can thus have an important effect on the prospects for manufacturing in such locations.

Studies of the locational patterns of Chicago industrial firms carried out by the Department of City Planning during the early years of the Daley administration show that, already by the late 1950s, the central area was losing manufacturing firms to outlying areas of the city and suburban communities (Department of City Planning 1960, 1961). According to these studies, firms leaving the central area in favor of other city locations were congregating along two industrial corridors extending northwest and southwest from the downtown area. City officials blamed economic factors such as high central area land prices and the obsolescence of multistory production facilities for these locational shifts. However, an examination of the Daley administration's capital budget for the late 1950s and early 1960s suggests that the City of Chicago was an active participant in the process.

Table 1 shows the administration's 1959–1963 budget for bridges and viaducts, street improvements, and sewers in three areas of the city: the central area (excluding the Loop), the northwest and southwest industrial corridors combined, and the Loop.[10] These are the kinds of public investments central city manufacturers required if they were to remain competitive with firms located in modern suburban facilities. Table 1 shows that the central area was highly underrepresented in two of the three categories of basic infrastructure projects—street improvements and sewer construction and repair—while the northwest and southwest corridors were overrepresented. Although comprising just under 30 percent of the total geographical area covered by the three industrial districts, the central area received no funding whatsoever for sewer improvements, 8 percent of funds allocated for street repairs, and only 16 percent of total investment dollars. Given this dearth of public investments for industrial infrastructure in the near-downtown area, it is not surprising that manufacturers began to seek new production space elsewhere.

By the 1970s, public capital improvements in the central area rose measurably, but by this time such projects were increasingly designed to leverage private commercial and residential investment rather than industrial development in this part of the city.[11] As Table 2 indicates, capital-investment priorities shifted in favor of both the Loop and non Loop portions of the central area by the late 1970s. Meanwhile, public spending for industrial infrastructure in the northwest and southwest industrial corridors, still used predominantly for manufacturing by then, fell by substantial amounts during the 1960s and 1970s. Ultimately, the pattern from the late 1950s onward became one of consistent neglect in the funding of capital improvements for industrial areas, while portions of the city perceived to be hubs of commercial and upscale residential development benefitted from heavy concentrations of public funds.

**Table 1.** Budgeted Capital Improvements
for Basic Infrastructure in Three Locations, 1959–1963

| District | Percent of Total Area | Bridges and Viaducts | Streets | Sewers | Total |
|---|---|---|---|---|---|
| Central Area (excluding Loop) | 27 | $14,300 | $730 | $ — | $15,030 |
| NW and SW Industrial Corridors | 69 | $35,660 | $8,490 | $32,665 | $76,815 |
| Loop | 4 | $5,700 | $100 | $1,020 | $6,820 |
| **Total** | **100** | **$55,660** | **$9,320** | **$33,685** | **$98,665** |

*Source:* Department of City Planning (1959).  *Note:* Dollar amounts are in thousands.

## Urban Development Action Grants

In addition to the private investment dollars leveraged through its capital improvements programs, the City of Chicago also influenced the trajectory of downtown redevelopment through several federally funded grant and loan programs. Beginning in 1978, the U.S. Department of Housing and Urban Development (HUD) initiated the Urban Development Action Grant (UDAG) program to help stimulate economic development in urban areas experiencing severe economic distress.[12] Private investors participating in the program received at least $1.00 in UDAG funds for every $2.50 in private investment committed to a proposed new development. City government played a key role in determining which projects received UDAG funding, since program eligibility requirements stipulated that private investors persuade city officials to sponsor their projects and submit applications to HUD on their behalf. Investors were also required to demonstrate that market forces alone were insufficient to make their projects workable.

Between 1979 and 1986, the City of Chicago was awarded fifty-eight UDAGs worth a total of $98 million. An analysis of the UDAG program carried out by the University of Illinois at Chicago reveals that a large share of UDAG funds were concentrated in Chicago's central area, many for the conversion of industrial loft buildings to various commercial and residential uses (Wright 1987). According to the study, 49 percent of Chicago development

**Table 2.** Budgeted Capital Improvements
for Basic Infrastructure in Three Locations, 1977–1981

| District | Percent of Total Area | Bridges and Viaducts | Streets | Sewers | Total |
|---|---|---|---|---|---|
| Central Area (excluding Loop) | 27 | $34,000 | $2,554 | $4,606 | $41,160 |
| NW and SW Industrial Corridors | 69 | $10,895 | $5,024 | $12,563 | $28,482 |
| Loop | 4 | $81,819 | $57,039 | $440 | $139,298 |
| Total | 100 | $126,714 | $64,617 | $17,609 | $208,940 |

*Source:* Department of Planning (1978). *Note:* Dollar amounts are in thousands.

projects relying on UDAG support from 1979 to 1986 were located in the Loop and surrounding area. In the South Loop, three of Printing House Row's twelve industrial loft buildings were converted to residential developments with the assistance of $6.8 million in UDAG funds. The nearby Dearborn Park and River City residential developments received another $5.1 million through the UDAG program (Wright 1987, 10). On the Near West Side, seven of nine UDAG-sponsored projects involved the conversion of industrial buildings to commercial lofts, with $4.2 million in UDAG funds leveraging a total of $43 million worth of private investment (Wright 1987,

15). According to the study's principal author, Patricia Wright, the absence of a coherent city policy for the sponsorship of UDAG-funded economic development projects enabled property developers to dominate the program in Chicago, causing funds to be concentrated in commercial and residential redevelopment projects in the central area (Wright 1987, 31).

## Industrial Revenue Bonds

The preoccupation of city officials with the promotion of commercial and residential growth in the downtown area of the city did not cause them to neglect manufacturing entirely. Beginning in 1977 under the administration of Richard J. Daley's successor Michael Bilandic, the Department of Economic Development began offering low-interest Industrial Revenue Bonds (IRBs) to assist companies seeking to relocate, to expand, or to improve their facilities within the city of Chicago. From 1977 to 1984, when changes in federal tax laws led to major cutbacks in the program, 102 Chicago firms received a total of $187 million in loans through the IRB program (Clemons, Giloth, and Tostado 1985, 17). Due to IRB guidelines that weighted the program in favor of manufacturers, 74 percent of IRB recipients were manufacturing firms (Clemons, Giloth, and Tostado 1985, 2).

The IRB program provided badly needed financial support for certain Chicago manufacturers, yet it also played a significant role in the deindustrialization of the central area. Program specifications placed a $500,000 minimum restriction on bond amounts, skewing the distribution of IRBs toward larger firms that could afford the bonds.[13] Smaller manufacturers, meanwhile, were denied access to credit. Sectors dominated by small- to medium-sized firms such as printing, apparel, and fabricated metals that made up the bulk of central area manufacturing establishments were underrepresented in the program (Clemons, Giloth, and Tostado 1985, 15). Although central area firms did receive a substantial share of total IRB dollars, bond recipients there were primarily larger firms from sectors such as primary metals and chemical and allied products with few strong ties to the near-downtown area. Not surprisingly, many such firms used the bonds to relocate elsewhere in the city, freeing up land for new commercial and residential development. Intentionally or not, IRBs thus became another tool in the city's effort to remove industry from the central area.

## Zoning for Commercial and Residential Redevelopment

Land-use plans, capital investments, and business subsidies all had an enormous impact on the trajectory of postwar economic development in Chicago's central area. However, the remaking of downtown Chicago could not have been accomplished without appropriate changes to the city zoning ordinance. Zoning laws give development plans their teeth, setting detailed guidelines for the types of land use permissible in a given area of the city. The Chicago Zoning Ordinance maps the city into separate districts for residential, commercial, and industrial uses, although the separation of categories is, in practice, rarely so neat. In theory, Chicago's zoning laws are intended both "to protect residential, business, and manufacturing areas alike from harmful encroachment by incompatible uses" and to "conserve and enhance" the value of private property, goals not always easily reconcilable (Committee on Buildings and Zoning 1955a, 3–4). When the two principles collide, the final interpretation of the city zoning ordinance is as likely as not to become an exercise in local power politics.

Chicago's first zoning ordinance was passed by city council on April 5, 1923. Since then, the council's Committee on Buildings and Zoning has produced two comprehensive amendments to the ordinance, first in 1942 and once again in 1957, two years after Richard J. Daley was elected mayor. The 1957 Comprehensive Amendment was inspired by many of the same fears and concerns that prompted the 1958 *Development Plan for the Central Area of Chicago,* namely, stagnation and falling property values in the Loop and growing blight in the surrounding communities.[14] Both the tone and provisions of the amendment closely anticipate the postindustrial thrust of the 1958 Development Plan. For the central area, zoning was to be a tool to regulate and encourage the construction of downtown office space (Meltzer 1963, 1). An interim amendment to the zoning ordinance adopted in 1962 extended this emphasis to residential development as well (Meltzer 1963, 3).

Central area manufacturers, by contrast, received little in the way of zoning protections or incentives under the new amendment because their exodus from the downtown area was viewed as a foregone conclusion. According to a 1952 study of industrial land use prepared by the Chicago Plan Commission in anticipation of the 1957 rezoning, "such features as obsolete buildings, inadequate space, congested streets, and surrounding blight have placed the Central Area in a poor position to hold existing industries or attract new ones" (Chicago Plan Commission 1952, 2). The report's principal recommendation was the rezoning for industrial purposes of 1,300 acres of largely vacant land in outlying areas of the city to foster long-term industrial development in portions of the city deemed more suitable for such activities.

Ultimately, the 1957 Comprehensive Amendment designated roughly half of the central area property devoted to manufacturing as one of three subtypes of commercial districts. Commercial districts are the most flexible of the city's four primary zoning classifications, allowing various types of office and residential development, in addition to light manufacturing. The argument by city planners was that land-use patterns were still unresolved in portions of the central area. Flexible zoning in such areas would give "market forces" time to develop before more definitive land-use controls were put into effect (Mayor's

Committee for Economic and Cultural Development 1966, 37–39). In practice, this left many central area manufacturers largely unprotected from developers hoping to profit from a change in land use, since many conversions from industrial to both office and residential development could take place in commercially zoned areas with no zoning changes whatsoever.

For firms engaged in heavy manufacturing, the 1957 rezoning had more immediate ramifications. All such enterprises unlucky enough to find themselves in areas rezoned as commercial or residential districts now became "nonconforming uses" under the 1957 Comprehensive Amendment. Business owners were required to cease operation within a limited time period or face condemnation of their property. This regulation had been included in the previous comprehensive amendment as well, but generous grace periods for phasing out nonconforming uses substantially weakened the provision's impact.[15] By 1957, the city's tolerance of "industrial nuisances" had waned considerably. Under the new amendment, nonconforming manufacturing uses in newly designated commercial or residential districts were given as little as four years to shut down (Committee on Buildings and Zoning 1955b, 48a–50a).[16]

The 1957 Comprehensive Amendment also introduced important changes in the methodology used for evaluating the nuisance-creating potential posed by a given manufacturing establishment. Previously, industries had been assigned to one of two types of manufacturing districts, based exclusively on the type of product produced. Light industrial activities such as printing and woodworking were permitted uses in one such district, while noisier, dirtier operations like chemical production were assigned to another. Under the new amendment, the type of product produced became irrelevant. Instead, new "scientific" performance standards were established using such criteria as noise, vibrations, and emissions as a means of segregating industrial uses. Three new types of manufacturing districts were established, the highest set of standards reserved for producers located near the boundaries of residential or business districts.[17]

Though hailed by city officials as a way of encouraging manufacturers to "clean house," manufacturers themselves protested the changes, arguing that the proposed new controls would ultimately drive industry out of the city (Babcock 1972, 100). These fears, as it turned out, were not unfounded. Higher performance standards faced by industries located in close proximity to commercially and residentially zoned property acted as a wedge for residential and commercial incursion into manufacturing districts. In the central area, as various borderline properties ultimately became unsuitable for manufacturing under the new ordinance or went on the market for other reasons, developers often found it relatively easy to acquire them, obtain a zoning change from the city, and redevelop them for commercial or residential uses (Giloth and Betancur 1988; Babcock and Larsen 1990). In each case, a new set of manufacturers suddenly found themselves on the boundaries of newly expanded commercial or residential zones, subject to—and quite possibly out of compliance with—a more stringent set of industrial performance standards than before. At that point, the process was set to begin all over again.

The new performance standards and reduced time periods for the elimination of nonconforming uses might not have posed such a threat to central area manufacturers if zoning changes were more difficult to procure. Such changes, however, have long been commonplace. Although the last comprehensive amendment to the Chicago Zoning Ordinance was drafted in 1957, city council has approved literally hundreds of petitions for minor amendments to the ordinance since then. Indeed, some of the heaviest concentrations of industrial loft conversions during the 1970s and 1980s took place in two areas, River North and the Westgate Mill area of the Near West Side, which were still zoned exclusively for manufacturing under the 1957 Comprehensive Amendment (Ludgin and Masotti 1985, 1986). By 1980, incremental changes to the zoning ordinance had removed the last restrictions against commercial or residential use in both of these districts, along with most of the remaining portions of the central area.

A petition for a change to the city zoning ordinance in a particular ward is typically introduced by the alderman of the affected ward, often at the request of a ward constituent. Following review and recommendations by the city zoning administrator and the Department of Planning and Development, the City Council Committee on Buildings and Zoning schedules public hearings on the proposed change. Final approval of the change requires a favorable vote of at least two-thirds of city council (Committee on Buildings and Zoning 1955b, 121a–123a).

Within Chicago city government, there is a longstanding tradition of deference to aldermen on matters affecting their individual wards. With respect to zoning issues, this means that an alderman's recommendation for a zoning change in his or her own ward will rarely be challenged by the Mayor's Office or by fellow council members (Gardiner and Lyman 1978). This tradition dates back at least to the years of the Daley machine. While Daley generally centralized decision-making on policies affecting the city as a whole, he recognized the importance of aldermanic discretion at the neighborhood level for purposes of machine-building. Regulatory relief in such matters as zoning decisions or building inspections, along with patronage appointments and city service provision, were the currency of politics during the machine years. Aldermen cemented party loyalties by selectively allocating such favors and rewards among ward constituents (Rakove 1975). As long as a particular alderman was loyal to the mayor and votes for the machine were being delivered in the ward in question, Daley was unlikely to interfere in something as minor as a zoning variance, particularly if it involved a change to a "higher and better" use of land.

In practice, the combination of aldermanic discretion and standards for amending the city zoning ordinance, "so vague as to provide no guidance to developers, the citizenry, or the decisionmakers," left the direction of central area zoning after 1957 largely in the hands of ward aldermen and private developers (Phillip Zeitlin Associates 1982, 94). Not until the mid-1980s would remaining central area manufacturers achieve sufficient organizational capacity to make a difference in city zoning policy. Until then, the steady, incremental conversion of central area manufacturing districts to new commercially and residentially zoned areas made a mockery of at least one of the city zoning ordinance's primary stated objectives—to protect residents, businesses, and manufacturers alike from incursion by incompatible land uses.

## The Chicago Rehabilitation Code

Efforts to convert near-downtown industrial loft buildings to housing or office space were given a significant boost in 1982, when the new Chicago Rehabilitation Code was incorporated into the city's building code. Before 1982, the City of Chicago did not have a rehabilitation code. Specifications for new construction, as well as the maintenance, repair, and rehabilitation of existing buildings, were all contained in one municipal building code. Building code regulations stem from concerns over fire protection, general safety, and hygiene. To the extent that they impose higher standards—and thus higher costs—for building rehabilitation, they act as a disincentive for the conversion of industrial loft space to alternative uses. By all accounts, the rehabilitation provisions of Chicago's building code were exceptionally high before the passage of the city's new rehabilitation code in 1982 (Metropolitan Housing and Planning Council 1980).

Ironically, the architect of Chicago's demanding building rehabilitation standards was none other than Richard J. Daley himself. Rigorous construction standards for building rehabilitation were initiated under the Daley administration and upheld through the mayor's largely successful efforts to institutionalize the policymaking process for updating the building code.[18] In 1964, Mayor Daley assembled a group of architects, engineers, building managers, and labor officials, along with representatives from the Department of Buildings, the Fire Department, and other city agencies to serve on his new Mayor's Advisory Committee for revising the building code (Jones 1985, 27). The committee provided a forum for various interested parties to reach negotiated solutions on code amendments. Its recommendations were submitted to city council with the endorsement of the mayor, which, during the Daley years, virtually ensured passage. Through his authority to appoint and to dismiss committee members, Daley exercised considerable power over the amendment process. At the same time, his lack of active participation allowed him to remain aloof from the politically controversial decisions taking place in the committee (Jones 1985, 34).

To a large extent, rigorous construction standards for building rehabilitation remained a fixture of building-code amendments under the Daley administration because most of the architects and developers represented on the Mayor's Advisory Committee came from large firms involved with the design and construction of new buildings downtown rather than from smaller firms focusing on the rehabilitation of existing buildings.[19] The large developers on the committee were, for the most part, indifferent to the rehabilitation provisions of the code. By contrast, committee members from city agencies such as the Fire Prevention Bureau, who saw the building code as an important vehicle for promoting fire safety and upgrading the city's housing stock, consistently argued for tough rehabilitation standards. With little opposition voiced by the private sector participants on the committee, revisions of the code during the 1960s and 1970s consistently incorporated the city bureaucrats' demands for stringent rehabilitation provisions (Jones 1985, 35–36).

During the Daley years, there was very little disruption to this exclusive bargaining system for amending the building code. Daley's control of patronage and the slating of candidates for office guaranteed broad-based support for his programs in city council. Disaffected rehabilitation contractors excluded from the Mayor's Advisory Committee could always take their concerns directly to the council, but the strong aldermanic support that Daley commanded discouraged them from doing so. Moreover, throughout most of Daley's tenure as mayor, groups favoring more lenient rehabilitation standards were largely disorganized and, for the most part, politically nonthreatening.

Shortly before Daley's death, however, coalition building among various rehabilitation forces began to occur. In 1976, the Ad Hoc Working Committee for Residential Rehabilitation was formed through the joint efforts of the Chicago chapter of the American Institute of Architects and the Chicago Rehab Network, a community organization involved with the rehabilitation of housing in low-income city neighborhoods (Metropolitan Housing and Planning Council 1980, 2). The committee issued a report in 1978 criticizing the rehabilitation provisions of the existing building code and calling for more lenient construction standards for residential rehabilitation (Ad Hoc Working Committee for Residential Rehabilitation 1978). During the next several years, the committee continued to broaden its membership base, eventually attracting such politically connected groups as the Committee for Legal Lofts, a coalition of architects and developers who together controlled five million square feet of central area loft space, including much of Printing House Row (Washburn 1981).

By 1979, the voices favoring relaxed rehabilitation standards had grown sufficiently loud that newly elected Mayor Jane Byrne was compelled to recognize them. Shortly after taking office in April 1979, Byrne assembled a thirty-member committee chaired by former building commissioner Joseph Fitzgerald to write what would become the city's first rehabilitation code. The committee submitted its final report to the mayor in October 1981. With Byrne's approval, the Chicago Rehabilitation Code was passed into law by city council in March 1982.[20]

Lacking the authority and centralized power base commanded by Mayor Daley, Byrne was unable to limit participation in the building-code revision process to the exclusive group represented in the Mayor's Advisory Committee for amending the code (Jones 1985, 39). The new rehabilitation code was a clear-cut victory for the one-time outsider coalition of rehabilitation groups and a major defeat for city bureaucrats concerned with fire protection standards and the upgrading of the city's housing stock. Previously, any developer wishing to convert a building to an alternative use had been obliged to bring the entire building up to modern code standards. Under the new code, only the remodeled portions of such projects had to meet modern construction standards. Fire exit requirements were liberalized as well, and the previous building height limitation of eighty feet for residential loft conversions was abolished. Finally, the new code authorized the mayor to appoint a seven-member board of appeals with the power to grant exceptions to code provisions. Significantly, no board members were to be drawn from the city bureaucracy.

Along with city bureaucrats, the other major losers in the debate over the new rehabilitation code were, of course, the small- to medium-sized manufacturers occupying much of the central area loft space in which the real estate community had recently taken such an interest. These manufacturers had been the unintended beneficiaries of city bureaucrats' longstanding insistence on stringent building rehabilitation standards. Strict code provisions had discouraged many industrial building owners from undertaking costly building conversions to higher-rent office or residential uses. By defending building safety standards, city bureaucrats were thus inadvertent participants in a deeper struggle over the nature of downtown production space.

However, once the coalition of rehabilitation groups gained access to the appropriate decision-making arena, forcing a public debate over the issue, the preoccupation of city bureaucrats with building safety alone meant that no one spoke publicly for the interests of the manufacturing community. The industries themselves, at this point still politically unsophisticated and largely disorganized, were hardly in a position to do so. Ultimately, the debate was cast as a dispute between meddlesome city bureaucrats and innovative developers seeking to bring life to a decaying downtown area.[21] Not only was this a confrontation city bureaucrats were unlikely to win, but the impact that the new rehabilitation code was destined to have on the future of downtown area industrial space went virtually unnoticed throughout the entire debate.

## Conclusion

Between 1955 and 1983, the central area of Chicago experienced an enormous economic upheaval. The mixture of industry, commerce, and low- to moderate-income residential communities that dominated the area in the early postwar years gave way to an entirely new agglomeration of corporate offices, business services, and upscale residential developments. Downtown area property values rose measurably, while centrally located industrial districts providing well-paying blue-collar jobs for city residents were dismantled piece by piece, block by block. By the time Chicago's last machine mayor, Jane Byrne, was defeated by Harold Washington in 1983, Chicago had assumed a prominent position in the hierarchy of global cities, its downtown the headquarters of twenty-six Fortune 500 companies and the location of the world's tallest building, the Sears Tower. In international banking, LaSalle Street was surpassed within the U.S. only by Wall Street, and Chicago's Board of Trade and Mercantile Exchange gave the city a decided edge over New York in commodities and futures trading (Squires et al. 1987, 38).

Urban political economists typically view the redevelopment of older industrial cities such as Chicago following World War II as a response to structural economic change. Downtown redevelopment and its counterpart, urban industrial decline, are said to be linked to a particular phase of capitalist development, featuring the hypermobility of capital, rapid technological change, and the persistence of regional and global variations in land and labor costs. Efforts to remake central business districts arise in response to structural economic shifts, taking place within the context of a division of labor between state and market under which private investors are afforded considerable autonomy. By most accounts, Chicago planning officials perceived a structural change in the city's economy from manufacturing to services and responded in kind with policy changes necessary to support economic growth on new terms.

Yet the narrative of downtown redevelopment presented in this chapter calls into question perspectives that draw such fine distinctions between politics and markets. The restructuring of Chicago's central area following World War II took place through the efforts of a progrowth alliance led by key segments of the downtown business community and city planning officials. Although structural economic changes were beginning to have an impact by the time this alliance was formed in the late 1950s, the evidence supporting a fundamental manufacturing-services shift at this early stage was, at best, slim. The more likely cause of the Daley administration's decision to embark on a downtown-oriented economic development strategy was ideological. City planners ultimately adopted the outlook of their allies within the business community, leading them to select a real estate-based growth strategy over potential alternatives.

The channeling of economic policy benefits into the hands of downtown property developers and other business leaders had to be legitimized in the eyes of neighborhood voters, who typically received few of the benefits of downtown growth and, in some instances, bore a disproportionate share of its costs. Part of the solution rested in machine politics. By structuring the electoral arena around patronage and selective incentives, machine politicians discouraged their constituents from identifying collectively as low- and moderate-income neighborhood residents threatened by economic development policies hostile to their interests. The other part rested in an ideology of privatism, whereby city officials argued forcefully that public policies supporting downtown redevelopment were formulated in response to well-defined patterns of private investment activity over which city government exercised little to no control.

As durable as this set of arrangements would prove to be, it was nonetheless crisis-prone. As we shall see in Chapter 4, growing tensions between the machine's governing and electoral coalitions and within the electoral coalition itself increasingly taxed the ability of machine leaders to hold the contradictions of growth politics in check. By the 1970s, near-downtown manufacturers, workers, and residents of neighborhoods decimated by industrial decline began to identify a common enemy in the progrowth alliance of city planning officials and downtown business elites. Increasingly, the individualistic politics of the machine gave way to coalition-building around a new set of policies designed to support an economically viable alternative to downtown redevelopment. Within this changing political context, possibilities for the construction of new regimes would begin to emerge.

# Chapter Three

# Rethinking Industrial Decline

## The Chicago Printing and Apparel Industries

I n the previous chapter, we saw how a progrowth alliance between city officials and downtown business leaders encouraged downtown redevelopment in postwar Chicago to follow a particular trajectory, one from which centrally located manufacturers were conspicuously absent. As yet, however, little evidence has been offered to suggest that there was a viable alternative to this. After all, city officials and their allies in the downtown business community justified the procorporate leanings of their redevelopment efforts by arguing that national and international economic trends marked the death of manufacturing in central cities. This argument rested on a seemingly firm empirical foundation: manufacturing employment began declining in Chicago and other major industrial cities shortly after the close of World War II. The possibility that the policies and programs described in Chapter 2 were simply nudging downtown area growth a little faster and more efficiently down the path it was destined to take cannot be dismissed out of hand.

This chapter asks two principal questions: First, to what extent did the central area of Chicago remain a viable site for industrial development in the years following World War II? Second, how specifically did public-policy decisions designed to foster commercial and residential redevelopment in the downtown area affect the prospects of central area manufacturers? The experiences of two prominent central area industrial sectors, the printing and apparel industries, will be analyzed to address these questions. These two sectors have been selected for a number of reasons. To begin with, they have long been among the top employers in the area. In 1962, central area printing establishments employed forty-eight thousand workers, over twice as many employees as any other sector there, while the apparel industry ranked third among central area employers with seventeen thousand workers (Real Estate Research Corporation 1970, 4). Taken together, employment in these two sectors alone accounted for 39 percent of all central area manufacturing employment in 1962.

In addition, these industries share certain features and exhibit certain patterns of behavior that distinguish them somewhat from many other types of manufacturers. In general, both printers and apparel manufacturers have shown more of a tendency to concentrate in the downtown and near-downtown areas of Chicago than industries from other sectors. As the following pages will suggest, this concentration stems in part from the relatively specialized products that the manufacturers of these two industries typically produce. In many cases, products are tailored to the specifications of downtown customers, and the manufacture of one item may involve a number of firms. Face-to-face consultation with downtown customers or subcontractors may be necessary at certain stages of the production process. Partly for this reason, producers in both sectors congregated at one time in readily identifiable districts. Chicago's printing and garment districts were, until quite recently, located within blocks of one another in the near-Loop area.

Put briefly, these two sectors appear to have had stronger ties to the central area of Chicago than any others, both before and after World War II. If the central area ultimately became an unprofitable or otherwise undesirable location for these producers independently of the downtown redevelopment efforts discussed in the previous chapter, it is unlikely that the experiences of manufacturers from other sectors would have been any different. Conversely, to the extent that the printing and apparel industries appear to have been viable industrial sectors undercut by unrepresentative public policies, it becomes possible to imagine a different scenario for downtown redevelopment than the one presented in Chapter 2. The hypothesis that politics played a decisive role in the deindustrialization of Chicago's central area becomes more plausible.

## The Chicago Printing Industry

Chicago's historical center of printing and publishing lies in an area of the South Loop bordered by Congress Parkway and Polk Streets to the north and south, and State and Clark Streets to the east and west (see Map 2). Between 1883 and 1912, Chicago's flourishing community of printing and publishing firms commissioned the design and construction of twenty-one loft structures and multifunction office buildings in the district, commonly known as Printing House Row. Several features of this area made it particularly attractive to the graphic communications industry. The first was the location of the Dearborn Street Railway Station at the district's southern boundary, providing firms with a direct link to producers and consumers nationwide. The second was the area's distinctive street layout, consisting of lengthy, narrow blocks unique to the downtown area. The loft structures

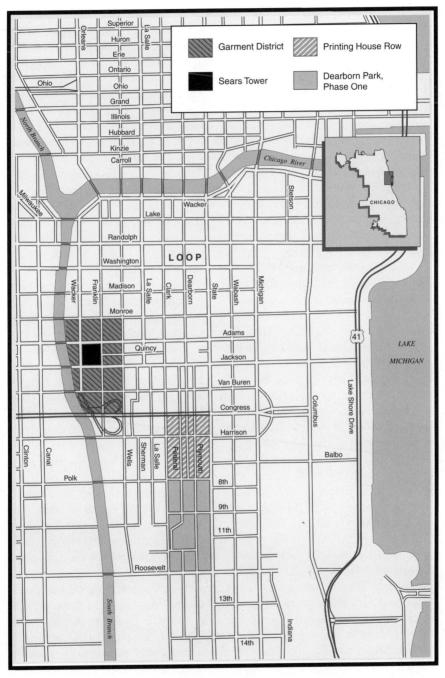

Map 2. Chicago Downtown Industrial Districts

built here were, by necessity, long and slablike, a feature that admitted a maximum amount of light into buildings and allowed long lines of presses to be arranged in an orderly fashion (Commission on Chicago Historical and Architectural Landmarks 1983).

Markets for Chicago's early printers and publishers varied substantially from firm to firm. Some companies benefitted from the nationwide growth in mail-order merchandising around the turn of the century. To help gain access to America's potentially huge and largely untapped rural markets, downtown retailers such as A. Montgomery Ward and Richard W. Sears hired Printing House Row firms to produce voluminous catalogues with vivid illustrations and detailed descriptions of store merchandise. Other Chicago printers specialized in the printing and publishing of inexpensive books and periodicals for mass consumption. Still others found work printing material for various social and political causes, such as the city's burgeoning labor movement (Commission on Chicago Historical and Architectural Landmarks 1983).

In the decades following World War II, as advances in transportation and communications encouraged certain Chicago manufacturers to relocate to outlying portions of the metropolitan area, much of the printing industry continued to exhibit a strong locational preference for its original South Loop home. By 1970, when the central area contained just 15 percent of the Chicago metropolitan area's total manufacturing employment, over 50 percent of the region's printing and publishing jobs were still clustered in this portion of the city (Real Estate Research Corporation 1970, 4). To a certain extent, this can be explained by the interrelationships that began to develop between the printing industry and the city's expanding corporate-financial sector following World War II. As the downtown areas of cities like New York and Chicago became home to growing concentrations of national and international corporate headquarters, law firms, advertisers, and financial and cultural institutions, the demand for printed products such as advertising brochures, lawyers' briefs, and concert programs increased accordingly. Printers serving markets like these typically operate under stringent time restrictions, making a central location near important downtown customers highly advantageous (Gustafson 1959, 163).

Printed goods also differ in important respects from the typical mass-produced commodities being manufactured increasingly on the urban periphery and beyond. Unlike standardized goods such as ball bearings or radio transistors, which manufacturers can generally produce in large quantities and then stockpile, most printed products are uniquely tailored to the detailed specifications of individual customers. This tends to create an ongoing need for consultation between printers and their customers, particularly at the pre-press stage of production. Layout, typesetting, and preparatory work for graphics and illustrations must typically be approved by the customer before a print job goes to press. The close and continual contact between printers and their customers required under these circumstances is best facilitated by the location of the two in close proximity to one another (Gustafson 1959, 164; Tobier and Willis 1981).

## Technological Change

During the 1960s and 1970s, the printing industry experienced a major technological upheaval that introduced new complications into the industry's locational patterns and preferences.[1] Until then, the method for printing letters and images, known as letterpress, had changed very little during the previous five hundred years. Printing was accomplished by inking a raised surface and pressing it onto paper. The setting of type was done on huge Linotype machines that cast heavy slugs of type from molten lead. Hot lead was dropped, one line at a time, into forms, which then had to be lifted and mounted on presses. For the printing of illustrations and photographs, special engravings requiring considerable time and skill had to be made. The lengthy and costly preparation necessary for letterpress printing jobs favored relatively long production runs with a minimum of graphics. In addition, since typesetting and printing had to be located in close proximity to one another (due to the weight of the lead used to set type), they were generally done by the same firm.

By the 1960s, letterpress was rapidly losing ground to a new method of printing called lithography (also known as offset printing). Instead of printing images by inking a raised surface, lithography uses photographic negatives to produce images on thin photosensitive metal plates chemically treated to attract ink. The plates, which are easily handled, are bent around cylinders on lithographic presses to print image after image in a continuous motion.[2] By 1984, letterpress accounted for just 17 percent of commercial printing revenues nationwide, while lithography's share had grown to 70 percent (Center for Urban Economic Development 1987, 18).

The introduction of lithography helped generate a further ripple of technological innovations in the printing industry, particularly within the prepress phase of production.[3] First, typesetting was increasingly computerized, a development that replaced hot type with computer-generated typewritten pages photographed and transferred to chemically treated plates. Computerized typesetting machines can produce either hard copy or digitized electronic images easily transmitted to distant locations via modem or satellite. This meant that the typesetting and printing of an image no longer had to take place within the same firm or, for that matter, the same city or country.

In addition, lithography greatly simplified the preparatory work necessary for the printing of multicolor graphics. Recall that under letterpress, the preparation of intricate metal engravings was necessary for the printing of graphic illustrations, a highly labor-intensive undertaking. In lithographic printing, by contrast, graphic images are simply photographed with special filters to separate them into four basic colors, and the resulting pieces of film are then realigned for reproduction. Together with new computer controls on presses that reduced the time required to set up individual press runs, innovations such as this ultimately helped cheapen the cost of small-batch, multicolor printing jobs considerably. The expansion of niche markets for multicolor work helped stimulate the growth of new firms specializing in the preparation of lithographic film and plates, known in the industry as printing trade shops.

During the early 1960s, the Richard J. Daley administration commissioned a series of studies examining the impact of technological change on a number of Chicago industrial sectors, including graphic communications. The printing industry study, carried out by a private consulting agency, Corplan Associates, concluded that the cost of much of the new, technologically advanced equipment associated with the growth of lithography would be beyond reach of most small firms (Corplan Associates 1964, 2). The study anticipated a "weeding out" of smaller, specialized shops and the consolidation of production in large (160–400 employees), vertically integrated companies sufficiently capitalized to keep abreast of the newest technological developments in the industry. Because production space in central area loft buildings was not well suited to the needs of such large firms, the future prospects for printing in Chicago were said to be grim, unless alternative space could be located outside the central area (Corplan Associates 1964, 3).

As it turned out, this forecast proved to be largely inaccurate. Technological change in the printing industry did not lead to a reintegration of the production process during the 1970s and 1980s, as Corplan had anticipated. To the contrary, just 20 percent of Chicago area printing establishments were fully integrated by the mid-1980s (Ranney and Wiewel 1988, 17). Among commercial printers, firms doing small-batch, multicolor work, while contracting out their prepress operations, became the fastest growing part of the business (Ranney and Wiewel 1987, 93). Within the prepress segments of the industry, small- and medium-sized typesetting establishments and trade shops showed the strongest growth, both nationally and in the Chicago area. Between 1967 and 1982, typesetting firms and trade shops recorded a 74 percent gain in total number of establishments nationwide (Ranney and Wiewel 1988, 15). Forecasts by the Illinois Department of Employment Security showed employment growing in Chicago area typesetting establishments and trade shops at a rate of 31 percent between 1982 and 1995, the highest growth rate of any segment of the printing industry (Ranney and Wiewel 1987, 46).

Technological innovations and the new market opportunities that accompanied them had important locational ramifications for the Chicago area printing industry. As small-batch, multicolor print jobs grew more affordable, downtown advertising firms became the largest customers for many Chicago printers. By the mid-1980s, 90 percent of Chicago printing establishments did at least some advertising work (Ranney and Wiewel 1987, 73). Due to demands for rapid turnaround and the need for face-to-face communication between printers and their customers in the production of advertising copy, printers specializing in these markets generally tended to cluster in the downtown area, oftentimes collaborating with one another on individual jobs. Moreover, because these firms were typically on the small side, with twenty or fewer employees, the relatively cramped production space available in central area loft buildings did not present the same efficiency problems it did for larger firms. In a 1987 survey of 320 Chicago printing establishments undertaken by researchers from the University of Illinois at Chicago, less than 40 percent of respondents expressed dissatisfaction with the layout and condition of their existing production facilities (Ranney and Wiewel 1987, 124).

Other segments of the industry, by contrast, responded to a far greater extent to the kinds of structural economic pressures identified in Chapters 1 and 2, relocating production facilities outside the city of Chicago where land and labor costs were substantially lower. Ironically, the same technological innovations that helped root certain industry segments more firmly in the downtown area made other segments more footloose. In particular, the ability to receive and to transmit digitized images via satellite or modem encouraged many larger commercial printers producing catalogs or periodicals for national or international markets to set up their press operations in low-cost suburban, rural, or Third World locations, even if much of their prepress work continued to be done by more centrally located typesetting firms and trade shops (Wiewel, Ranney, and Putnam 1990).

## Displacement

At roughly the same time that technological advances in lithographic printing were fueling the growth of centrally located commercial printers, typesetters, and printing trade shops specializing in small-batch, multicolor work, these same industry segments began to experience real estate pressures associated with downtown commercial and residential redevelopment. The Daley administration's efforts to revalorize central area property and protect the investments of downtown retailers and corporations by surrounding the Loop with stable residential communities helped create a market for residential and commercial loft space, the same loft space being used at the time by printers and apparel manufacturers in the downtown area. Beginning in the mid-1970s, developers began purchasing industrial buildings in Printing House Row and elsewhere in the central area, converting them to back office space or condominiums, and selling or leasing the rehabilitated space for anywhere from two to six times the going price commanded for industrial use.

By 1986, after a flurry of loft conversion activity during the late 1970s and early 1980s, Printing House Row no longer housed a single graphic communications establishment.

In reality, the fate of the printers, typesetters, binders, and other graphic communications firms on Printing House Row had been largely sealed several decades earlier when the Daley administration, working closely with the Chicago Central Area Committee (CCAC), issued its *Development Plan for the Central Area of Chicago* in 1958. As we saw in the previous chapter, the plan called for extensive redevelopment in the South Loop and the Near South Side, including the construction of a new federal-government center, housing for middle-income families, and a new University of Illinois campus on a 130-acre site encompassing Printing House Row and underutilized railroad land south of the Loop. When unfruitful negotiations with railroad company owners caused the city to seek an alternative campus site in 1960, plans for Printing House Row and the surrounding area were temporarily put on hold. However, the city had, by that time, already sent a clear message that it would support efforts to redevelop this area for nonindustrial purposes. Prices for unimproved loft space in the Printing House Row district increased sharply during the 1960s. As Table 3 indicates, land values at the corner of Dearborn and Harrison Streets (the district's center) were stable between 1950 and 1960 but jumped from $7.00 to $17.00 per square foot during the following ten-year period.

For most industrial properties in Chicago, an increase of this magnitude would be highly unlikely unless the sellers had obtained a zoning change from the city, assuring purchasers they would be able to develop the property

**Table 3.** Land Values in and near Printing House Row, 1950–1990

| Location | 1950 | 1960 | 1970 | 1980 | 1990 |
|---|---|---|---|---|---|
| Corner of Harrison and Dearborn Streets *(Printing House Row)* | $6.25 | $7.00 | $17.00 | $22.00 | $70.00 |
| Corner of Harrison and Wells Streets *(three blocks west of Printing House Row)* | $4.50 | $5.00 | $10.00 | $12.00 | $40.00 |

*Sources:* Olcott (1950, 1960, 1970, 1980, 1990).   *Note:* Amounts represent dollars per square foot.

for higher-rent, nonindustrial uses. However, industrial property on Printing House Row, like much of the industrial property elsewhere in the central area, was zoned C3, which allows a mixture of light industrial, commercial, and residential uses. No zoning changes were required to convert the industrial space in this area to residential lofts. This meant that property values in the Printing House Row district automatically reflected their "highest and best use," assuming the city's willingness to provide infrastructure and other public support necessary for nonindustrial redevelopment was not in question. Given the Daley administration's stated preferences for residential and institutional development in the South Loop area, it is no surprise that by the 1960s land speculators began to bet on a change in land use in Printing House Row.

Although redevelopment plans for the South Loop and the Near South Side remained in limbo for well over a decade following publication of the 1958 Development Plan, the CCAC never abandoned its commitment to a large-scale development south of the Loop. In 1973, plans for the massive new Dearborn Park middle-income housing development were announced as part of the CCAC's Chicago 21 Plan, which was intended once again to protect the value of downtown real estate by gentrifying the neighborhoods immediately surrounding the Loop. The project's developers, the Chicago 21 Corporation, eventually agreed on a site directly south of Printing House Row, between Polk Street and Roosevelt Road (see Map 2). The City of Chicago enthusiastically supported the proposal, committing $7.74 million in city funds for infrastructure improvements, a new school, and two public parks for the first phase of Dearborn Park alone (Hollander 1987).

Several years after plans for Dearborn Park were announced, a group of developers led by Chicago architect Harry Weese began quietly acquiring property on Printing House Row. By 1979, the group had purchased five industrial buildings and spent millions of dollars rehabilitating the loft space for residential and commercial use. The new conversions would, in the words of one developer, create "a fresh green ribbon" between the Loop and the new Dearborn Park housing development, helping to further rejuvenate the South Loop area (Ziemba 1976). Weese himself would go on to chair the influential Committee for Legal Lofts, one of the most prominent groups represented in the coalition of civic organizations that successfully pressured the Jane Byrne administration to relax the city's building-code standards for loft conversions in 1982.[4] In addition to easing building rehabilitation standards, city officials agreed to spend $1.5 million for infrastructure improvements and the construction of a public park in Printing House Row (Hollander 1987). To top it all off, the city agreed to sponsor Urban Development Action Grant applications to finance the conversion of three industrial buildings in the district, providing Weese's development group with $6.8 million in investment funds (Wright 1987).

Although city officials insisted that the buildings were underutilized and functionally obsolete as sites for manufacturing (see Commission on Chicago Historical and Architectural Landmarks 1983, 8–9; Department of City Planning 1958, 8), a 1987 study of loft-conversion activity on Printing House Row carried out by the University of Illinois at Chicago suggests otherwise. The study's author successfully located and interviewed representatives from forty-nine of the ninety-six printing firms that had left Printing House Row since 1970.[5] Sixty-seven percent of respondents reported they had been pressured to vacate their existing production space in Printing House Row, through excessive rent increases, breaking of leases, and harassment (Pruska-Carroll 1987, 21). Half the firms contacted had moved to other locations in the central area following displacement from Printing House Row. Many emphasized the financial hardship involved in relocation and the difficulty of securing alternative, suitably located production space. Seventy percent of respondents indicated an ongoing preference for a near-downtown location (Pruska-Carroll 1987, 24).

Even more important than the time and expense involved in finding alternative production space in the downtown area was the disruption of important subcontracting and networking relationships among firms located in close proximity to one another. These relationships, built and reinforced through years of face-to-face contact among manufacturers, helped create a certain entrepreneurial dynamism relatively unique within agglomerations of small competitive firms. One commercial printer located in the same Printing House Row loft building for thirty-seven years described these interrelationships to me in the following terms:

> It was a perfect building for a small printer such as I. We had a very large ink company [in the building]. Then on the eleventh floor we had Mackin's Bindery, and we would send our folding, cutting, and trimming up there. I had a two-color press, twenty-three inches by thirty-six inches. If I had eight-and-a-half by eleven work I'd farm it out to Ad Litho next door or Campaign Press on the seventh floor. We'd follow a line of reciprocity. Campaign Press would have some work that was twenty-three by thirty-six inches—too large for their presses—so we would do that work for them. Campaign Press, Ad Litho, and RLA Press were all both customers and suppliers. So there was reciprocity all over the building. It was quite advantageous to have everybody in the same building. (Maar 1996)

Small commercial printers without well-developed typesetting or binding capabilities were able to save time and expense by utilizing the services of other firms in the same building. According to the same printer,

> When we got a job off the press, we would just roll it over to the freight elevator on a press dolly and send it upstairs to the eleventh floor [for binding]. If I

were sending it out to an outside bindery, we'd have to put it on a skid and then band it with a steel band. All that takes time. So the building was a great advantage. (Maar 1996)

Roughly half the printers who relocated from Printing House Row during the 1970s and 1980s moved into buildings several blocks west or south of the district (Pruska-Carroll 1987, 26). Redevelopment pressures, however, were never far behind. In recent years, industrial buildings in many of these areas have become attractive targets for commercial and residential conversions as well, and some printers are now being uprooted for a second time. While I was in Chicago doing research during the winter of 1996, I discovered one such building in the process of conversion to residential lofts. The story of its transformation from working to living space provides a vivid illustration of the way in which downtown redevelopment can destabilize the market for industrial loft space.

The building, a twelve-story, turn-of-the-century loft structure, is located three blocks west of Printing House Row on West Harrison Street in the South Loop. During its peak years of industrial use in the 1940s, the building housed sixty-seven industrial tenants, forty-three of which were engaged in either printing or related activities (Winters Publishing Co. 1942). By the time loft conversion activity began nearby on Printing House Row in the 1970s, it was still occupied mainly by printers and providers of ancillary services, many of whom had been there for twenty-five years or more.

In 1982, the building changed ownership for the first time in several decades. It is unclear what the buyer's intentions were, but there are signs that he purchased the building for speculative purposes. According to tenants, building maintenance deteriorated rapidly after he assumed ownership and remained substandard for the duration of his tenure as building owner. The freight elevator was in a chronic state of disrepair, forcing tenants to rely on the smaller passenger elevator for deliveries. On several occasions, both elevators were simultaneously out of service. Eventually, firms started to move out. By 1992, when the building changed hands once again, occupancy had fallen below 50 percent and many intrabuilding subcontracting and networking relationships had been destroyed.

In the meantime, property values in this area of the Loop had begun to accelerate sharply. Like Printing House Row, this area was zoned C3, meaning that land prices here automatically incorporated the effects of the nearby loft conversion activity in Printing House Row and the new Dearborn Park housing development. Table 3 shows that land values at the corner of Harrison and Wells Streets, where the building is located, rose from $12.00 to $40.00 per square foot between 1980 and 1990. Land speculators here could more than triple the value of their investments simply by holding onto real estate for eight to ten years and then reselling it at inflated prices. These prices virtually guaranteed that a change in land use from industrial to nonindustrial would accompany any real estate transaction here, since rents for industrial tenants were far too low to support the property taxes and building mortgages on such costly real estate.

By winter of 1996, the new owners were busily converting the building to one and two bedroom residential lofts, at prices ranging from $145,000 to $320,000. By then, all existing industrial tenants had received notices that their leases would not be renewed, and only seven printing firms remained in the building. Three of these firms formerly occupied loft space in Printing House Row and were now being forced to move for the second time in fifteen years or less. All but one of the seven had successfully located new production space elsewhere in the central area. Most firms were moving several blocks further west, just across the Chicago River. However, unless strong steps are taken to curb the pace of redevelopment activity in this part of the city, it will be only a matter of time before these printers are once again forced to relocate.

## Decline

With the reduction of industrial loft space in Printing House Row and elsewhere in the downtown area, the number of printing establishments in the central area of Chicago fell sharply during the 1980s and early 1990s. Table 4 shows the magnitude of this drop: altogether, firms engaged in commercial printing, typesetting, and printing trade services in the downtown area decreased in number by nearly 50 percent between 1981 and 1993. These numbers appear to reflect industry decline within, not movement away from, the central area of the city. Between 1979 and 1985, Chicago printing employment located in this part of the city *increased* from 50 percent to 60 percent (Illinois Department of Employment Security 1979, 1985). Many

**Table 4.** Printing Establishments in the Central Area of Chicago, 1981 and 1993

| Industry Segment | 1981 | 1993 | Percent Change |
|---|---|---|---|
| Commercial Printers | 312 | 160 | -49 |
| Typesetters | 64 | 36 | -44 |
| Trade Shops | 25 | 20 | -20 |
| **Total** | **401** | **216** | **-46** |

*Sources:* Influential Contacts, Ltd. (1981); Inside Contacts (1993).
*Note:* Includes Standard Industrial Classification (SIC) categories 275, 2791, and 2795.

Chicago printers apparently still preferred a central location but were increasingly incapable of surviving there.

It would be unfair to blame this decline entirely on real estate pressures accompanying downtown redevelopment. By the 1980s, Chicago area printers were wrestling with various other difficulties as well. Most importantly, the rapid pace of technological change in the industry eventually created financing problems for some firms too small to afford state-of-the-art equipment (Ranney and Wiewel 1987). In addition, printing employers faced a growing shortage of skilled labor by this time, caused by declining membership in the industry's two principal labor unions, the International Typographical Union (ITU) and the Graphic Communications International Union (GCIU), and by the breakdown of the union apprenticeship programs (Wiewel, Ranney, and Putnam 1990).

Even though displacement pressures alone cannot fully account for the decline of centrally located printing establishments in recent years, the loss of the industry's spatial compactness is critical. As we saw in Chapter 1, firms located in industrial districts elsewhere have developed collective solutions to common problems such as labor and equipment shortages, in some cases sharing tools, workers, and information with nearby establishments (Brusco 1982; Sengenberger and Pyke 1992; Kristensen 1992). These relationships appear to be built, to a great extent, on the mutual trust that eventually develops among district members as a result of repeated reciprocal exchanges (Lorenz 1988; Granovetter 1985). Spatial proximity among firms increases opportunities for these exchanges to occur, thus fostering trust among district-member firms to the extent they perceive such exchanges to be mutually beneficial (Harrison 1992).

In Chicago, printing firms displaced by the pressures of downtown redevelopment have thus far shown a strong tendency to seek alternative production space elsewhere in the central area. Yet while the majority of Chicago's printing establishments remain in the downtown area, the concentration of firms is much less pronounced than it was twenty-five years ago when Printing House Row still served as the nucleus of Chicago's graphic communications industry. Opportunities for subcontracting and networking relationships among firms still exist, but a good deal of the synergy produced by repetitive, face-to-face interactions among printers, customers, and suppliers has no doubt been lost. Conditions that might have facilitated cooperative problem-solving among firms on other issues have been seriously undermined as well.

## The Chicago Apparel Industry

The history of the Chicago apparel industry parallels that of the city's printing industry in a number of important ways. By 1925, Chicago apparel manufacturers had concentrated in a tightly knit cluster several blocks northwest of

Printing House Row along the east bank of the Chicago River (see Map 2). Like the printing industry, the spatial concentration of apparel firms in the downtown area was caused principally by uncertainties and rapid fluctuations in the market for the industry's output. The importance of fashion to many segments of the apparel industry, and the inability of producers to predict in advance which lines of clothing would generate the greatest enthusiasm among buyers, placed limits on the consolidation of production in large, self-contained factories. It also encouraged manufacturers to locate near the city's large downtown department stores in order to keep themselves abreast of the continuously changing fashion preferences of retail clothing buyers (De Meir-leir 1950, 127–128).

While firms in Chicago's garment district were generally quite small, with ten or fewer employees, there were also a number of large factories employing one hundred or more workers (Magee 1930, 97). At times of peak demand, the district's smaller firms could be pressed into service as contractors for large manufacturers, allowing such firms to respond to seasonal fluctuations in the market without expanding their own productive capacities (Carsel 1940, 7–8). At other times, small manufacturers worked either independently or as contractors for "jobbers" in the district, the latter of whom generally handled the design, purchasing of fabric, and sales of their garments themselves but contracted out the actual sewing.

This set of arrangements provided the Chicago apparel industry with the flexibility necessary to respond quickly to extremely volatile, unpredictable markets. The output of successful lines of clothing could be rapidly increased without a corresponding expansion in the productive capacity of individual firms, while less successful lines could be quickly discontinued with minimal costs. Through contracting and subcontracting relationships, overall production in the district easily shifted in favor of those garments for which demand was strongest. The spatial concentration of firms facilitated contracting and subcontracting among manufacturers and jobbers by providing the face-to-face contact necessary for such relationships to develop and mature. It also reduced the time and transportation-related cost penalties of subcontracting and cut down on the distance retail buyers had to cover when visiting the showrooms of Chicago apparel manufacturers (Magee 1930, 91).

Spatial concentration was important, not only for the synergy of the garment district itself but also for the viability of individual firms. By 1910, the International Garment Workers Union had made significant gains among the employees of Loop apparel-manufacturing firms. Hoping to escape what many perceived as an increasingly unfavorable business climate, numerous firm owners began to set up shop in one of two locations several miles outside the Loop, each featuring large pools of nonunion, immigrant laborers (Magee 1930, 82). In the long run, however, this strategy proved to be disadvantageous. According to historian Keith McClellan,

Experience showed that to have a central location was far more important in the garment industry than to achieve small wage differentials. Peripheral firms found that being isolated from contractors and jobbers reduced "face-to-face" confrontations and resulted in a loss of business. . . . By 1920, the number of clothing manufacturing firms located outside the Loop had declined markedly, and by 1928 the industry was more heavily concentrated in the Loop than ever before. (McClellan 1966, 34)

## Postwar Industry Restructuring

Concentration among Chicago apparel manufacturers in the Loop garment district continued during the 1930s and early 1940s. Following World War II, however, developments in clothing production and new market opportunities for some types of apparel firms introduced changes in the locational preferences of certain segments of the industry. To begin with, even though the volatility of fashion and difficulties of mechanizing the production of clothing from soft, limp fabrics have always made the clothing industry somewhat resistant to mass-production techniques, U.S. apparel manufacturers went further in that direction than ever before (or since) during the postwar years (Kenyon 1964). Postwar prosperity and greater public acceptance of casual, informal clothing reduced pressure for manufacturers to differentiate themselves on the basis of style (Helfgott 1959, 77). Instead, with the encouragement of large downtown retailers, many clothing manufacturers moved to capture scale economies by producing standardized lines of clothing in long production runs (Zeitlin and Totterdill 1989, 157). Such firms tended to be large and relatively self-contained. This, together with the low design content of their product lines, led manufacturers like these to seek lower-cost production space outside the city center. In Chicago, new concentrations of apparel firms began to emerge on the Near West Side, while manufacturers producing for more fashion-sensitive segments of the market continued to cluster in the city's original garment district several blocks away in the West Loop area (De Meirleir 1950, 127–128).

Ultimately, however, apparel manufacturers that had neglected design in order to achieve scale economies found themselves ill-prepared to respond to several important changes in U.S. apparel markets during the 1970s. First, even with standardization, clothing production continued to be highly labor intensive, with materials handling accounting for up to 80 percent of the total time involved in the production of a garment (Hoffman 1985, 372). Once Third World countries acquired the relatively unsophisticated technology and skills for large-batch, standardized garment production, their comparatively lower labor costs enabled them to undercut U.S. producers by wide margins. By 1980, labor costs represented 35 percent of the total cost of a typical garment manufactured in the U.S. and only 7 percent of a similar garment produced in an Asian newly industrializing country such as Taiwan or Hong Kong (Hoffman 1985, 373).

Large domestic clothing producers were also caught off guard by the recessions accompanying the oil price hikes of the 1970s The growing instability of domestic demand during the 1970s, together with rising competition from imports, made it increasingly difficult for many U.S. clothing manufacturers to achieve the sales volumes necessary to amortize the large investments they had made in plants and equipment during the 1950s and 1960s. Table 5 shows the impact of these two new conditions on the eight major segments of the Cook County apparel industry. Firm closures and relocations during the 1970s caused declines in employment in virtually every segment of the industry. Job losses were particularly heavy in standardized industry segments most susceptible to import penetration, such as women's and children's undergarments and girls', children's, and infants' outerwear.

**Table 5.** Apparel Employment in Cook County, 1970 and 1980

| Industry Segment | 1970 | | 1980 | |
|---|---|---|---|---|
| | Firms | Employees | Firms | Employees |
| Men's, Youths', and Boys' Suits, Coats, and Overcoats | 26 | 6,331 | 12 | 2,500–9,999* |
| Men's, Youths', and Boys' Furnishings, Work Clothing, and Allied Garments | 36 | 1,378 | 20 | 1,078 |
| Women's, Misses', and Juniors' Outerwear | 88 | 3,613 | 59 | 2,139 |
| Women's, Misses', Children's, and Infants' Undergarments | 16 | 1,525 | 5 | 719 |
| Hats, Caps, and Millinery | 19 | 445 | 15 | 473 |
| Girls', Children's, and Infants' Outerwear | 9 | 120 | 0 | 0 |
| Miscellaneous Apparel and Accessories | 24 | 1,172 | 22 | 500–599* |
| Miscellaneous Fabricated Textile Products | 246 | 5,502 | 173 | 4,655 |

*Source:* Robinson (1985).   *Exact amounts are withheld to avoid disclosing data for individual companies.

U.S. apparel manufacturers were, however, not the only ones to feel the pressure of global economic changes in clothing markets. Domestic clothing retailers eventually discovered that the sourcing of low-cost, standardized garments from Third World producers could not compensate for the increasingly sluggish domestic demand for clothing by the 1970s. As a result, retailers began to make new demands on their suppliers, emphasizing fashion, quality, and rapid turnaround times as a means of defining and responding quickly to new market niches. According to economists Jonathan Zeitlin and Peter Totterdill,

> While price remains important, particularly at the lower end of the market, the struggle for competitive advantage has come to center increasingly on retailers' and manufacturers' efforts to target specific groups of consumers defined in new ways; to seduce customers with attractive, fashionable garments; and to respond rapidly to short-term trends in the sales of individual product lines. (Zeitlin and Totterdill 1989, 162)

The growing fragmentation of mass markets for clothing during the 1980s favored manufacturers capable of producing relatively wide ranges of styles and flexible enough to switch production between clothing lines in response to short-term sales trends. With bar-coding now providing instant access to sales-performance data on entire store inventories, retailers were generally much less willing to place advance orders in large quantities. Retail buyers who during the 1960s and 1970s finalized most of their orders with suppliers at the beginning of each fashion season were by the mid-1980s oftentimes staggering the bulk of their purchases over the course of each season (Costigan 1996). According to Zeitlin and Totterdill, these developments created new advantages for centrally located domestic clothing producers and disadvantages for Third World manufacturers:

> Lead times are too long, minimum production runs too large, quality control too difficult, and the capital costs of stocks too high to make sourcing in the Far East worthwhile for many of the more fashion-sensitive types of garment. . . . Physical proximity is also important for collaboration between retailers and suppliers in range development and rapid adjustment of production to sales. (Zeitlin and Totterdill 1989, 167)

In Chicago and other fashion centers, the segment of the apparel industry in the best position to respond to these new conditions was a small but growing community of designer/manufacturers and contractors who typically occupied downtown area loft space (Department of Economic Development 1987, 7). Designer/manufacturers generally employ a small staff of cutters and sewers to produce display garments for their showrooms and to handle small orders, but much of their production work is ordinarily contracted out. In an industry where uncertainty reigns, this arrangement reduces risk and increases flexibility for all parties concerned. Designers can temporarily increase production when orders rise by hiring additional contractors. In turn, contractors are free to accept orders from more than one designer, when necessary. To a great extent, designer/manufacturers have taken the place of jobbers, who performed a similar role in Chicago's garment district during the prewar years. The major difference between the two is that designer firms often target a far more specialized, identifiable segment of the market than the typical jobbers did. According to Dorothy Fuller, vice president of the Chicago Apparel Center,[6]

> These firms are small, very focused, and probably priced a little higher than the average but with something rather special to sell. We have, for example, a couple of companies that do hand painting—hand painted silk gowns, dresses, costumes. They're expensive and they're very special, very identifiable, and their business is probably $3 million. There are also a whole group of designers whose business is under $1 million. (Fuller 1996)

By the 1980s, some designer firms were beginning to utilize computer-aided design (CAD) systems as a way of expanding their garment styles and decreasing turnaround times from concept to delivery. CAD systems reduce much of the time and effort involved in creating patterns, the basic building blocks of apparel manufacture. Patterns are used as templates for the cutting of fabric and must be prepared for each component (such as a collar or a sleeve) of a particular garment. Before computerization, clothing designers had to mark out patterns by hand in the full range of sizes being produced. The patterns for one style alone could easily number in the hundreds, and the process of grading each pattern up and down to produce multiple sizes was extremely time-consuming (Hoffman 1985, 375). Computerization eliminated the need for much of this work. Designer/manufacturers using CAD systems simply make one set of patterns for each garment, enter the specifications into the system, and watch while the computer automatically generates a full set of additional patterns for each size specified by the operator. This frees designers to spend more of their time producing new clothing styles rather than grading patterns to produce multiple sizes of existing styles. It also allows them to ship orders two to three weeks faster than they otherwise could, at considerable cost savings (Liametz 1996).

Despite new market opportunities and technological advances reducing the cost penalties of small-batch clothing production, the performance of Chicago's centrally located designer/manufacturers during the past decade has not been strong. By the mid-1990s, there were very few of these firms left in the central area, for reasons to be explored shortly. According to one comprehensive Chicago area business directory, only 66 apparel manufacturing establishments were located in the entire central area in 1995, down from 135 in 1981 (Inside Contacts 1995). To get a better idea of the characteristics of this segment of the industry and the reasons for its decline, I selected a random sample of the sixty-six remaining firms for a brief telephone questionnaire. Although these manufacturers were, for the most part, considerably less eager to share information than the printers with whom I spoke, I was still able to interview representatives from twenty of the sixty-six firms.

In general, the results of the survey suggest that, although designer/manufacturing firms have declined in numbers, they are still the types of apparel manufacturers most likely to be found in the near-downtown area. Moreover, such firms continue to exhibit strong attachments to this part of the city despite real estate pressures that have forced many firms to relocate one or more times within the past fifteen years. Thirteen of the twenty firms surveyed (65 percent) indicated that the manufacturing of designer wear was an important part of their business. Most of these firms were relatively small, employing twenty or fewer workers. In addition, fifteen firms (75 percent) reported that a central location was either moderately important or very important to their companies. The primary reasons given were proximity to contractors and customers and convenience of transportation. Seventeen of the twenty firms (85 percent) either contracted out work to, or accepted work from, other manufacturers. Finally, thirteen firms (65 percent) reported they had found it necessary to relocate at least once in the past fifteen years due to rent increases, building demolitions, or building conversions to new nonindustrial uses.

In many ways, the designer/manufacturer segment of the Chicago apparel industry resembles the segment of the Chicago printing industry that began to emerge in the 1970s, when technological innovations in lithographic printing began to make small-batch, multicolor print jobs economically feasible. Both groups have taken advantage of new technologies to reduce the cost penalties that typically accompany production in short runs, allowing them to tap into new, previously inaccessible market niches. Both have also made use of extensive subcontracting relationships to reduce risks and increase flexibility. This, in turn, helps explain the tendency of firms in both industry segments to cluster in industrial districts located near downtown customers. However, both groups have ultimately lost many of the benefits of spatial proximity through displacement pressures associated with downtown commercial and residential redevelopment. For the Chicago apparel industry, these pressures appeared earlier and carried more severe consequences than they did for the Chicago printing industry.

## Displacement

The Chicago garment district first began to experience the pressures of downtown redevelopment shortly after World War II, when planners routed the new Congress and Dan Ryan Expressways through the West Loop and Near West Side as part of the city's efforts to link Chicago's central business district with the outlying portions of the metropolitan area. The construction of the Congress Expressway alone led to the demolition of 250 structures in the Loop and on the Near West Side, including 157 commercial buildings (Sturdy 1949). The new freeway cut a path through the southern edge of the downtown garment district, extending west through the heart of the Near West Side, where many of the industry's less fashion-conscious manufacturers had begun to locate following World War II. Altogether, some 3,000 apparel industry jobs were lost between 1948 and 1958 due to displacement caused by freeway construction (Center for Urban Studies 1966, 60). Job losses were concentrated among Near West Side apparel firms, but five loft buildings in the downtown garment district occupied primarily by apparel manufacturers were also destroyed. The city made no effort to secure alternative production space for displaced manufacturers elsewhere in the garment district, and many uprooted firms that did not go out of business altogether moved to new locations in other parts of the metropolitan area (Center for Urban Studies 1966, 60).

Like Printing House Row, the demise of Chicago's garment district was also written into the Daley administration's 1958 Development Plan for Chicago's central area. As late as 1960, over 50 percent of Chicago apparel manufacturers were still concentrated in an area of the West Loop bordered by Monroe Street and Congress Parkway to the north and south, and Wells Street and the Chicago River to the east and west. Table 6 indicates that 116 of Chicago's 221 apparel manufacturing firms were located within these boundaries in 1960. Under the 1958 Development Plan, both this area and

**Table 6.** Concentration of Apparel Firms in the
Chicago Garment District, 1951–1981

| Location | 1951 | 1960 | 1970 | 1981 |
|---|---|---|---|---|
| Apparel Firms Citywide | 369 | 221 | 148 | 130 |
| Firms Located within Garment District | 183 (50%) | 116 (52%) | 57 (39%) | 26 (20%) |

*Sources:* Manufacturers News, Inc. (1951, 1960, 1970); Influential Contacts, Ltd. (1981).
*Note:* Includes SIC categories 231–237.

adjoining properties to the north were to be integrated more extensively into the central business district (Department of City Planning 1958, 7). Ideally, the mix of relatively low-intensity commercial and industrial land uses that made up much of the area between Wells Street and the Chicago River would be replaced by high-rise office buildings, boosting downtown property tax revenues and creating the construction jobs that the Daley administration relied upon to shore up its support from the building trade unions.

**Table 7.** Land Values in and near the Chicago Garment District, 1950–1980

| Location | 1950 | 1960 | 1965 | 1970 | 1980 |
|---|---|---|---|---|---|
| Corner of Franklin and Van Buren Streets *(Garment District)* | $8.50 | $8.50 | $12.00 | $27.00 | $60.00 |
| Corner of LaSalle and Van Buren Streets *(Central Loop)* | $16.00 | $20.00 | $29.00 | $45.00 | $70.00 |
| Corner of Jackson and Desplaines Streets *(Near West Side)* | $5.00 | $8.00 | $10.00 | $11.00 | $13.00 |

*Sources:* Olcott (1950, 1960, 1965, 1970, 1980).    *Note:* Amounts represent dollars per square foot.

By the mid-1960s, however, even though redevelopment activity was proceeding at a rapid pace east of Wells Street, developers had made fewer inroads into the western portions of the Loop. Table 7 shows that property in the heart of the garment district was still being priced for low-density industrial and commercial uses in 1965, at $12.00 per foot, while land values just two blocks east in the central Loop were more than double that amount. Wells Street, also serving as the north-south route for the city's elevated commuter rail line in the west Loop, appeared to represent a psychological barrier for the real estate community. Investors seemed reluctant to cross this line as long as opportunities for new office-tower construction in the heart of the central business district continued to present themselves. Eventually, city planners became convinced that a large development project was necessary in the West Loop to serve as a visual anchor and solidify investor confidence in the area.

In the late 1960s, Sears, Roebuck and Company informed city officials that it was planning to consolidate its administrative facilities—at the time spread over various Chicago area locations—in one large downtown high rise office building it wanted to construct (O'Connor 1975). Company plans called for a 110-story, 1,450 foot headquarters building, taller than any other structure in the world. Sears was interested in a West Loop location and had identified a site along Franklin Street between Adams and Jackson. The property was situated within the garment district, and two buildings housing primarily apparel firms were located on the site. However, assuming the building owners could be persuaded to sell, there was another more pressing obstacle. The parcel of land Sears wanted to develop was bisected by Quincy Street, meaning the company would have to build two towers next to one another instead of one massive high-rise building. Sears was unwilling to do this.

In 1969, Sears chairman Gordon Metcalf met privately with Mayor Daley to seek the mayor's support for the transfer of this block of Quincy Street to Sears, Roebuck and Company, emphasizing the vast number of construction jobs the project would generate and the prestige Chicago would enjoy as home of the world's largest building (O'Connor 1975, 137). The administration eventually agreed to a deal: it would recommend the sale of Quincy Street to Sears at a relatively high price of $2.8 million, or $130.00 per square foot. However, the city would absorb the $1.2 million cost of rerouting water and sewer lines beneath the street, effectively reducing Sears' purchase price to $77.00 per square foot. As Daley biographer Len O'Connor observed, this was a "bargain basement price" for a public thoroughfare in downtown Chicago (O'Connor 1975, 137).

City of Chicago Corporation Council Raymond Simon prepared an ordinance reflecting the above agreement. With Mayor Daley's stamp of approval, it sailed through the City Council Committee on Streets and Alleys. According to O'Connor,

> Without the imprimatur of His Honor the Mayor, this deal would have been dumped into the Rules Committee, the bottomless pit into which all anti-administration measures in Chicago City Council are cast. Presented to the full council as a mighty architectural prize, giving Chicago—with the John Hancock Center built and the Standard Oil Building already under construction—three of the five tallest structures on earth, there was no dissent when the ordinance was presented for vote. (O'Connor 1975, 137)

The *Chicago Sun-Times* reported Mayor Daley's reaction to the new development as follows:

> Daley called [Sears Roebuck and Co.] "one of the most humane [corporations] because of its interest in people and helping cities find answers to social problems." He said the building will constitute a "boost for the area" and expressed

the hope that other firms will move into the West Side area and rehabilitate it. (*Chicago Sun-Times,* 6 March 1969)

Mayor Daley was not to be disappointed. Land speculation and redevelopment activity in the West Loop area began to accelerate even before Sears broke ground in 1970. Tables 6 and 7 show the impact of these new development pressures on the garment district during the 1970s. As property values at the corner of Franklin and Van Buren Streets, just one block south of the Sears Tower development, increased to $60.00 per square foot by 1980, the concentration of Chicago apparel firms located in the garment district fell to just 20 percent. As in Printing House Row, no zoning changes were required to redevelop this property for nonindustrial purposes. Most of the new development here, however, involved land clearance and construction of massive new high-rise office buildings rather than the adaptive reuse of existing buildings favored by developers in nearby Printing House Row. By 1980, very few of the turn-of-the-century loft buildings that once lined the south ends of Franklin Street and Wacker Drive (formerly Market Street) were left, and the area had ceased to function as an identifiable garment district. In 1988, the building housing the last remaining apparel firms in the district was demolished to build a parking garage for downtown office workers.

The reduction of loft space in the Chicago garment district during the 1970s and 1980s, at roughly the same time that changes in clothing markets were beginning to create new opportunities for small, flexibly specialized apparel firms emphasizing design and innovation over economies of scale, came at an inopportune time for Chicago's newly developing community of designer/manufacturers. Although many apparel firms were able to find affordable space elsewhere in the central area, companies were generally much more isolated from one another than they had been before. This isolation carried significant costs in terms of lost networking opportunities, easy access to contractors and suppliers, informal intraindustry technical assistance, and other advantages associated with the location of firms in close proximity to one another. As New York Fashion Council President Gerald Shaw argued in a 1985 letter to Mayor Edward Koch complaining of the impact of redevelopment pressures on New York City's garment district,

> This industry can only thrive while having in close physical proximity manufacturers (including not just selling activities, but also designing, purchasing, and shipping), textile vendors and the ancillary, critical trimming makers, machinery maintainers, and freight forwarders. Scattering any of these all over the five boroughs destroys the synergy unique to the life of our industry. (Lebow 1985)

It is impossible to say how this segment of the Chicago apparel industry might have fared had city officials responded more evenhandedly to the interests of downtown real estate developers and central area manufacturing establishments. The industry has faced a number of important challenges apart from real estate pressures, including the financing of expensive CAD equipment, competition from rising numbers of illegal sweatshops, and increasingly liberal foreign trade policies for clothing products. An apparel industry task force created by the Harold Washington administration during the 1980s helped focus attention on certain of these issues, with some success. In April 1995, for example, a shared-use CAD facility was opened in the Chicago Apparel Center to provide small designer firms with access to costly technologies they cannot afford to purchase themselves. However, another goal of the task force—the resurrection of a needle trades district in the central area of the city—has thus far proved more elusive. It remains to be seen whether recent efforts to support the industry can succeed without the less tangible but still important benefits of spatial clustering.

## Conclusion

The redevelopment of postwar Chicago, as we saw in the previous chapter, took place through the efforts of a progrowth alliance, or "growth machine," led by city officials and downtown business leaders. The ideological underpinning of this redevelopment strategy was a narrative of urban economic restructuring and industrial decline embraced by city officials, business elites, and scholars alike. The central propositions of this narrative, including the rising mobility of capital, the growing obsolescence of cities as viable locations for manufacturing, the division of labor between state and market, and the equation of economic growth with real estate development and rising property values, all pointed to one conclusion: that downtown redevelopment would necessarily become the linchpin of citywide economic growth.

The case studies of the Chicago printing and apparel industries presented in this chapter and the story of downtown redevelopment told in Chapter 2 both seem to call aspects of this narrative into question. Even more importantly, perhaps, they show how it legitimized a particular strategy for downtown redevelopment, where viable alternatives existed. As this chapter illustrates, segments of both the printing and apparel industries responded differently to technological change and industry restructuring following World War II. Large, vertically integrated firms used assembly production to achieve scale economies, producing low-priced goods for mass markets and shifting production to low-cost locations outside city limits. However, smaller, vertically *dis*integrated firms achieved economies of scope through the use of flexibly specialized machinery and subcontracting arrangements. Interrelationships among manufacturers, suppliers, and subcontractors and the need to locate in close proximity to downtown customers helped root these industry segments in Chicago's downtown area.

The behavior of the latter types of manufacturers is difficult to square with the assumption of most urban political economists that mobile firms choose locations chiefly on the basis of factor costs. Printers and apparel manufacturers in Chicago's printing and garment districts developed longstanding networking relationships with subcontractors and other manufacturers. Firm owners passed along job referrals to and exchanged information with nearby competitors because they knew, based on past experience, that their neighbors would reciprocate. These relationships, based on nonmarket values like mutual trust and cooperation, could not be easily reproduced elsewhere. Production was embedded in a social context that was situated, in turn, within a particular geographical setting.

This set of arrangements helped shelter certain manufacturers from the effects of global economic restructuring. By competing more on the basis of quality, specialization, and rapid turnaround times than on the basis of price, centrally located printers and apparel manufacturers avoided direct competition with large, vertically integrated shops using low-cost land and labor to manufacture inexpensive, standardized products. Nevertheless, such competitive strategies were of little value in fending off real estate speculators acting within an institutional context in which the principal of "highest and best use" determined land-use priorities. Measures to protect central area manufacturers from real estate pressures would have caused downtown area property values to suffer. In the eyes of downtown business leaders and their allies in city government, any such efforts would have been viewed as fundamentally antigrowth.

Undergirding the downtown redevelopment plans of Chicago's progrowth alliance was an ideology of privatism. City officials insisted throughout that they were acting within a division of labor between state and market in which private investment decisions largely determined the course of central area restructuring. By maintaining that city planning efforts were formulated in response to, not in conjunction with, market-based activity, city officials could claim that their activities were essentially nonpolitical. By all indications, centrally located printing and apparel manufacturers found such arguments convincing. I asked representatives from twenty firms (thirteen apparel, seven printing) that had been displaced through redevelopment pressures whether, to the best of their knowledge, public policy had played any particular role in the events that had forced them to relocate. Nineteen of the twenty answered this question negatively. As they saw it, their problems began and ended with the interests on the part of their former landlords in obtaining the highest available returns on their property. Not only that, many seemed to find the question puzzling, as if the answer should have been obvious to someone with the credentials I claimed to own.

Given these perceptions, it is not surprising that Chicago printers and apparel manufacturers offered little in the way of resistance when confronted with real estate pressures caused by commercial and residential redevelopment activity. Because land speculators and property developers were understood to be exercising legitimate property rights, political mobilization was simply not viewed as a sensible course of action. As we shall see in Chapters 5 and 6, however, manufacturers on Chicago's Near North Side behaved much differently when confronted with similar pressures during the late 1980s and early 1990s. When piecemeal changes to the city zoning ordinance began to threaten viable industries by reducing acreage zoned for industrial use in this portion of the city, manufacturers there forged alliances with neighborhood residents, community-based organizations, labor unions, and key city officials in what would prove to be a successful bid for government protection. For this to occur, a number of critical changes had to take place in Chicago politics. These changes are the focus of the following chapter.

Mayor Richard J. Daley leading the NAACP Independence Day parade down State Street, 1963. African-American voters provided critical support for the Daley machine during the 1950s and much of the 1960s. (Chicago Historical Society, ICHi-24729)

City officials view an architect's model of the 1958 *Development Plan for the Central Area of Chicago*. The plan called for extensive land-use changes in the central area, including the replacement of near-downtown industrial districts with middle- and upper-income housing. From left to right: Clifford Campbell, Deputy Commissioner, Department of City Planning; Mayor Richard J. Daley; James C. Downs, consultant to the mayor; Ira Bach, Commissioner, Department of City Planning. (Chicago Historical Society, ICHi-24726)

South Dearborn Street in the Printing House Row district, 1890s. The signage reflects the diversity of graphic communications firms and related business services that clustered in the district. (Chicago Historical Society, ICHi-20719)

An industrial loft building housing a Chicago apparel manufacturing firm, 1920s. Beginning in the 1970s, developers began converting buildings like this to residential and office space. (Chicago Historical Society, HB-TR-280-8. Photograph by Raymond Trowbridge)

Workers laying patterns at the firm of Hart Schaffner and Marx in the Chicago garment district, 1952. (Chicago Historical Society, ICHi-24111)

Laying of foundation forms for construction of the Sears Tower in the garment district, November 8, 1970. Mayor Daley played a key role in the site assembly process by endorsing a proposal authorizing the sale of one block of Quincy Street to Sears, Roebuck and Company. (Chicago Historical Society, ICHi-26994. Photograph by Eudell H. Greene)

Women from the Harrison-Halsted community on the Near West Side march on City Hall to protest plans for the demolition of hundreds of neighborhood homes and businesses to make room for a new University of Illinois campus, April 26, 1961. Although efforts to save the community were unsuccessful, Richard J. Daley and future Chicago mayors would be forced to contend with an increasingly vocal neighborhood movement from the 1960s onward. (Reprinted with permission, *The Chicago Sun-Times* ©1996)

Police shooting at a sniper at the corner of Division Street and Clybourn Avenue during civil unrest following the assassination of Martin Luther King Jr., April 6, 1968. Mayor Daley's handling of the disturbance, including orders to Chicago police that suspected looters and arsonists be shot on sight, fueled the mayor's growing unpopularity among African-American Chicagoans. (Chicago Historical Society, ICHi-24421. Photograph by T. Kneebone)

Inauguration of Harold Washington as mayor of Chicago, April 29, 1983. Just behind Washington is former mayor Jane Byrne. (The Chicago Public Library, Special Collections Division. Photograph by Willy Schmidt)

Mayor Harold Washington shakes hands with workers during a tour of Farley Industries on Chicago's Near South Side, July 16, 1987. Washington was a strong proponent of industrial retention. (The Chicago Public Library, Special Collections Division)

Mayor Richard M. Daley announcing his administration's support for the establishment of Planned Manufacturing Districts (PMDs) in the Goose Island and Elston Corridor portions of the North River Industrial Corridor, June 14, 1990. The districts are intended to preserve land for industrial development by calling a halt to the rezoning of industrial property for new commercial or residential uses. Daley had been critical of PMDs during his election campaign one year earlier. (Reprinted with permission, *The Chicago Sun-Times* ©1996. Photograph by Amanda Alcock)

*Chapter Four*

# Community Economic Development and the Crisis of Machine Politics

The growth machine formed by Chicago city officials, downtown business elites, and labor leaders was the rule, not the exception, in postwar urban politics. In cities across the nation, similar alliances sought to revitalize and expand downtown business districts, open up low-income and working-class neighborhoods to the new middle class, build freeways, sports facilities, convention centers, and university campuses, and otherwise intensify land use and increase property values (Molotch 1976; Logan and Molotch 1987; Stone 1976; Mollenkopf 1983). Higher land values appeared to hold something for everyone—greater returns on the investments of landowners, an expanding tax base for the city, and growth in construction jobs for the building trade unions. Realizing these benefits required policies designed to transfer property into the hands of those willing to develop it to its fullest potential. Particularly in the downtown areas of large cities, this oftentimes meant rearranging land-use patterns to encourage new commercial, institutional, and middle- to upper-class residential development in areas occupied by industry and lower-income residents (Hill 1983; Mollenkopf 1983; Judd 1983; Fainstein, Fainstein, and Armistead 1983).

If the redevelopment strategies of growth machines were similar from city to city, so were the ideologies used to legitimize them. The benefits of growth, according to local business and government leaders, ultimately extended to all city residents in one form or another (Elkin 1985; Clavel and Wiewel 1991, 4). Developing property for its "highest and best use" created job opportunities and enhanced the city's fiscal position, easing the tax burden on middle-class homeowners and other city residents and providing revenues for redistribution to lower-income neighborhoods. In any case, economic development strategies were highly constrained by the market. Debate over the substance of economic development policy was thus both unnecessary and counterproductive. In Chicago and other major cities, this message was driven home by the leading area newspapers, which together with major downtown banks, department stores, utility companies, and real estate developers, formed the nucleus of urban growth machines (Molotch 1976; Logan and Molotch 1987; Feagin 1983; Shlay and Giloth 1987).[1]

Growth coalitions proved to be politically vulnerable in some cases, however, mainly because the costs and benefits of growth were unequally distributed, the former falling primarily on lower-income neighborhoods targeted for urban renewal and the latter accruing principally to downtown developers, corporations, and their employees, many of whom lived (and voted) in the suburbs. In Chicago and elsewhere, resistance to the growth machine came first in the form of self-preservation efforts by community residents whose neighborhoods were slated for large-scale clearance and renewal. On Chicago's South Side, for example, a neighborhood group called The Woodlawn Organization waged a high-profile campaign against the University of Chicago's urban renewal plans for the Hyde Park/Woodlawn area in the early 1960s (Fish 1973). Soon afterward, neighborhood activists from the Near West Side picketed City Hall and staged a sit-in at Mayor Daley's office to protest plans for the destruction of their community in order to make room for a new University of Illinois campus (Rosen 1980).

Isolated protests such as these were not always successful in blocking renewal projects, but they did force city officials and other members of local growth coalitions to divert resources into efforts aimed at maintaining social peace in the neighborhoods (Stone 1976, 1989; Fainstein, Fainstein, and Armistead 1983). Once neighborhood groups began to act in concert, however, these efforts were not always enough. During the early 1970s, for example, community organizations from white ethnic, black, and Latino neighborhoods in Chicago set aside longstanding antagonism to work together against the proposed Crosstown Expressway, which included plans for the destruction of over three thousand units of housing on the city's Northwest and Southwest Sides. With the project embroiled in controversy, Illinois Governor Dan Walker withheld state funding and plans for the expressway ultimately collapsed (Shearer 1973). A proposal for a 1992 world's fair in Chicago met with a similar fate, due once again to the opposition of a broad-based coalition of neighborhood organizations (Shlay and Giloth 1987; McClory 1986).

Such protest efforts marked the beginnings of a new variant of urban political conflict, pitting business and government leaders against community-based organizations oftentimes acting outside of formal political channels and institutions (Boyte 1980; Perlman 1976; Karapin 1994; Bennett 1989). In many cases, projects orchestrated by growth coalitions served as rallying points for community opposition (Elkin 1985; Fainstein and Fainstein 1983). The growing sophistication of these opposition efforts turned many of them into credible political forces. By the 1980s, neighborhood activism in cities across the nation had significantly compromised the ability of urban growth coalitions to unilaterally dominate local development agendas (Mollenkopf 1983; Abbott 1987; Hartman 1974; DeLeon 1992).

To some extent, the development of Chicago's neighborhood movement fits this model of urban conflict, which portrays cities as divided between supporters and opponents of downtown growth. However, this chapter raises an additional suggestion as well. Within Chicago's emerging neighborhood movement lay the seeds of something more than simple protest. By the early 1980s, a new coalition of neighborhood organizations had begun to form, not so much in opposition to growth as in favor of an alternative set of economic development priorities to those being advanced by the city's traditional growth coalition of business, labor, and government leaders. Generally speaking, these priorities included job creation over real estate development, the promotion and retention of industrial jobs over service-sector jobs, and neighborhood development over downtown development. In time, the ideas and practices generated from within this movement formed a coherent alternative to the corporate-center strategy of the growth machine. I call this alternative the "local-producer strategy" due to its emphasis, above all, on the preservation of neighborhood productive capacity.

The coalition forming around a local-producer strategy began to mature as Chicago was entering a period of regime instability and change. From the late 1960s onward, the political machine led by Mayor Richard J. Daley appeared increasingly fragile with each passing election. When Daley died in 1976, it was clear that future Chicago mayors would enjoy nowhere near the level of centralized power and authority that Daley had commanded for the previous twenty years. As this chapter will show, imperatives to forge new electoral and governing coalitions on the part of two of Daley's successors, Jane Byrne and Harold Washington, created an opening for a new coalition of neighborhood-based economic development advocates to become a significant new voice in Chicago politics.

## Building a Neighborhood Economic Development Agenda

The history of Chicago's neighborhood economic development agenda is rooted, in part, in the organizing efforts of the late Saul Alinsky and the style and philosophy of neighborhood organizing he helped to popularize in the city.[2] Alinsky began his organizing career in 1939 in the same Back of the Yards neighborhood chronicled by Upton Sinclair in *The Jungle* and eventually shifted his attention to other low- and moderate-income black, Latino, and white ethnic communities across the city during the 1950s and 1960s, particularly those experiencing racial transition. By the late 1970s, Chicago had roughly one hundred active neighborhood organizations founded by Alinsky or one of his followers (Joravsky 1990, 3).

Alinsky's primary organizational goal was to create independent bases of power in the city's neighborhoods, an objective no doubt influenced by the functioning of mainstream political institutions under Chicago's Democratic machine. As Chapter 2 showed, the machine was able to preserve its fragile electoral coalition of white ethnic and African-American neighborhood supporters while focusing economic development policies on the downtown area only by keeping substantive policy issues outside the scope of electoral politics. The latter objective was accomplished primarily through a quid pro quo arrangement in which patronage appointments, city services, and other discretionary resources were utilized to generate neighborhood support for the machine. Alinsky realized that only by building autonomous, community-based institutions that paralleled and ultimately rivaled those of the machine could the collective needs and concerns of Chicago's low- and middle-income neighborhood residents begin to be addressed. As one veteran neighborhood activist put it, Alinsky's organizations were essentially "governments in exile" (Joravsky 1990, 7).

Alinsky's organizational strategy, which he honed on the Back of the Yards neighborhood and then applied elsewhere as well, contained four key components.[3] First, existing community institutions such as churches, labor unions, and block clubs served as the building blocks of his organizations. Second, fusing these institutions into one body with a collective outlook was accomplished by organizing people around concrete, readily identifiable issues, not "abstract, mountain-top moralizing" or vague ideological pronouncements. Third, Alinsky organizations were consumer-based, calling for a redirection of goods and services in favor of low-income and working-class residential neighborhoods. Finally, organization victories were achieved through confrontational tactics designed to goad reluctant public officials and other targets into acting in the interests of the neighborhood.

This approach was effective to a point, but it also contained certain built-in limitations. The emphasis on immediate, tangible issues identifiable at the neighborhood level helped build strong organizations but left more fundamental concerns, such as racism and community power relations, unaddressed. As Harry Boyte points out,

> Alinsky's approach, for all its militancy and iconoclasm, could finally fit into the traditional interest-group form of American politics, in which different powerless groups accept the "givens" of income distribution and corporate structure and compete for scarce but expanding resources through the use of whatever tactics they can devise. (Boyte 1980, 52)

To some extent, the parochialism fostered by the Alinsky model of neighborhood organizing helped perpetuate the system of "city trenches" that have long divided the neighborhoods of cities like Chicago along racial and ethnic lines (see Katznelson 1981). In white ethnic neighborhoods experiencing racial transition, Alinsky organizations oftentimes played gatekeeper roles, focusing on community stabilization efforts designed to preserve the ethnic character of the neighborhoods they served (Squires et al. 1987, 137; Joravsky 1982).

As the 1960s were drawing to a close, these shortcomings grew increasingly apparent to many Chicago neighborhood activists, and a number of coalition-building efforts were undertaken to help bridge racial and ethnic cleavages. Several multiracial organizational networks, including the West Side Coalition and the Metropolitan Area Housing Alliance, formed in opposition to the "block-busting" and redlining of racially changing neighborhoods by unscrupulous real estate agents and banks (Metzger and Weiss 1988, 8–9).[4] Another citywide coalition, the Citizens Action Program, was established to challenge a utility rate hike requested by Commonwealth Edison, the local power company, during the autumn of 1969. Following this successful campaign, Citizens Action Program focused its efforts on such issues as redlining and the proposed Crosstown Expressway discussed earlier in the chapter (Shearer 1973; Pavlos 1975). Finally, the Chicago Central Area Committee's Chicago 21 Plan for the redevelopment of the central area served as a rallying point for coordinated opposition by a number of centrally located neighborhood organizations during the early 1970s (Betancur, Bennett, and Wright 1991).

Each of these campaigns united organizations from black, Latino, and white ethnic neighborhoods around a common agenda, demonstrating the power of coalition-building and the interests shared by all three communities. The fight against redlining, for example, helped reveal the political and institutional roots of neighborhood deterioration, leading many whites to redirect their anger away from African Americans to banks, real estate brokers, and machine politicians (Squires et al. 1987, 139). Through collective action, racial and ethnic divisions among the neighborhoods grew somewhat less hardened over the years, and the lines of conflict came to reflect a deepening division between the city's growth coalition of downtown business and government leaders and the neighborhood residents, workers, and small business owners locked out of meaningful opportunities for participation in the city's decision-making structures (Gills 1991; Mier and Moe 1991). Yet as long as these coalition-building efforts represented voices of protest alone, they could have little impact on the city's overall planning and development agenda other than perhaps to forestall certain pet projects advanced by civic leaders. To do more than that would require the neighborhoods to articulate an alternative set of practices and ideas to those emanating from downtown.

## Economic Crisis and the Rise of the Local-Producer Strategy

The consumer-based, protest-oriented approach of Alinsky-style organization-building was developed within a particular economic context, one in which the availability of well-paying manufacturing jobs was a reality for many working-class Chicagoans, particularly those from the city's white ethnic neighborhoods. Although growth in industrial employment within the city of Chicago began to taper off following World War II, it was not until the 1970s and early 1980s that manufacturing jobs experienced a sharp decline. Table 8 lists Chicago manufacturing employment by sector for the years 1958, 1972, and 1983. Citywide manufacturing employment grew from 329,000 to 389,000 between 1958 and 1972, an average increase of just over 1 percent per year. From 1972 to 1983, however, the situation worsened considerably, with total manufacturing employment falling by 131,000 jobs, an overall decline of 34 percent.

In many cases, sectoral declines were interrelated, downturns in major end-use sectors such as steel, for example, leading to widespread layoffs and plant closures among local supplier industries. Makers of machinery and machine tools were particularly hard hit by the decline of the Chicago area steel industry during the 1970s and early 1980s (Midwest Center for Labor Research 1989, 4). Such ripple effects also extended to neighborhood banks, grocery stores, and small shopping malls, where laid-off workers from steel and steel-

**Table 8.** Manufacturing Employment in the City of Chicago,
1958, 1972, and 1983

| Industries | 1958 | 1972 | 1983 |
|---|---|---|---|
| Lumber, wood, furniture | 8,171 | 15,300 | 9,821 |
| Stone, clay, and glass | 3,670 | 4,900 | 3,797 |
| Primary metals | 25,033 | 31,100 | 14,185 |
| Fabricated metals | 34,232 | 48,000 | 28,070 |
| Nonelectrical machinery | 30, 290 | 36,200 | 20,760 |
| Electrical machinery | 49,625 | 46,800 | 25,539 |
| Transportation equipment | 5,660 | 12,100 | 7,574 |
| Instruments and misc. | 22,738 | 30,500 | 16,464 |
| Food and kindred products | 51,127 | 50,900 | 41,795 |
| Apparel and allied products | 21,436 | 18,200 | 9,063 |
| Paper, printing, publishing | 55,148 | 71,900 | 54,675 |
| Chemicals, petroleum, coal | 11,803 | 13,000 | 14,452 |
| Other nondurables | 10,099 | 10,100 | 11,817 |
| Total | 329,032 | 389,000 | 258,012 |

Sources: Department of City Planning (1960); U.S. Bureau of the Census (1976);
Illinois Department of Employment Security (1983).

related industries formerly spent and invested their wages. University of Illinois economist Joseph Persky estimated that the loss of 20,000 Chicago area steelworker jobs in 1979 ultimately resulted in an additional 10,000 job losses within the next year (Squires et al. 1987, 30). Area housing markets were affected as well. Between 1970 and 1980, Chicago lost an estimated 5 percent of its rental housing stock, or 40,145 units (Weiss and Metzger 1989, 142).

The downward spiral of Chicago's working-class neighborhoods during the 1970s was cast into sharp relief by the urban renaissance taking place in the downtown area, led by the record-setting pace of office-building construction in the Loop. Economic development plans published during the 1970s and early 1980s under the Richard J. Daley and Jane Byrne administrations anticipated a restructuring of the city's economic base from manufacturing to services and proposed downtown-oriented policies and programs designed to accommodate such a shift (Chicago Central Area Committee 1973; Department of Planning 1982). However, the service sector was proving itself unreliable as a source of job creation. Although Loop employment posted a modest gain of 11,574 jobs between 1972 and 1983, the number of nonmanufacturing jobs citywide actually declined by 45,000 during this period (Illinois Department of Employment Security 1984; Clavel and Wiewel 1991, 19).

Table 9 shows the impact of industrial decline and a lackluster service-sector performance on employment in five working-class Chicago neighborhoods during the 1970s and early 1980s. Between 1972 and 1983, employment in these five neighborhoods alone fell by over 63,000 jobs, resulting in a combined average job loss of 35 percent. By 1982, the city's overall unemployment rate had risen to a postwar high of 17 percent (Squires et al. 1987, 43). In addition, due to declining unionization rates and the low productivity of many of the new service-sector jobs, Chicagoans who did have jobs were oftentimes working for less. As a result, average real incomes fell from $20,894 in 1969 to $18,776 in 1979, a decrease of 10 percent (Squires et al. 1987, 41).

**Table 9.** Employment in Five Chicago Community Areas, 1972 and 1983

| Community Area | 1972 | 1983 | Percent Change |
| --- | --- | --- | --- |
| Stockyards | 46,026 | 24,963 | -46 |
| Pilsen | 37,070 | 24,295 | -35 |
| Garfield Park | 35,304 | 20,886 | -41 |
| Wicker Park | 34,571 | 24,641 | -29 |
| Logan Square | 21,253 | 16,025 | -25 |

*Sources:* Illinois Department of Employment Security (1972, 1983).

In May 1981, as the crisis was drawing to a head, the *Chicago Tribune* responded with a four-part series entitled "Chicago: City on the Brink." *Tribune* economics correspondent R. C. Longworth seemed to identify the problem accurately: manufacturing employment in the city's neighborhoods had gone into a free fall, and service sector job opportunities in the Loop and elsewhere in the city were not picking up the slack. However, those called upon by Longworth to propose solutions were primarily business leaders, academics, and city planning officials, not representatives from the neighborhoods themselves. The remedies offered were predictable, ranging from greater public support for downtown redevelopment, to tax holidays and regulatory relief as a means of attracting new industries, to University of Chicago sociologist Gerald Suttles' suggestion that the unemployed be encouraged to leave the city altogether. According to Suttles,

> I don't think you should give anybody any incentive to stay where there is no hope of employment. Our incentives ought to be concentrated on getting them to move elsewhere. . . . We can be human but we have to say, "Look, it doesn't make any sense to keep you here." (Longworth 1981)

The combination of economic decline and dissatisfaction with outsider-defined solutions such as these ultimately led many community-based organizations to broaden their agendas from protest and advocacy around improved service delivery and community self-preservation to the actual rebuilding of neighborhood economies (Betancur, Bennett, and Wright 1991; Wright 1992; Clavel and Wiewel 1991, 25–27). A conceptual shift began to occur, through which neighborhood activists came to perceive their communities increasingly as sites for both consumption and production (McKnight and Kretzmann 1984). In African-American neighborhoods, this shift dovetailed with ideas that had been emerging from the more militant factions of the civil-rights movement since the 1960s, emphasizing black cultural and political autonomy and community self-reliance (Gills 1991, 43). By the late 1970s, community development corporations (CDCs) from black, Latino, and white ethnic areas of Chicago were experimenting with a variety of local development initiatives, including housing rehabilitation, small-business development, and efforts to assist and retain existing neighborhood retail and industrial establishments.

The funding requirements of these new undertakings encouraged CDCs to forge new partnerships with municipal government agencies, which typically acted as brokers for federal-funding programs designed to promote community development. Housing development groups received assistance from the HUD Section 8, Rental Subsidy Program, which supported the construction or rehabilitation of 8,976 housing units in Chicago between 1975 and 1980 (Metzger and Weiss 1988, 28). Beginning in 1980, housing

CDCs could also apply for HUD self-help grants, worth upward of $100,000 each (Slonka 1981; Betancur, Bennett, and Wright 1991, 205). Both housing and business development organizations received funding through HUD's Community Development Block Grant (CDBG) program, established in 1974 to provide support for economic development projects in low- and moderate-income communities (Wright 1992; Betancur, Bennett, and Wright 1991). Finally, many business development CDCs took advantage of the Small Business Administration Section 503 Certified Development Company Program to help build their business loan-packaging capabilities (Metzger and Weiss 1988, 28–29).

Programs such as these boosted the capacity of neighborhood organizations to pursue community-based economic development efforts, but they also forced organizations to struggle with new tensions between community organizing and community development. The confrontational negotiating style favored by Alinsky was generally not the most effective way for organizations to secure a greater share of CDBG funds and other economic development resources from local public officials, yet local discretion in the use of federal economic development funds meant that community pressure in one form or another was essential. In many cases, this proved to be a difficult balance to strike (Capraro, Ditton, and Giloth 1985, 40–44; Mott 1984).

Although early community economic development efforts in Chicago were limited primarily to housing rehabilitation and the development of small-business ventures (Mier and Wiewel 1983; Slonka 1981), by the early 1980s a growing number of organizations also began providing assistance to, and advocacy on behalf of, small- to mid-sized neighborhood industries (Mier and Moe 1991; Mier, Wiewel, and Alpern 1992). The latter efforts were prompted chiefly by the growing realization on the part of community economic development practitioners that high-paying blue-collar jobs yielded larger economic multipliers than the employment provided by most other types of neighborhood development efforts (Lemonides 1984). Some of the most creative, experimental approaches to neighborhood economic development that blossomed in Chicago during this period involved the efforts of these industrial development organizations (IDOs). Space does not allow for an exhaustive review of these efforts here. However, a brief look at a number of organizations and strategies provides a useful cross section of this segment of Chicago's neighborhood economic development community.

Beginning in the early 1980s, the growing shortage of affordable, centrally located production space for both new and established manufacturers led a number of Chicago industrial development organizations to initiate efforts to develop small-business incubators, typically using older industrial loft buildings in near-downtown areas of the city (Auerbach 1980a; Community Workshop on Economic Development 1987; Capraro, Ditton, and Giloth 1985).

Business incubators provide low-cost production space and business services for small, start-up industries, generally for a limited duration. The most successful of these projects was begun in 1981 by a West Side organization, the Industrial Council of Northwest Chicago (ICNC), which used a $1.7 million grant from the Economic Development Administration of the U.S. Department of Commerce to develop a small-business incubator in a largely abandoned multistory industrial building on the city's Near West Side.

According to ICNC executive director Ken Govas, some of the primary advantages offered to incubator firms included low rents of between $1.50 and $1.75 per square foot and access to shared administrative services. In addition, ICNC support staff acted as intermediaries among incubator companies and outside institutions, helping to foster cooperative peer relationships among tenant firms and providing access to other institutions critical to the success of newly established businesses, such as local banks, technical assistance providers, and government agencies. By 1985, nearly half the companies located in the incubator had developed customer/supplier relationships with other incubator firms. There was also some cooperative bidding on jobs and some sharing of employees. During the first four years of its operation only four companies failed, while total employment increased to five hundred workers (Govas 1995).

The fostering of cooperative and collaborative relationships among manufacturing firms located within close proximity to one another became a growing priority for other Chicago industrial development organizations as well during the early and mid-1980s. These efforts sometimes targeted specific industrial sectors, such as metalworking or woodworking. In 1985, for example, a North Side organization, the Jane Addams Resource Corporation (JARC), began operating a consortium of metalworking firms that grew from eight to twenty-five members during the first three years of its operation. North Side metalworking establishments faced a number of challenges by the mid-1980s. Most were small- to medium-sized "job shops," producing components for nearby original equipment manufacturers (OEMs) such as Playskool, Sunbeam, and Stewart-Warner. During the late 1970s and early 1980s, many of the area's larger OEMs began to source elsewhere or to relocate out of the city altogether, forcing North Side metalworkers to broaden their customer bases (McCormick 1994). For many, this required technological upgrades, improved quality standards, and much greater attention to marketing than before, all costly undertakings involving considerable risk for small, cash-poor manufacturers (Vindasius 1988).

The networking relationships fostered through JARC's metalworking consortium enabled member firms both to share the risks and costs associated with industry restructuring and to expand market opportunities (Vindasius 1988). According to JARC executive director Michael Buccitelli, informal networking among owners and operators of small job shops is commonplace. However, a broker like JARC can help expedite and cement such relationships, leading in some instances to highly structured cooperative undertakings such as new product development. As Buccitelli explains,

> We do see a lot more sharing of ideas and solutions [among consortium member firms]. Somebody from a small job shop will go over to another job shop or consortium member that we've introduced them to to see how they've acclimated. . . . Certain companies network more than others because of their proximity to one another. A couple of consortium members located on the same block have been collaborating on new product development ideas, subcontracting to one another, maybe borrowing materials or purchasing materials from each other. A lot of these kinds of relationships are certainly developing. (Buccitelli 1995)

Other Chicago industrial development organizations pursued place-specific rather than sector-specific industrial-advocacy approaches. One such strategy that proved to be particularly effective was pioneered in 1982 by a Northwest Side organization, Greater North Pulaski Development Corporation (GNPDC). GNPDC focused its efforts on revitalizing a small, visibly deteriorating industrial district in the Humboldt Park area of the Northwest Side. Following Alinsky, organization staff members formed a broad-based advisory committee including area manufacturers, neighborhood residents, representatives from community organizations and nearby churches, academics, real estate brokers, and the ward alderman to draft a development plan for the area (Center for Urban Economic Development 1983; Lemonides 1984). The broad base of community participation helped mobilize aldermanic support for the plan, leading to commitments on the part of the city to provide public infrastructure and improve city services in the area during the following year (Lemonides 1984). The project eventually became the model for one of the Harold Washington administration's key industrial programs, the Local Industrial Retention Initiative (Lemonides 1995).

Experimentation such as this both required and helped facilitate considerable learning and capacity-building on the part of many Chicago industrial development organizations. In many cases, as the policy implications of their industrial outreach efforts began to unfold, organizations broadened their efforts to include stronger advocacy roles. For example, a Near North Side organization, the Local Economic and Employment Development (LEED) Council, was established in 1982 partly to improve employment linkages between residents of the Cabrini-Green public-housing development and nearby manufacturers in the North River Industrial Corridor (Ducharme 1991). However, organizers soon discovered the area's manufacturing base was being threatened by the conversion of industrial buildings and industrially zoned property to residential and commercial uses. As a result, LEED Council staff members began to channel their efforts into a major organizing drive among area manufacturers designed to raise public awareness of such land-use conflicts and to pressure the city to take steps to preserve the area's concentration of high-paying manufacturing jobs (Ducharme 1991; Giloth and Betancur 1988).[5]

## Coalition-Building among Community Development Corporations

In general, both industrial development organizations and other community-based economic development and housing organizations that formed during the 1970s and early 1980s tended to be much more open to coalition-building, networking, and the sharing of resources and information than the older, more turf-conscious, Alinsky-inspired organizations had been (Gills 1991, 45). From the mid-1970s onward, a considerable amount of formal and informal networking among such groups began to take place, in many cases bridging racial, class, and philosophical divides (Mier and Moe 1991; Mier, Wiewel, and Alpern 1992). This made it possible for the new insights into community development and industrial retention provided by experiments such as those described in the previous section to be disseminated among a wide range of neighborhood development groups. It also made the city's corporate-center strategy for downtown redevelopment the subject of a growing challenge from an increasingly vocal chorus of neighborhood organizations rapidly coming together around an alternative set of economic development practices and ideas.

Neighborhood housing development organizations were among the first community development groups to unite formally, establishing the Chicago Rehab Network in 1976. The coalition's initial efforts involved providing technical assistance to local housing groups and acting as a liaison to programs offered by the Chicago Department of Housing (Metzger and Weiss 1988, 27–28; Auerbach 1980b). By the late 1970s, the Rehab Network had also become a vocal policy advocate for community-based housing initiatives, pressuring the city for greater community participation in public-housing developments, use of the city's own land inventory for low- and moderate-income housing, and targeting of capital improvements to leverage private investment in affordable housing (Auerbach 1980b; Gills 1991).

Economic development groups coalesced in two citywide umbrella organizations, the Chicago Association of Neighborhood Development Organizations (CANDO) and the Community Workshop on Economic Development (CWED), formed in 1979 and 1982, respectively. CWED, the more policy-oriented of the two groups, played a key role in Harold Washington's 1983 mayoral campaign discussed later in the chapter. CANDO began as a coalition of neighborhood-based business development groups working to preserve neighborhood retail strips by engaging in policy advocacy and providing a variety of services, such as loan packaging and assistance with storefront modernization, to its membership organizations. By the early 1980s, as its membership base grew increasingly preoccupied with efforts to halt neighborhood industrial decline, CANDO expanded its focus to include advocacy and technical assistance for neighborhood industrial development organizations (Chicago Association of Neighborhood Development Organizations 1994; Mier, Wiewel, and Alpern 1992).

The advocacy efforts of these new coalitions and the new experimentation in neighborhood economic development they supported helped broaden the downtown-versus-the-neighborhoods debate from a conflict focused predominantly around questions of redistribution and neighborhood preservation to one in which the substance of economic development policy also became a subject for legitimate public discussion and debate. According to former Harold Washington administration officials Robert Giloth and Robert Mier,

> The antinomy of neighborhood versus downtown—a long-standing, urban grass-roots metaphor—was transformed in Chicago and elsewhere in the 1980s to portray a new set of development choices: manufacturing versus the service economy; blue-collar jobs versus low-wage McJobs; job generation versus real estate development; industrial expansion versus downtown growth; credit-starved neighborhoods versus the growth of the finance industry; targeted local hiring versus regional business climate; and minority/female business versus efficiency. (Giloth and Mier 1989, 185)

By the time of the 1983 mayor's race, the growing strength, sophistication, and political mobilization of Chicago's neighborhood development community posed a significant challenge to the political power and influence of the city's progrowth alliance and its ability to continue to define economic development in terms beneficial primarily to its own member organizations and institutions. Increasingly, proponents of downtown development were forced to defend their economic programs against a coherent local-producer strategy for neighborhood redevelopment evolving from within the neighborhoods themselves. Nothing demonstrated this growing vulnerability more convincingly than Harold Washington's successful neighborhood-backed campaign to unseat the growth machine's candidate of choice in the 1983 Democratic primary, incumbent mayor Jane Byrne.

## The Jane Byrne Anti-Coalition

Ironically, Byrne herself had initially been a key beneficiary of the growing political mobilization occurring within lower- and middle-income Chicago neighborhoods. Byrne, a Daley protégé and former cochair (with Daley) of the Cook County Democratic Central Committee, had entered the 1979 mayor's race against incumbent Mayor Michael Bilandic, selected by Democratic Party insiders to serve the remainder of Mayor Daley's term following Daley's death of a heart attack in 1976. Bilandic's political strategy paralleled that of his predecessor. Under the Bilandic administration, the narrow governing coalition of business and labor leaders, city bureaucrats, and machine politicians that had dominated policymaking under Daley's tenure as mayor remained largely intact, while patronage appointments and other discretionary favors were deployed to maintain electoral support in the neighborhoods (Rakove 1982).

For some time now, however, the electoral component of this strategy had been showing signs of increasing strain. To begin with, a number of groups excluded from the machine's governing coalition had begun to demand collective benefits and a greater voice in the public-policy debate, while the machine continued responding to them as individuals, if at all (Ferman 1991). Blacks, in particular, energized by the civil-rights movement and Martin Luther King Jr.'s marches and organizing efforts in Chicago during the mid-1960s, grew more vocal in their demands for equal access to housing and educational opportunities. Mayor Daley, unwilling to jeopardize his support among white ethnics, responded by appointing anti-integrationists to the Chicago Housing Authority (CHA) and the Board of Education, defending the Chicago Police Department against accusations of discriminatory hiring and promotion practices, and issuing his infamous "shoot to kill" orders to Chicago police during the riots following King's assassination in the spring of 1968 (Ferman 1991, 53; Kleppner 1985, 84–85). As a result of actions like these, voter support for machine candidates in the city's predominantly African-American wards declined precipitously from the late 1960s onward (Kleppner 1985, 75).

Neighborhood organizations, whose constituencies included a racially and ethnically diverse range of low-income and working-class communities, represented an additional base of support for a potential challenge to the machine. Although Chicago's neighborhood movement had yet to coalesce around a coherent neighborhood agenda by the time of the 1979 mayor's race, growing community demands for access to decision-making bodies and a greater share of municipal service dollars and economic development funds further undermined the machine's ability to mobilize neighborhood support through the provision of particularistic benefits (Ferman 1991).

For that matter, a number of the key resources that the machine had traditionally utilized to reward its supporters were by this time in decline anyway. Most importantly, political firing was declared unconstitutional in 1972 in the first of the Shakman Decrees, jeopardizing the Cook County Democratic Central Committee's control over an estimated 21,500 patronage jobs (Erie 1988, 152–153).[6] In addition, federal urban social programs, which machine politicians had relied upon heavily to reward and to co-opt minorities, experienced major cutbacks under the Carter administration from 1977 to 1980

(Erie 1988, 184–186). The loss of these key resources, combined with growing militancy on the part of neighborhood groups and minorities, significantly reduced party loyalties during the 1970s.

Jane Byrne entered the 1979 mayor's race with no organization or precinct workers and little money. However, she well understood the machine's weaknesses and attacked Bilandic where he was most vulnerable, making strong overtures to the neighborhoods and campaigning actively in the city's black wards. Throughout the winter of 1979, Byrne appeared regularly at block-club meetings, church services, and community celebrations in African-American neighborhoods on the city's South and West Sides. She called, in somewhat unspecific terms, for the establishment of neighborhood planning councils and increased funding for neighborhood-based economic development and affordable housing programs. She criticized the level of public support that the Bilandic administration had provided for downtown redevelopment, promising a more balanced pattern of development between downtown and the neighborhoods under a future Byrne administration (Reardon 1990, 54–55; Kleppner 1985, 115).

Byrne's campaign received a number of unexpected boosts. First, the winter of 1979 was unusually harsh, the total season snowfall of eighty-seven inches more than doubling that of an average Chicago winter. For most of the month of January, many side streets remained impassable, garbage was left uncollected, and Chicago Transit Authority (CTA) buses and trains ran hours late. Then, in late January, CTA officials decided to improve service to its suburban commuters by closing six inner-city stops in predominantly black neighborhoods during the morning and evening rush hours. After four days of protests and the threat of a civil-rights suit, the CTA reversed its decision, but the political fallout from the incident would continue to dog Bilandic for the remainder of the election campaign (Rakove 1982; Kleppner 1985, 112–113).

In addition, despite slim margins of victory for machine candidates in the previous two mayoral primaries, Bilandic and his supporters initially saw Byrne's candidacy as so frivolous that they did not even bother to recruit a black or liberal challenger to divide the antimachine vote among several opposition candidates. As Byrne's candidacy gained momentum during the snowy winter of 1979, the shortsightedness of this decision became obvious, but by that point it was too late to remedy the situation. The 1979 Democratic mayoral primary thus shaped up as a two-way contest between a politically vulnerable incumbent and a challenger whose appeal was based more on the rising antimachine sentiment shared by growing numbers of Chicagoans than on a well-articulated agenda for governing the city (Rakove 1982).

On February 27, 1979, the machine's slated candidate for mayor was defeated at the polls for the first time in a half century, as Byrne edged out Michael Bilandic in the Democratic mayoral primary by the slim margin of 16,775 votes (Kleppner 1985, 104). Black voters vented their anger at

Bilandic by rallying behind Byrne, handing her majorities in fourteen of the city's sixteen predominantly black wards. Byrne also outpolled Bilandic in the mostly white ethnic wards of the Northwest Side and the white middle-class wards along the lakefront. Several months later, she trounced her Republican opponent Wallace Johnson in the general election, winning 82 percent of the popular vote (Holli 1995; Ciccone 1979).

## Planning and Development Policy under the Jane Byrne Administration

Following Byrne's triumph over the machine, a wave of euphoria swept over the low-income and working-class neighborhood wards that formed the base of her electoral coalition, as it appeared that the mayor's office had fallen into the hands of someone committed to balancing their interests against those of the city's downtown business and political leadership. Indeed, a number of Byrne's initial acts as mayor gave her supporters cause for optimism. At Mayor Byrne's request, Northwestern University Professor Louis Masotti formed a broad-based transition team of academics, public administrators, and municipal reformers to prepare a four-year plan for reforming city government (Reardon 1990, 52; Holli 1995, 169). Soon after the election, Byrne also took the first steps toward implementing her campaign promise to establish neighborhood planning councils, awarding the Chicago consulting firm of John A. Melaniphy Associates a $600,000 contract to conduct a needs assessment of the city's seventy-seven community areas and prepare a feasibility study examining various approaches to community planning (Reardon 1990, 56).

Yet the high hopes of Byrne's neighborhood supporters were quickly dashed. The new mayor soon reversed her support for neighborhood planning councils with substantive decision-making powers. The release of the Melaniphy report was suppressed, and Professor Masotti's transition team was ultimately given the cold shoulder by the new administration (Holli 1995, 169; Reardon 1990, 56). In the meantime, Byrne undertook steps to strengthen the administration's ties with members of the city's traditional power structure. She watched quietly in the aftermath of the election as the Democratic machine's leadership in city council awarded key committee chairmanships to its most ardent supporters, taking no action to secure leadership positions for her own backers in city council. She soon developed close working relationships with prominent machine aldermen such as Eddie Vrdolyak and Edward Burke, individuals she had singled out during her election campaign as part of an "evil cabal of men" unsympathetic to the needs of the city's neighborhoods (Kleppner 1985, 117; Reardon 1990, 49–51).

Byrne also moved quickly to mend fences with members of the downtown business community, some of whom had expressed concern over her antibusiness campaign rhetoric (Gruber 1979).[7] Over the opposition of historical preservationist groups and neighborhood organizations that had supported her election bid, Byrne sought approximately $120 million in direct subsidies and tax abatements for a major redevelopment project in the North Loop she had criticized during her election campaign (Bennett et al. 1988). She supported the developers of Presidential Towers, a $200 million, 2,346-unit upscale housing development on the Near West Side, by helping to arrange an insured, low-interest $158 million federal mortgage and a low-interest $180 million construction loan financed through the sale of tax-exempt bonds (Ferman and Grimshaw 1992).[8] Finally, she gave the administration's backing to plans for a 1992 Chicago world's fair, spearheaded by former Commonwealth Edison utility executive Thomas Ayers with the support of other key members of Chicago's growth coalition. The proposal, which sparked the mobilization of a citywide coalition of opposition groups, involved an estimated cost of between $885 million and $1 billion and called for the razing of viable community areas and businesses on the city's Near South Side (Shlay and Giloth 1987).

Efforts such as these were consistent with the policies articulated in the major planning document issued by the Byrne administration, the *Chicago 1992 Comprehensive Plan,* which committed the administration to using its financing powers and controls over land use and public infrastructure to support the plans and objectives of the downtown business community (Department of Planning 1982). The plan represented a ten-year redevelopment program for the city, culminating in the 1992 Chicago World's Fair. Its vision of Chicago in the year 1992, like earlier economic development and land-use plans published during the Richard J. Daley administration, was that of the postindustrial city, driven by the growth of its finance, trade, and service industries downtown.

While expressing a commitment to the retention of manufacturing jobs in the neighborhoods, Mayor Byrne supplied few supportive resources or programs. Of a total of $163 million budgeted for citywide economic development expenditures in the Byrne administration's 1981–1985 Five Year Capital Improvements Program, $70 million (43 percent) alone was targeted for redevelopment projects in the Loop (City of Chicago 1981). Meanwhile, in an apparent attempt to shore up her electoral standing in low- and moderate-income communities, Byrne channeled CDBG funds into traditional services such as street cleaning and snow removal instead of economic development projects, continuing the machine's tradition of currying favor with its lower-income and working-class constituencies through service provision and other localized benefits (Rich 1993, 200).

## Interpretations of the Byrne Administration

Mayor Byrne's alliance with the downtown business community and machine leadership in city council following an election campaign in which she promised a more equitable distribution of resources and policies seems consistent with the views of most contemporary urban political economists, who, as we saw in Chapter 1, tend to be largely pessimistic about the long-term prospects of neighborhood-based governing regimes. City officials lack the authority to rule by themselves, a situation that leads them to seek partnerships with nongovernmental actors in possession of resources necessary for governing (Stone 1989; Elkin 1985; Stone, Orr, and Imbroscio 1991). Although many resources and activities are essential for the well-being of cities, the need for economic growth to provide jobs and to maintain tax revenues means that *economic* resources are particularly valuable (Stone 1993; Fainstein 1990). According to political scientist Clarence Stone, the concentration of economic resources in the hands of the downtown business community produces a "strong tug" toward some form of business/government alliance and gives populist regimes a "built-in tendency towards instability" (Stone 1987b, 286–287). Campaign promises for fairness and equity in city planning and policymaking tend to dissipate quickly once the election is over and the need for policies to support downtown development becomes evident (Stone 1987b; Elkin 1985; Logan and Molotch 1987).

A number of explanations for Byrne's behavior in the aftermath of her election victory have been advanced, some of which are consistent with this kind of reasoning. For example, Holli (1995) and Reardon (1990) have both emphasized the city's deteriorating fiscal position in the late 1970s. Shortly after Byrne assumed office, her financial advisors discovered a previously undisclosed $100 million deficit in the city budget. Public revelation of the deficit caused Standard and Poor's to lower Chicago's general obligation bond rating from AA to A-, and Byrne is said to have been forced away from a redistributive agenda under pressure from the city's creditors to demonstrate her administration's commitment to restoring the city's fiscal integrity.

It has also been suggested that Byrne's electoral coalition of blacks, lakefront liberals, and Northwest Side white ethnics was too diverse to refashion into a governing coalition, leaving Byrne with little alternative but to seek alliances with the very elements of Chicago's power structure she had run against during her election campaign (Rakove 1982; Ferman 1991; Kleppner 1985, 118). According to political scientist Milton Rakove,

> [Byrne's electoral coalition] could only come together for winning an election or, rather, defeating an incumbent. It was not a coalition with which Byrne (or anyone else) could govern the city, unless she was prepared to undertake drastic changes in the thrust of public policies. And if she did that, she would immediately alienate segments of the coalition, since they had contradictory ideas of what should be done and inherently conflicting interests. (Rakove 1982, 230)

Each of these arguments would be more convincing if it were not for the fact that Harold Washington, faced with similar pressures and constraints after assuming the mayor's office in 1983, behaved much differently than Byrne. Washington's electoral coalition of blacks, Latinos, and lakefront liberals was similar in its diversity to that of his predecessor, yet, unlike Byrne, Washington forged a governing coalition that included each of these groups. Moreover, he did so despite inheriting a $121 million budget deficit from the Byrne administration and facing a disappointing B+++ Standard and Poor's debt rating for much of his tenure as mayor.[9]

The key explanation for Byrne's behavior lies not so much with the city's budgetary position or with "irreconcilable differences" among members of her electoral coalition, although each of these pressures was certainly a contributing factor. More importantly, Byrne and her supporters had simply made no attempt to develop a positive program for governing the city once she was in office. Her electoral coalition was an "anti-coalition," united around its dissatisfaction with the Bilandic administration's downtown-oriented policies and neglect of neighborhood concerns but lacking a shared consensus around an alternative set of governing principles.[10] Such a consensus was not an impossible one to achieve, as the following discussion of Harold Washington's mayoral campaign illustrates. It would, however, require both a stronger commitment to the neighborhoods than Byrne appears to have held and a well-orchestrated effort by the neighborhoods themselves to advance a coherent economic development policy agenda of their own. Not until the 1983 mayor's race would such an agenda become clearly recognizable.

## CWED and the Harold Washington Mayoral Campaign

Jane Byrne's insensitivities to the needs and interests of the lower-income and working-class communities largely responsible for her 1979 election victory fueled a growing sense of outrage among these constituencies, as it became increasingly evident that the new mayor had no intention of delivering on her campaign promises for more fairness and equity in city government. This frustration was compounded by newly elected President Ronald Reagan's policy of "New Federalism," which featured cutbacks in federal funds for community development and social services, and a market-based approach centered around the creation of "enterprise zones" to address the problems of disinvestment and deindustrialization in urban communities. Neighborhood activists protested the budget cuts and voiced concerns that the tax breaks and regulatory relief offered to firms within the new enterprise zones would encourage destructive competition among inner-city communities (Giloth and Mier 1989).

In early 1982, a church-based civic organization called the Community Renewal Society invited several hundred representatives from Chicago-based neighborhood organizations to a conference whose purpose was to develop a citywide neighborhood response to the enterprise zone legislation then under consideration in the Illinois state legislature. At the conference, it became clear that, in addition to the critique of enterprise zones, there was an interest in developing a positive set of policy alternatives based on the new community development efforts with which neighborhood organizations from across the city had been experimenting (Mīer, Wiewel, and Alpern 1992). At this point, no such agenda had yet been advanced in Chicago on a citywide basis. As one conference participant put it,

> There's a sense in which this enterprise zone idea made us aware, for the first time, of what a policy gap there was. Didn't we have a set of ideas about how to develop communities and create jobs that would put this to shame? So we sort of got backed into understanding what a policy void there was. At that point in the early 1980s, the first CDCs had only been in existence for probably ten years, so it wasn't like there was a huge, decades-long set of experiences. The idea that you could knit together practices that were being invented in community development, kick it up to another level and say, "What policy implications might there be here?" was a new idea. (Kretzmann 1996)

During the next eight to ten months, organization leaders continued to meet on a regular basis, eventually uniting formally as the Community Workshop on Economic Development (CWED). A key purpose of the meetings was to produce a policy statement that incorporated the experiences and policy concerns of both organization leaders and their constituencies. By late summer of 1982, the main principles and recommendations of the CWED policy statement had been put into writing (Community Workshop on Economic Development 1982).[11] The document identified seven primary goals and seventeen specific policy recommendations through which these goals were to be implemented. Included were calls for greater community ownership and control over economic resources, more community involvement in the planning of economic development programs, policies designed to promote full employment, and a shift of public resources in favor of neighborhood development projects. "Top-down" solutions to community development were explicitly rejected in the statement's preamble, which stated:

> During the past two decades, community-based organizations throughout Chicago have accumulated a vast store of knowledge and experience about economic development. Their understanding of programs that have been successful or unsuccessful, combined with direct information about community needs and strengths, provides them with the expertise and perspective necessary for the design of appropriate policies that can foster self-sustaining economic development in existing Chicago communities. This point also leads to the conclusion that communities must participate actively in locally initiated and controlled planning for community economic development. (Community Workshop on Economic Development 1982)

At the same time that CWED-member organizations were building a consensus around the principles contained in the CWED policy statement, many black Chicagoans were beginning to mobilize around an additional set of concerns more specific to African Americans. In July 1982, Mayor Byrne capped a series of high-profile snubs of the black community by replacing two African-American members of the Chicago Housing Authority with whites, tipping the balance of the authority from a black majority to a white majority (Kleppner 1985, 136–146). In response, a wide range of community organizations led by Jesse Jackson's Operation PUSH formed the People's Coalition to Boycott ChicagoFest, a week-long outdoor music festival sponsored by the Mayor's Office of Special Events. The boycott seemed both to energize and to galvanize the black community, cutting across longstanding divisions and ultimately fueling a voter registration drive launched earlier in the summer (Rivlin 1992). By November 1982, black voter registration since the 1979 mayoral election had increased by 127,000, while voter registration among white Chicagoans rose by only 1,656 during the same period (Kleppner 1985, 148).

The success of the drive convinced many African-American leaders that the mayor's office was within their grasp (Mier and Moe 1991; Rivlin 1992). The favored candidate among black Chicagoans was Harold Washington, at the time a U.S. Congressman from the 1st Congressional District on Chicago's South Side. Washington had strong ties to many of the city's black neighborhood organizations, but he was also well-known and well-liked by progressive whites. On November 10, 1982, after considerable prodding by neighborhood activists and African-American political leaders, he formally announced his entry as a candidate in the upcoming Democratic mayoral primary scheduled for the following February.

Washington quickly appointed two individuals active in CWED, Hal Baron and Kari Moe, to leadership positions on the campaign's Research and Issues Committee, where the central policy proposals of the campaign platform were to be developed. At Baron's suggestion, Washington agreed to forego the conventional approach to issues development, which was to assemble a small group of "experts" compatible with the candidate's politics to write position papers. Instead, roughly fifteen issues teams staffed by ten or more individuals each were designated to conduct research and write papers on specific topics such as energy, housing, transportation, neighborhoods, and economic development. The papers drafted by each team were published collectively as the "Washington Papers," the campaign's central policy document (Mier and Moe 1991).

The economic development issues team included a number of additional CWED participants and ultimately served as a gateway for certain key ideas and proposals voiced in the CWED policy statement to find their way into the Washington Papers.[12] One of the most important of these ideas was the argument that job creation, *not* real estate development, should be the long-term goal of economic development policy. Public policy had operated for years under the assumption that these two goals were synonymous—that employment opportunities for Chicago residents were an obvious corollary of policies that encouraged the development of property for its "highest and best use." In severing the connection between the two and identifying job creation as the long-term policy objective, the Washington Papers set the stage for a more open public debate over the shape of the city's economic future. In cases where the land-use preferences of commercial or residential property developers and those of manufacturers conflicted, for example, property values would no longer represent the sole standard against which public decisions would be determined and evaluated. This was a radical departure from the reigning ideology of Chicago's progrowth alliance. Other priorities voiced in the Washington Papers—including full employment, an emphasis on neighborhood development over downtown development, and a commitment to retaining traditional manufacturing industries—promised a similar departure from the economic development policies, practices, and ideological claims of previous governing coalitions.

The Washington Papers were important as well because they provided the campaign with a positive set of governing principles. The broad-based, participatory framework through which the campaign issues papers were developed helped bring together the diverse strands of Washington's electoral coalition around a common agenda for governing the city. It meant that Washington's electoral coalition, unlike that of Jane Byrne, would be more than an anti-coalition, united in its dissatisfaction with the status quo but lacking a coherent set of positive policy alternatives. Ultimately, many of the key ideas, policies, and programs appearing in the Washington Papers—including the emphasis on jobs over real estate development—were reproduced in the Washington administration's economic development plan, *Chicago Works Together: 1984 Chicago Development Plan* (City of Chicago 1984). Policies articulated in the Washington Papers and the 1984 Chicago Development Plan not only helped to establish the administration's economic development agenda but also could be conveniently held over the administration's head by members of the Washington coalition when the pressures of governing began to push the administration in less progressive directions (Ducharme 1991).

Not surprisingly, the Washington Papers did not play well within the city's downtown business community, which divided its support between Washington's two rivals in the Democratic mayoral primary, Jane Byrne and Richard M. Daley, the eldest son of the late mayor. It was a campaign marked by deep divisions along class and racial lines. In an editorial entitled "White Business and Black Mayors," *Crain's Chicago Business* openly questioned whether the city's white business establishment could work with an African-American mayor.

[Washington] has to win the support of a basically suspicious business community, which in the final analysis, is as it should be. Rep. Washington comes from a neighborhood—culturally and politically—that is foreign and forbidding to white business people. They harbor a very real fear that they will be unable to deal with Rep. Washington's administration because they don't know the territory, and they fear also that they'll be unwelcome. (*Crain's Chicago Business*, 13 December 1982)

Speaking on behalf of the Byrne campaign to an assembly of two hundred Northwest Side precinct captains, Democratic Party Chairman Eddie Vrdolyak was considerably less subtle, urging his troops on with the following words: "It's a racial thing. Don't kid yourself. I'm calling on you to save your city, to save your precinct. We're fighting to keep this city the way it is" (Rivlin 1992, 155).

In the end, Washington's narrow victories in the Democratic primary and general election several months later were due to the mobilization of many of the same forces responsible for Jane Byrne's upset over Michael Bilandic in the 1979 mayor's race. Voter turnout among blacks in the 1983 general election was a remarkable 85 percent, with 99 percent of those votes cast for Washington over his white Republican challenger, Bernard Epton. Washington also received 82 percent of the Latino vote and up to one-third of the white vote in the north lakefront wards (Rivlin 1992, 196–197).

With Harold Washington's election victory in the spring of 1983, the community development agenda seemed to have come full circle. What had begun as a set of practices and ideas within neighborhood development organizations, whose policy implications were collectively debated and hammered out in the forum provided by CWED, had now penetrated the mayor's office on the wings of the Washington campaign. However, few neighborhood activists were naive enough to believe that Washington's victory marked an end to the longstanding political influence held by the various members of Chicago's growth machine. For most, it was clear that Washington's governing agenda would ultimately involve some form of compromise between the downtown business leadership, the administration, the machine faction of city council, and community leaders. As Washington was sworn in as mayor of Chicago on April 29, 1983, neighborhood activists waited anxiously to see what form that compromise would take.

## Conclusion

Chicago's governing arrangements, remarkably stable for decades following the election of Richard J. Daley in 1955, fell increasingly into crisis by the early 1980s. It was a crisis at once economic, social, political, and ideological. Court rulings that declared political patronage unconstitutional and cutbacks in federal aid to cities undermined the ability of the machine to re-ward its supporters in the neighborhoods and discourage group mobilization around collective demands. In addition, the contrast between the deindustrial-ization and soaring unemployment rates in the neighborhoods and the row-upon-row of glistening office towers rising in the Loop threatened to open the city's role in downtown redevelopment and economic restructuring to greater public scrutiny and debate. Finally, the failure of the downtown service sector to provide jobs for displaced manufacturing workers undermined the credibility of arguments that all Chicagoans benefitted from economic devel-opment policies focused primarily on revitalizing the central business district.

These developments combined to fuel a neighborhood movement whose base was, by this time, already well-established. They also helped expand the residential base of the movement to include growing numbers of manufac-turers and other community business establishments that, like neighborhood residents, were shut out of the closed decision-making process fostered by the politics of downtown growth. The outreach efforts of industrial devel-opment organizations like Jane Addams Resource Corporation, the Indus-trial Council of Northwest Chicago, and Greater North Pulaski Develop-ment Corporation represented a turning point for the neighborhood movement in Chicago, helping to redefine the relationships of neighbor-hood manufacturers to one another, to the community, and to city govern-ment. As a result, the downtown-versus-the-neighborhoods debate shifted onto new terrain. The significance of neighborhoods as production sites was incorporated into the neighborhood critique of the growth machine, and the existing residential/consumer base of the movement was expanded to include a strong producer component as well. Calls for redistribution be-came liberally supplemented with new demands for balanced growth, as a local-producer strategy for neighborhood redevelopment emerged to chal-lenge the practices and ideologies of the progrowth alliance.

The Jane Byrne victory of 1979 provided an indication of the new political possibilities. However, it was not until four years later, when Harold Wash-ington was elected mayor, that Chicago would experience a fundamental regime change. Under Washington, the alliance between business and gov-ernment leaders was replaced by a new governing coalition in which neigh-borhood organizations figured prominently. "Balanced growth" would be-come the centerpiece of Washington's economic development platform, and downtown business elites and their allies would be forced into a debate with neighborhood activists over how that concept should be operationalized. In the context of this debate, the beginnings of a citywide industrial policy would emerge. The following chapter explores these beginnings.

# Chapter Five

# The Battle for the Near North Side

A s we saw in Chapter 1, urban political economists provide compelling reasons for the dominance of land-based interests in city politics. Key among these is the argument that city officials and landed interests both share an overriding concern with the intensification of land use (Molotch 1976; Logan and Molotch 1987; Domhoff 1983, 166–173). Property owners want to attract "higher and better" uses to enhance the value of their real estate holdings, while city officials require healthy rates of economic growth to boost tax revenues and provide jobs for city residents. Efforts to rearrange and intensify land use accomplish each of these objectives by increasing the city property-tax base and creating temporary construction jobs and new forms of permanent employment. Capital mobility cements the alliance between city officials and landed interests, since both groups share an interest in attracting mobile investors to maintain high-intensity land uses and neither can achieve this goal without the cooperation of the other (Elkin 1985, 1994).

According to most urban theorists, alliances of this nature are the pervasive type of governing coalition in contemporary cities not simply because they are mutually beneficial but also because few viable alternatives exist. Nonbusiness groups like neighborhood associations may hold useful organizational resources, but these are no match for the substantial economic holdings of landed interests and their allies in the downtown business community (Stone 1989, 1993). City officials must promote economic growth, and the pressures of global economic restructuring and deindustrialization have, by most accounts, made the growth machine's corporate-center strategy for downtown redevelopment the only game in town (or, at least, the only *winnable* game). Under these circumstances, even administrations with a progressive bent can do little more than redistribute some of the benefits of downtown growth in favor of low- and moderate-income neighborhoods (Dreier and Erlich 1991; Turner 1992; Wong 1988).

For decades following World War II, Chicago's governing arrangements conformed well to this model. Yet the election victory of Harold Washington in 1983 seemed to represent a potential turning point. Washington had incorporated themes from community economic development circles—like balanced growth, jobs over real estate, and manufacturing over services—into his election campaign. Such themes set up a potential conflict with the real estate-based growth coalition's goal of rising property values, since the preservation of well-paying manufacturing jobs required that land values and property taxes remain affordable for industrial users. Indeed, as the case studies of the printing and apparel industries in Chapter 3 illustrate, land speculation was perhaps the central cause of industrial displacement in Printing House Row and the Chicago garment district. By drawing a distinction between jobs and real estate development and prioritizing the former, Washington set his administration on a new course in which land-based interests suddenly found themselves in the unfamiliar position of political outsiders.

If the arguments and assumptions of contemporary urban political economy are correct, however, property developers and their progrowth allies should not have remained outsiders for long. Faced with difficult choices between growth and redistribution, Washington would have found himself drawn increasingly into alliance with members of the business community holding the economic resources necessary for governing. Fortunately, certain events that transpired during the Washington years provide useful empirical evidence with which to test this proposition. Shortly after Washington assumed office, significant conflict erupted on the city's Near North Side between property developers seeking to redevelop industrial space for new commercial and residential uses and manufacturers attempting to maintain a foothold in this area of the city in the face of intensive real estate speculation. The city's zoning policy became an arena of political conflict, and the administration was forced to make hard choices between a real estate-based development strategy backed by powerful members of the city's downtown growth coalition and a jobs-based development strategy supported by a coalition of manufacturers, workers, and neighborhood organizations.

This chapter questions whether the dynamics of that conflict, the administration's response, and the alternative political and economic possibilities to which it pointed can be grasped within the framework provided by contemporary urban political economy. Contrary to the scenario painted in much of the literature today, the options that policymakers faced forced them to choose not between growth and redistribution but between two growth strategies benefitting different segments of the community. Moreover, the choice between these growth strategies was made politically through an expansion of the city's controls over land use, not through Darwinian competition in the marketplace. The following narrative portrays urban economic restructuring as open-ended and politically contested, suggesting that opportunities for meaningful development choices continue to exist within the context of global economic change.

## The Harold Washington Administration: Broadening the Economic Development Debate

Studies of community power have often shown how economic elites dominate the public agenda at the expense of low- and moderate-income city residents or workers by limiting the scope of legitimate public debate over redistributive or regulatory questions or by preventing conflict from arising in the first place (Crenson 1971; Bachrach and Baratz 1962; Gaventa 1980). However, power relations may also be a factor in determining the range of public debate over economic development strategies themselves. Chicago mayors Richard J. Daley, Michael Bilandic, and Jane Byrne each presided over narrow governing coalitions dominated by a select group of land-based interests drawn from the downtown business community. The use of public policy to support the commercial and residential downtown redevelopment agenda of this segment of the business community was possible, in part, because of a narrow public decision-making process in which the proponents of alternative development strategies did not participate in any significant form.

As we saw in the previous chapter, Harold Washington's electoral coalition included a diverse group of community-based organizations advocating, among other things, a local-producer strategy for neighborhood redevelopment. An important part of this agenda, as articulated in the Community Workshop on Economic Development (CWED) policy statement and later in the "Washington Papers" themselves, was the argument that traditional Chicago industries could survive under the appropriate political conditions and that city government should expand its one-dimensional focus on downtown growth to include greater attention to the needs of city manufacturers. While mindful of the need to maintain the confidence and support of the downtown business community, Washington nevertheless undertook a number of steps during his first term in office that helped place these concerns within the parameters of legitimate public discourse. Taken together, these steps helped create a fertile political climate for manufacturers threatened by nearby commercial and residential redevelopment to demand and receive protection from city government.

To begin with, Washington placed a number of community leaders in prominent positions within the city bureaucracy. The key appointment was that of Robert Mier as Commissioner of the Department of Economic Development (DED). In 1978, Mier had helped establish the Center for Urban Economic Development at the University of Illinois at Chicago, a think tank and technical-assistance provider for community-based organizations. Mier was also a founding member of CWED and helped draft the economic development platform of the "Washington Papers." Mier's appointment, together with those of other community-minded academics and neighborhood advocates such as Robert Giloth, Arturo Vazquez, and Kari Moe, created outposts in the bureaucracy where elements of an industrial policy could be articulated and advanced.

In May 1984, the Washington administration released its economic development plan, *Chicago Works Together: 1984 Chicago Development Plan* (City of Chicago 1984). As we have seen earlier, the development plans issued by the Richard J. Daley and Jane Byrne administrations had focused overwhelmingly on real estate development, with particular emphasis placed on the downtown and near-downtown areas of the city (Department of City Planning 1958; Department of Planning 1982). In keeping with the policy objectives identified in the "Washington Papers," the Washington administration's plan prioritized job creation over real estate development and emphasized the need to retain traditional manufacturing industries in the city's neighborhoods. The plan played an important role in framing the economic development policy debate in Chicago during the Washington years. For example, one of the major downtown civic organizations, the Commercial Club of Chicago, subtitled its own development plan released in December 1984 "Jobs for Metropolitan Chicago" (Commercial Club of Chicago 1984).

One aspect of the Washington administration's strategy for retaining manufacturing jobs involved the creation of task forces for two prominent Chicago industries, steel and apparel, and the funding of a printing industry task force convened by the Center for Urban Economic Development at the University of Illinois. While the efforts of each task force culminated in a number of significant policy innovations, one of their most important functions was to help defeat the common perception that all manufacturing in Chicago was either dead or dying (Giloth and Mier 1989). Each task force produced a substantial research paper and a smaller document that summarized the research findings and outlined policy recommendations. In each case, researchers successfully identified key industry segments seemingly unaffected by the decentralizing pressures of global economic restructuring (see Markusen 1985; Robinson 1985; Ranney and Wiewel 1987). For example, the printing industry task-force report pointed out how technological innovations had opened up new markets for small, centrally located graphic communications firms for whom face-to-face communication with downtown customers was essential, making this one of the strongest industry segments (Center for Urban Economic Development 1988). The administration helped generate publicity and support for task-force findings by issuing press releases and holding briefings for editors from the major Chicago newspapers, local labor leaders, and city council members in conjunction with the release of individual task-force reports (Mier 1986).

Finally, the Washington administration significantly boosted the organizational capacity of a number of industrial development organizations through the Local Industrial Retention Initiative (LIRI), introduced in 1983 by DED Commissioner Mier. The LIRI program, modeled after Greater North Pulaski Development Corporation's target area industrial improvement project described in Chapter 4, funded industrial development organizations to organize manufacturers around policy issues of concern to neighborhood industries. Previously, city economic development officials had attempted to address the concerns of manufacturers by contacting them individually and then developing solutions to industry problems within the bureaucracy. By contrast, the Washington administration's LIRI program created a central planning role for manufacturers themselves, providing them with both a strong sense of ownership of the process and an organizational presence with which to pressure the city to make good on commitments for funding, infrastructure, and other assistance (Reardon 1990, 165–170). In 1983, LIRI's first year, four groups received a total of $76,000 in CDBG funds. By 1987, the number of LIRI groups had grown to eight, while the program's annual budget had increased to $387,500 (Mier, Wiewel, and Alpern 1992, 90).

## Industrial Displacement:
## Identifying the Problem and Developing a Solution

One of the LIRI organizations that the Washington administration began funding early in its first term was a Near North Side industrial development organization called the Local Employment and Economic Development (LEED) Council. One of the most diverse areas of the city, the Near North Side is home to the affluent residential community of Lincoln Park near the lakeshore, the Cabrini-Green public housing development, and the largest industrial corridor on Chicago's North Side. Founded in 1982 as a unit of the New City YMCA, LEED Council was established in part to help neighborhood residents and businesses design a community economic development strategy that would link the low-income residents of Cabrini-Green with employment opportunities in the nearby North River Industrial Corridor (Ducharme 1991, 225).

The North River Industrial Corridor encompasses 566 acres of land, roughly half of which lie within the northern portion of Chicago's central area, the rest extending for another several miles along the Chicago River to the northwest. The boundaries of the corridor are, roughly, Wellington and Chicago Avenues to the north and south, and Clybourn Avenue and the Kennedy Expressway to the east and west (see Map 3). Twenty-seven industrial sectors are represented in the corridor, with major employers including primary and fabricated metal products, printing and publishing, rubber and plastics, and food products (Department of Planning and Development 1992, 15).

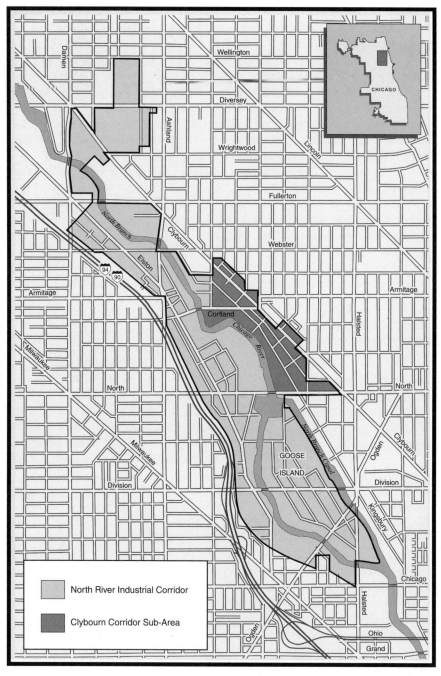

Map 3. North River Industrial Corridor with Clybourn Corridor Sub-Area

In 1986, industrial firms located within the North River Corridor employed roughly 16,000 manufacturing workers, representing somewhere between 8 and 10 percent of Chicago's total manufacturing jobs at the time (Ducharme, Giloth, and McCormick 1986, 18). Until 1983, the zoning classifications for the entire corridor were either M1, M2, or M3, dividing the corridor into light, medium, and heavy manufacturing districts. Apart from its industrial zoning, a number of other characteristics had long attracted manufacturers to this area of the city, including its proximity to the central business district, waterway access to the Great Lakes and the Mississippi River via the Chicago River, and a rail spur from the Soo Line Railroad (Department of Planning and Development 1992, 11–14).

Yet the North River Corridor also had features that would eventually make it attractive to nonindustrial users as well. In particular, portions of the corridor contained concentrations of the multistory industrial loft buildings that real estate developers in areas nearby had recently begun to target for conversion to more lucrative commercial and residential uses. Although such activities were still generally concentrated closer to the Loop by the time LEED Council was founded in 1982, a recent flurry of loft conversions just south of the North River Corridor in the River North area suggested that redevelopment was, by this time, poised to strike. Between 1977 and 1984, over seven thousand manufacturing and durable wholesaling jobs were lost in River North, many the result of adaptive reuse of the area's numerous industrial loft buildings for nonmanufacturing purposes (Giloth and Betancur 1988, 284).

In 1983, developers Tem Horowitz and Robert Matthews approached forty-third ward alderman Martin Oberman with the first request for a rezoning of industrial property in the North River Corridor. The developers wanted to convert a vacant piano factory on Clybourn Avenue to residential lofts and needed the property rezoned from manufacturing to residential in order to proceed with their plans. LEED Council staff members quickly organized companies near the proposed Clybourn Lofts development, most of whom were opposed to the zoning change due mainly to fears that noise and odors produced by nearby industries would provoke complaints from the new loft dwellers. In response, the developers agreed that all loft purchase agreements would include a clause indicating the buyers understood they were purchasing property in a manufacturing area. LEED Council ultimately withdrew its opposition to the development, and Alderman Oberman agreed to support the zoning change.

During the next two years, however, development hit Clybourn Avenue and its immediate surroundings at a brisk pace. Oberman's office received no less than seven additional requests for zoning changes on sizeable parcels of land, and the remaining industrial buildings on Clybourn Avenue soon became interspersed with a growing number of upscale stores, restaurants, movie theaters, and several additional residential developments (Joravsky

1988). Property values in the area soared, and before long nearly every industrial building on the market was being priced for conversion to residential or commercial uses, at values two or more times the going industrial rate (Ducharme 1991, 228).

The rapid pace of redevelopment soon began to compromise the industrial integrity of the area along Clybourn Avenue. Rising property values priced existing manufacturers out of the market for expansion space and discouraged outside manufacturing firms from moving into the area. They also led to sizeable property-tax increases; in 1984, tax assessments in the North River Corridor rose by an average of 100 percent, boosting industry operating costs (Ducharme, Giloth, and McCormick 1986, 24). In addition, the doubts manufacturers harbored about the likely tolerance of their new residential neighbors for the sounds and smells of industrial development were quickly confirmed. Oberman's office was soon bombarded with complaints from the new loft dwellers, and companies feared lengthy and expensive court battles would inevitably follow (Joravsky 1988). Ultimately, redevelopment began to have a chilling effect on industrial investment activity along Clybourn Avenue, as uncertainties about the future of the area led more and more firms to defer expenditures for plant and equipment (Ducharme 1991, 228–229).

Despite the claims of real estate developers to the contrary, the redevelopment activity that hit Clybourn Avenue during the mid-1980s was not a simple expression of market forces. Rather, the city's zoning laws and practices favored the real estate community. To begin with, the Chicago Zoning Ordinance offered little protection to manufacturers because zoning changes were, in most cases, relatively easy to procure. In principle, changes to the zoning ordinance required the approval of at least two-thirds of city council. In practice, however, aldermen held sway over such decisions within their own wards. This practice, as we saw in Chapter 2, has its origins in Chicago's machine-style political tradition. Zoning variances were one of a wide variety of selective incentives used by ward politicians to cement party loyalties, and aldermen learned to respect one another's boundaries where such matters were concerned to avoid possible retaliation and threats to their own political fiefdoms. The relative absence of bureaucratic hurdles to overcome helped fuel real estate speculation along Clybourn Avenue. Because investors were confident that their requests for zoning changes would be processed with few hassles, M-zoned property was soon being priced at commercial or residential rates even before the variances had actually been granted (Ducharme, Giloth, and McCormick 1986, 22–23).

Piecemeal changes to the city zoning ordinance did more than simply destabilize property values along Clybourn Avenue, however. Since the last comprehensive revision of the Chicago Zoning Ordinance in 1957, manufacturers located near commercial or residential districts have faced more restrictive operating standards for noise, vibrations, and odors than manufacturers with no commercial or residential neighbors.[1] The rezoning of a nearby M-zoned land parcel to allow residential or other nonindustrial uses could thus place a given manufacturing establishment out of compliance with the zoning ordinance, even if it had been there long before any nonindustrial types of land use were established nearby.

This provision of the zoning ordinance was introduced following a wartime boom in manufacturing, during which time citywide manufacturing jobs increased from 403,000 in 1939 to 615,000 in 1954 (McDonald 1984, 10). Concerned about the nuisance-creating potential of the rapid industrial expansion, legislators established industry performance standards as a way of stemming further incursion of heavy industry into residential and commercial areas of the city (Babcock 1972). Now that the tables were turned, however, and the problem was residential and commercial encroachment upon industrial areas, the performance standards became a weapon that real estate developers could utilize in their efforts to rearrange land use along Clybourn Avenue.

In late 1984, staff members from LEED Council and the Research and Development Division of the city's Department of Economic Development began a joint research project on the issue of industrial displacement on Chicago's Near North Side. At this point, the notion that industry needed or desired protection from city government had won few converts within the Washington administration. However, Robert Giloth, Deputy Commissioner of the Department of Economic Development under Washington and eventual head of the department's Research and Development Division, had had firsthand experience with the issue during his tenure as executive director of the Eighteenth Street Development Corporation, a Near South Side community development corporation, during the 1970s. The efforts of Giloth and other community activists had helped persuade officials in the Jane Byrne administration to reject a developer's plan to convert a cluster of nineteen industrial buildings in the Pilsen community of the Near South Side to a mixed-use commercial and residential development (Giloth and Menashe 1981).

The research team, led by Giloth and LEED Council Executive Director Donna Ducharme, published its findings in a 1986 report, *Business Loss or Balanced Growth: Industrial Displacement in Chicago* (Ducharme, Giloth, and McCormick 1986). The study documented job losses resulting from loft-conversion activity in River North from 1978 to 1985 and argued that a similar fate awaited blue-collar workers in the North River Industrial Corridor if existing redevelopment trends were allowed to continue. Using the economic development priorities voiced in the "Washington Papers" and the administration's 1984 Chicago Development Plan as leverage for their arguments, the authors of the study charged that city government support for the rezoning of industrial property was inconsistent with the administration's commitment to balanced growth. The report concluded with a recommendation that areas of the city experiencing industrial displacement be designated as "protected industrial districts" in which further zoning changes from manufacturing to commercial or residential designations would be prohibited.

The study proved to be significant for a number of reasons. First, it helped sensitize administration officials to the issue of industrial displacement, both within the Department of Economic Development and elsewhere in the bureaucracy. Even more importantly, it made a major impression on forty-third ward alderman Oberman, whose approval of rezoning requests until that point had helped feed the real estate speculation occurring along Clybourn Avenue. After reading a draft of the report in late 1985, Oberman called a moratorium on further zoning changes in the forty-third ward portion of the North River Industrial Corridor and appointed a task force composed of representatives from LEED Council, the Departments of Planning and Economic Development, and the alderman's office to develop a comprehensive strategy for achieving a balance among the different sets of interests competing for space in the area.

Understanding Oberman's sudden concerns for the plight of Clybourn Avenue manufacturers requires a brief digression on the somewhat unique characteristics of forty-third ward politics. Once a machine stronghold, the forty-third ward eventually became one of the city's handful of independent wards as the area's working-class German ethnics were displaced by an influx of middle-class professionals in the late 1960s and early 1970s (Fremon 1988, 281–288). The new ward residents were typically employed in the corporate and financial sectors downtown and, unlike their predecessors, did not generally depend on ward politicians for patronage jobs and other individual favors. Since the early 1970s, this has left aldermen representing the forty-third ward more free than their counterparts in the city's machine wards to focus their attention on policymaking, which is ultimately what their middle-class constituents want and expect. All this does not mean that Oberman was oblivious to the political opportunities that his support for rezoning requests along Clybourn Avenue provided. It does mean, however, that once a conflict arose, he was more willing than most Chicago aldermen to consider the issue from a policy rather than a machine-building perspective.[2]

In early 1986, Oberman's task force on industrial displacement began to hold monthly meetings with Near North Side manufacturers as part of its efforts to help resolve the land-use conflicts occurring in the North River Corridor. The meetings served two key purposes. First, they gave the issue of industrial displacement further credibility within city government by providing administration officials with firsthand accounts of the pressures manufacturers were experiencing in the area. Second, they helped build a sense of commitment among manufacturers to the process of devising a solution, increasing the likelihood that they would weather the time-consuming organizing work that would necessarily be a part of any long-term political settlement (Ducharme 1991, 230–231).

In July 1986, the task force recommended that a Protected Manufacturing District (PMD) be established in the eastern portion of the North River Industrial Corridor between Clybourn Avenue and the Chicago River (the "Clybourn Corridor"), where most of the real estate speculation that had buffeted the area in the previous several years had been concentrated (see Map 3). The new district would consist of a core zone, where manufacturing would be the only permitted land use, and an exterior buffer zone, where a mixture of commercial and industrial uses would be allowed in order to buffer the heavier manufacturers in the district's core from the residential development taking place outside the boundaries of the PMD. No further residential development whatsoever would be allowed within the new district. Nearly two years later, Oberman's successor as alderman of the forty-third ward, Edwin Eisendrath, would use the recommendations of the task force as the basis for a Protected Manufacturing District ordinance introduced into city council under his name.

## Building the Coalition

During the two-year period between the issuance of the task-force report and the introduction of the PMD ordinance into city council, LEED Council engaged in a monumental organizing drive designed to identify and secure bases of support for the initiative within the community in order to provide sympathetic public officials with a sufficiently broad political base from which to act. Part of this time was spent crafting and gaining city council approval of a PMD enabling ordinance, which provided the legislative guidelines for the establishment of protected manufacturing districts in specific areas of the city (Ducharme 1991, 232). While adding extra time to the process, passage of the enabling ordinance meant that future campaigns to create additional PMDs in areas besides the Clybourn Corridor could be developed within a clear legislative framework, simplifying the process considerably.

Support for the Clybourn Corridor PMD involved considerable risk for public officials. Real estate developers active in the area made a persuasive case, arguing that their proposals brought life to declining and obsolescent industrial areas by refurbishing underutilized and abandoned buildings. According to developers, loft rehabilitations and other commercial and residential redevelopment projects represented the highest and best use for the property, while PMDs were politically misguided efforts to restrict property rights and interfere with market forces.[3] As Tem Horowitz, developer of Clybourn Lofts, argued in 1986, "These buildings are basically fossils. Cities live. If the economics push the industries out, it is for the good of the city" (Barry 1986).

The position of the real estate community was reinforced by a series of articles and editorials published in the *Chicago Tribune* from 1986 to 1988 praising the efforts of property developers in the Clybourn Corridor and characterizing LEED Council and supportive city officials as antigrowth and antidevelopment. The *Tribune*'s high-profile campaign against the PMD made LEED Council's organizing work all the more critical to the success of the initiative, as media criticism left public officials increasingly reluctant to carry the initiative forward before strong support among a broad and diverse segment of the community had been mobilized. According to LEED Council's Donna Ducharme, "What we had to do was to cast the issue widely enough that lots of different types of people could find a way to hang their hats on it" (Ducharme 1995).

## The Manufacturers

At the center of the coalition backing the Clybourn Corridor PMD were, naturally enough, the Clybourn area manufacturers themselves. Companies supported the PMD for different reasons. Some businesses, like segments of the printing industry described in Chapter 3, required near-downtown locations for proximity to customers, suppliers, and subcontractors and were not enticed by the cash incentives being dangled by commercial or residential developers interested in acquiring their property. Others had major investments in heavy machinery and equipment, making relocation costs prohibitive. One specialty steel producer whose equipment included a 6,000-ton forging press calculated it would need to sell its land for at least $90.00 per square foot in order to relocate (Goff 1988). Even the priciest real estate on Clybourn Avenue was only going for half that amount in the mid-1980s.

Organizing the companies and building a commitment to the process on the part of firm owners and representatives proved to be difficult and time-consuming work. Most had never been involved in a grassroots political campaign such as this, and many were initially skeptical it would succeed. Ultimately, however, a number of company representatives emerged as forceful and articulate spokespersons on behalf of the PMD, testifying at hearings, writing letters to city officials, and presenting their cases in the local and national media. One firm even hired a publicist. For many of these manufacturers, the campaign marked a significant shift in the way they perceived and interacted with city government. As one Washington administration official observed at the time,

> What you're seeing in the Clybourn area for the first time in Chicago is the energizing of the manufacturing sector and its entry into the public policy debate. They've had their collective consciousness raised about the importance of public policy to their continued existence—something the real estate developers who opposed the PMD have always known. (Goff 1988)

Still, support for the initiative among Clybourn Corridor manufacturers was not unanimous. As property values continued to escalate during the mid-1980s, some firms with weaker ties to the area wanted the freedom to cash in their real estate holdings at commercial or residential rates, if they so chose. A number of companies that had supported the PMD when it was first proposed in 1986 had become vocal critics of the initiative by 1988.[4] Although such firms were clearly in the minority, the *Tribune* chose to emphasize the split between those firms supporting and those opposing the PMD in its coverage of the controversy.[5]

## The Community

Neighborhood organizations of various kinds were a second key component of the PMD coalition. Along with LEED Council, three additional North Side industrial development organizations—Jane Addams Resource Corporation, Greater North Pulaski Development Corporation, and North Business and Industrial Council—became strong supporters of the initiative. In addition, both of Chicago's citywide community economic development umbrella organizations—the Community Workshop on Economic Development (CWED) and the Chicago Association of Neighborhood Development Organizations (CANDO)—provided critical support for the campaign in various ways.[6] A number of resident-based organizations from low- and moderate-income neighborhoods bordering the North River Industrial Corridor also joined forces with the coalition. Their concerns were twofold: if redevelopment continued to move westward, gentrification would threaten both the livelihoods of community residents employed in nearby industries and the integrity of lower- and middle-income residential neighborhoods.

Support sometimes came from unexpected places. Once the new commercial development along Clybourn Avenue began to cause growing traffic congestion and parking problems, some of the middle- and upper-income residents living east of Clybourn Avenue in Lincoln Park began to see their industrial neighbors in a more favorable light. Sensing an opportunity to broaden the coalition still further, LEED Council held a meeting with several resident-based neighborhood organizations from the Lincoln Park area, including the Concerned Allied Neighbors, Sheffield Neighbors, and the RANCH Triangle Association, in September 1986. The proposed ordinance was revised to accommodate a number of concerns raised by organization members, and each of these groups ultimately chose to back the initiative (Department of Economic Development 1988, 11).

Along with the Clybourn Corridor companies and neighborhood organizations supporting the PMD, labor also played a significant role in the coalition. Because LEED Council relied heavily on the companies themselves to educate their workers and mobilize them on behalf of the PMD, support from labor was strongest among workers whose employers backed the initiative, while

workers employed by companies opposed to the measure were typically less
enthusiastic. Ultimately, the Chicago Federation of Labor became a strong
proponent of the initiative, allowing LEED Council to reach some workers in
companies that were not members of the PMD coalition. Altogether, roughly
ten union locals eventually identified themselves as supporters of the PMD
(Ducharme 1995).

## The Administration

The final major component of the PMD coalition was the Washington administration itself, whose endorsement of the initiative was critical for a number of reasons. For one thing, the enabling legislation made city council approval of the PMD contingent upon the Plan Commission's
recommendations. More importantly still, support for the initiative on the
administration's part would send a strong signal to both developers and manufacturers that the city was serious about protecting industry on Chicago's
Near North Side. Without a strong, unambiguous message from the administration, the ordinance alone would probably not be enough to stop real estate speculation and convince manufacturers to make a commitment to the
area. As one dubious Clybourn area manufacturer noted, "I don't know if
[the PMD] can provide meaningful protection in light of the way ordinances
get changed so easily" (Goozner 1986).

For much of the controversy, however, Washington himself remained officially silent on the issue, refusing to take a public stance either for or against
the PMD. This comes as no real surprise, since the controversy was clearly
pulling the administration in two different directions. On the one hand, the
initiative was consistent with a number of themes Washington had articulated
during the previous several years, prioritizing jobs over real estate development, neighborhoods over downtown, and traditional blue-collar industries
over service sector and high-tech employment strategies. Also, a number of
organizations backing the proposed ordinance were key members of the
Washington coalition. On the other hand, support for the initiative risked
upsetting the administration's already tenuous relationship with the downtown business community and left Washington susceptible to the kinds of
antigrowth charges the *Tribune* tended to level whenever the focus of the administration's economic development policies began to stray too far from
downtown. As Chicago's first African-American mayor, Washington was particularly sensitive to the antidevelopment charge.

For a long time, the administration's response to this dilemma was to play
both sides of the fence, approving zoning changes from industrial to nonindustrial designations while taking certain steps to support manufacturers, including funding LEED Council's antidisplacement work.[7] While couched in
the rhetoric of balanced growth, this strategy simply produced confusion

over the city's policy stance on the question of industrial displacement, as the following memorandum from DED Commissioner Robert Mier to Community Relations Director Jane Ramsey appears to suggest:

> The Protected Manufacturing District (PMD) ordinance and policy is coming under increasing criticism from the *Tribune* and development community. If it is passed, the *Tribune* and other media could portray the Mayor as anti-growth or anti-development. To counter this, we need a coordinated strategy to prevent this from happening while, at the same time, placing the Administration out front on the PMD issue. One thing that could help is for the Mayor to be involved with some type of manufacturing investment in the Goose Island/Clybourn Corridor. . . . The announcement of some type of industrial expansion will help convince the public that our PMD policy makes sense. In addition, it would be helpful if we could identify the Mayor with some type of major "yuppie" development. For instance, we could create a lot of fanfare around a project representing the 5 billionth dollar of commercial and residential development in the central area. . . . By having the Mayor identified with both of these processes—industrial expansion and boom time—we can perhaps begin to deal with the difficult public perception that balanced growth is not only possible but is happening, now. (Mier 1987a)

Ultimately, the administration's willingness to take a strong stand against industrial displacement proved to be contingent on the strength and diversity of the political base that had been mobilized around the issue in a given situation. As LEED Council's Donna Ducharme recalls, "The administration people talk about [the PMD] now like it was their idea and they always wanted to do it, but for a long time they were very hesitant to move forward on it. Every step of the way, I would have to organize a broader base for them to stand on to get them to take the next step" (Ducharme 1995).

Two high-profile zoning controversies that took place in the North River Industrial Corridor during 1986 and 1987 when public debate over the PMD was beginning to gather momentum help illustrate Ducharme's point. The first involved the proposed conversion of a former scrap smelting plant on Goose Island to a mixed-use, commercial/residential development. Plans for the development, to be called River Lofts, were officially unveiled in September 1986. Goose Island, a 160-acre island in the city's forty-second ward formed by a split in the Chicago River immediately south of the proposed Clybourn Corridor PMD, was zoned exclusively for heavy industry at the time. To proceed with their plans, the developers would need a zoning change from manufacturing to a business or commercial designation. Due to the parcel's riverfront location, Plan Commission approval was required.

Both the administration and forty-second ward alderman Burton Natarus initially gave their blessings to the project. However, LEED Council soon discovered there was significant opposition to the development on the part of Goose Island manufacturers. A rapid organizing drive of area industries conducted by LEED Council staff members led to a series of meetings between city officials and Goose Island manufacturers, during which manufacturers expressed their reservations about the River Lofts project and reiterated their opposition to the developers' request for a zoning change. Because of the manufacturers' protests, the rezoning application was continued before the Plan Commission for nine successive months. During this time, administration officials also began to express reservations about the development, drawing harsh editorial criticism from the *Tribune*.[8]

In July 1987, an agreement was finally reached. The Plan Commission decided to support the zoning change, but only after the project's developers agreed to numerous concessions designed to mollify the concerns of Goose Island manufacturers. Most importantly, the development company promised to limit its activities on Goose Island to the River Lofts project alone and agreed to support the passage of a future Goose Island Protected Manufacturing District ordinance to ensure that the rest of the island would remain industrial for years to come. Due largely to effective community organizing on the part of LEED Council, the administration had taken its firmest stance yet in support of North Side manufacturers threatened by nearby commercial and residential development.

Just one month before the River Lofts agreement was finalized, another development company announced plans for what would soon become a second high-profile zoning controversy in the North River Industrial Corridor. In this case, the development firm of Centrum Properties wanted to demolish a complex of vacant industrial buildings on a seventeen-acre parcel at the northern end of the corridor and redevelop the site as a shopping center and retail strip, to be called Riverpoint Center. Again, both the site itself and the surrounding land parcels were zoned for heavy manufacturing only. To carry out its plans, Centrum needed the area rezoned for commercial use. The large size of the parcel and riverfront location meant, once again, that Plan Commission approval was necessary.

While outside the proposed Clybourn Corridor PMD, the size of the project and its location within a contested area of the North River Industrial Corridor made this case a litmus test of the administration's policy stance on North Side industrial/commercial/residential land-use conflicts. In a September 1987 memorandum to DED Commissioner Robert Mier and Planning Commissioner Elizabeth Hollander, Deputy Planning Commissioner David Mosena wrote,

> It's a great site, good for industrial, but prime land for retail. In fact, it's because it's such a great retail site—near a growing yuppie market—that whatever we choose to do, it will really give off a clear message that will have an effect on

the marketplace in that area. . . . The stakes are high—real money stands to be lost. Everyone is watching to see what happens. Whichever message comes out of this decision, it will be the most powerful message yet from the City. (Mosena 1987a)

The negotiations over the River Lofts development on Goose Island had helped strengthen the administration's resolve to protect the integrity of North Side industrial districts threatened by redevelopment pressures. While still publicly silent on the PMD question, city officials initially expressed reservations over Centrum's proposal. One administration official quoted in *Crain's Chicago Business* insisted, "We're ready to go to war over this. It would send a bad signal. People would wonder if it's possible for the city to stop rezoning of industrial land in the future if it can't stop this" (Goff 1987). In response, the *Tribune* stepped up its editorial pressure, unleashing one of its harshest attacks yet against the administration's efforts to curb industrial displacement on the city's Near North Side:

> Mr. Washington has let his economic planners embark on a zany crusade to snuff out commercial and residential growth in areas that they—these insulated City Hall planners—have decreed should be reserved for manufacturing. Investors who want to convert abandoned old factory buildings into job-producing, tax-producing commercial complexes are told no, take your money to some other city. And don't think they won't, if Chicago continues this perverse ideological nonsense. (*Chicago Tribune*, 28 September 1987, sec. 1, p. 14)

In September 1987, the city began negotiating with Centrum over the future of the proposed retail center. Centrum insisted that the highest and best use for the site was commercial and offered to contribute to a linked development program in exchange for the city's approval of the zoning change (Mosena 1987b). Already by this point, the administration's commitment to retaining the site for future industrial users appeared to be wavering, although officials continued to voice reservations about the project publicly. From the city's standpoint, the problem with opposing this particular project outright was the lack of organized opposition to the proposed development among nearby manufacturers and neighborhood groups. Unlike Goose Island, neither LEED Council nor any other North Side industrial development organization had created a strong organizational presence around the issue of industrial displacement in this area of the North River Corridor. Without the solid backing of nearby manufacturers, the city's opposition to the development could be easily characterized as antigrowth. Conceding that a denial of the rezoning would represent a sizeable risk for the administration, Deputy Planning Commissioner Mosena wrote in a late September memorandum to Commissioner Hollander,

The retail market of west Lincoln Park is real, neighborhood organizations to the east support the shopping center, and the depth of our industrial support against the shopping center is weaker than it was in the Clybourn PMD or Goose Island. On the other hand, support of this rezoning without qualification puts this industrial area totally up for grabs and amounts to no policy from the City for this area. (Mosena 1987b)

By November 1987, the administration's strategy had changed completely. Opposition to the zoning change had been dropped from consideration, and the question now was how to announce approval of the project while inflicting as little damage as possible on the proposed PMD ordinance. Here once again, the lack of strong community organizing around the issue of industrial displacement in this area of the city proved to be the decisive factor. Initially, there was some discussion of making the announcement within the context of a moratorium on further zoning changes in the thirty-second ward portion of the North River Industrial Corridor, where the Centrum development was to be located. Like the settlement reached with the developers of the River Lofts complex on Goose Island, this would help quell speculation among area manufacturers and property developers that this particular zoning change was simply the first of many to follow. However, Greg Longhini, Manager of Industrial Land-Use Policy in the Department of Planning, counseled against this approach. In a November 1987 memorandum to Deputy Commissioner Mosena, Longhini argued,

Inconsistency is difficult for all of us to proceed with. Case-by-case analysis is tough. However, to map out an area for a moratorium, without a study or community planning process, could lead to difficulties, such as our rationale. . . . Donna [Ducharme] has never concentrated west of the river. We don't know what the industrialists would say. In a nutshell, we don't know our political base there very well. (Longhini 1987)

Two days later, the Department of Planning issued a press release announcing its recommendation that Centrum Properties' petition for a zoning change be approved. There was no mention of a moratorium on future zoning changes in the thirty-second ward, although weaker language expressing the city's commitment to preserving the overall industrial "character" of the area did appear. For its part, Centrum promised to require all tenants of its new Riverpoint Center to make use of the city's First Source jobs program, targeting low- and moderate-income Chicagoans, in filling their new retail positions, and agreed to develop an industrial project elsewhere on the North Side.

Ironically, it was the city's decision to drop its opposition to Riverpoint Center that finally pushed the administration off the fence on the issue of the proposed PMD ordinance. By this time, the coalition of manufacturers, neighborhood organizations, and labor unions supporting the initiative was largely in place. Fearful that the Centrum announcement would send the wrong message to both the manufacturing and real estate communities, the administration acted quickly during the following weeks to counter any perceptions that the city's commitment to safeguarding the interests of North Side manufacturers was wavering. A bus tour of the Clybourn Corridor—to include Mayor Washington and top administration officials, labor and community representatives, and members of the local news media—was hastily arranged. During the tour Washington finally made it official: his administration would support the passage of a Protected Manufacturing District ordinance to help shelter Near North Side manufacturers from the pressures of nearby commercial and residential redevelopment. To counter charges by developers that the Near North Side was no longer a viable area for manufacturing, Washington also used the opportunity announce plans for a new industrial park on Goose Island.

The cases of River Lofts and Riverpoint Center illustrate the importance of coalition-building between manufacturers and neighborhood organizations around the issue of industrial displacement. Both sites were situated in the midst of viable industrial areas, surrounded by manufacturers threatened by the proposed conversion of nearby land parcels to new uses incompatible with industrial development. However, only in the case of the River Lofts development on Goose Island did neighborhood activists step in to organize area manufacturers around a collective response to redevelopment pressures. A strong, united manufacturing presence on Goose Island gave sympathetic Washington administration officials the ammunition they needed to deflect charges by real estate developers that the area was no longer desirable for industrial use.

Manufacturers near Centrum Properties' proposed Riverpoint Center, by contrast, were located in an area of the city where community organizations had not yet allied themselves with neighboring industrial firms. Resistance to the developers' plans on the part of nearby manufacturers was, accordingly, weak and sporadic. Because profitable manufacturers failed to stand up in sufficient numbers to demand protection from the city, opposition to the development on the part of Washington officials seemed to give credence to the antigrowth charges being leveled at the administration by real estate developers and their allies. Lacking sufficient evidence in this case to refute such claims, administration officials quickly fell in line with Centrum's demands.

## The PMD Controversy after Washington

Mayor Washington's decision to end his long public silence on the PMD and to announce his support for the initiative appeared to represent the last and, in some ways, most significant link in the PMD coalition. However,

LEED Council and its allies on the Near North Side quickly suffered a major setback. Just three weeks after visiting the Clybourn Corridor and endorsing the PMD proposal, Washington collapsed suddenly and died at his desk in City Hall, the victim of a massive heart attack.

Washington's death ignited a fierce power struggle between the Washington and machine factions of city council over the city's future political leadership. The acting mayor was, by law, to be chosen from among the council's fifty aldermen. Eugene Sawyer, a soft-spoken black alderman with former ties to the machine, emerged as the compromise choice for mayor. Sawyer immediately pledged to remain faithful to Washington's neighborhoods-oriented policy agenda, but his history as a loyal machine foot soldier dating back to the 1950s caused many to question his sincerity. Media commentaries on the likely fate of Washington's policies called the future of the Clybourn Corridor PMD initiative an open question.

Although acting mayor Sawyer quickly announced his support for the PMD, the city's commitment to providing meaningful protection for North Side manufacturers continued to be called into question in the following months. In the spring of 1988, developer Duncan Henderson approached the city with plans to convert a former Ludwig Drum factory in an industrial area just west of the North River Industrial Corridor to a mixed-use, work/live development. The residential component of the project meant the site would have to be rezoned from its present manufacturing designation to allow Henderson to proceed with his plans. Ward Alderman Terry Gabinski, a machine loyalist, supported the development. Although several nearby labor and resident-based community organizations were critical of Henderson's plans, the area was not officially served by any of the city's LIRI groups or any other industrial development organization. Opposition to the project by area manufacturers was consequently weak and ineffective, much as it had been in the case of Centrum Properties' Riverpoint Center development several months earlier. In July 1988, the Plan Commission somewhat reluctantly approved the zoning change.

Also that spring, a North Side automobile dealer, Hanley Dawson, began negotiations to purchase a six-acre site within the core zone of the proposed Clybourn Corridor PMD. The company wanted to relocate its automobile dealership to the site and asked that the parcel's existing M3 zoning designation be changed to allow the new commercial development to go forward as planned. No rezonings within the core zone of the proposed PMD had been entertained since the PMD map had entered the public domain over two years earlier. Fearful of the message that an exception for Hanley Dawson, one of the city's largest automobile dealers, would convey, Planning Commissioner Elizabeth Hollander strongly urged Sawyer to oppose the development. In an April 1988 memorandum to the mayor, Hollander argued,

> The entire development community—commercial, industrial, and neighbor-
> hood organizations—are familiar with the PMD concept, and many with the
> map. In other words, re-zoning to allow in Hanley Dawson could create a
> firestorm within the community that is actively pursuing a PMD policy to pre-
> serve and create meaningful jobs. . . . If Hanley Dawson does not receive firm
> word from the City and from Alderman Eisendrath that their proposal is not
> sufficient to justify a re-zoning, serious damage could be done to the proposed
> PMD ordinance coming up before the Council. (Hollander 1988)

Hollander's recommendations seemingly fell on deaf ears. According to media accounts, Hanley Dawson was able to persuade a top Sawyer advisor to
intervene on its behalf (Goozner 1988a). By the time forty-third ward alderman Eisendrath introduced the PMD ordinance into city council early that
summer, the boundaries of the core zone had been redrawn to accommodate
the auto dealer's wishes.

During this time, however, the base of community support around the
PMD continued to expand. In the months following Washington's death, the
proposed ordinance was the subject of numerous articles and commentaries
in both the local and national media. A number of local publications, including *Crain's Chicago Business*, the *Reader*, and, on occasion, the *Chicago Sun-
Times*, played important educational roles, helping to offset the *Tribune*'s
one-dimensional coverage of the issue. Feature stories on Clybourn Corridor
companies such as Finkl Steel, a highly profitable, 109-year-old steel foundry
employing more than 400 workers, presented Chicagoans with a more nu-
anced portrait of industrial decline than many had previously been exposed
to. People began to learn that not all manufacturers were leaving Chicago for
the same reasons. As Charles Finkl, chairman of the steel company that bears
his name, argued in a *New York Times* cover story in December 1987, "It's
one thing to lose basic industries to international forces beyond our control.
But it's another thing to force healthy industries out of the city through un-
wise and piecemeal zoning policies" (Schmidt 1987).

The educational role played by the media was complemented by studies of
the Clybourn Corridor carried out during the summer of 1988 by the Department of Economic Development, the Mayor's Office of Employment and
Training, and an independent research team led by Peter Creticos and
Northwestern University business professor Louis Masotti. The studies contained similar findings: each concluded that the economic contribution to
Chicago's economy made by Clybourn Corridor manufacturers far out-
weighed that made by the retail and other service-sector establishments increasingly populating the area. Two of the studies focused on employment
multipliers, concluding that the higher value added by manufacturing workers, along with their relatively higher wages, allowed such individuals to

support up to twice as many additional jobs as did retail employees (Sandro 1988; Creticos and Masotti 1988). The third study included a direct comparison of employment, wages, and taxes paid by the industrial and nonindustrial firms in the Clybourn Corridor, at the time more or less evenly divided between the two. The results, reproduced in Table 10, show that for each variable considered, the industrial firms outperformed their nonindustrial counterparts by sizeable margins (Department of Economic Development 1988).

**Table 10.** Employment, Wages, and Taxes Paid
by Clybourn Corridor Business Firms, 1988

|                          | Industrial  | Nonindustrial |
|--------------------------|-------------|---------------|
| Number of firms          | 31          | 29            |
| Total employment         | 1,701       | 451           |
| Total payroll (millions) | $38.9       | $4.8          |
| Average wage             | $22,900     | $10,700       |
| City taxes paid          | $1,367,000  | $404,000      |

*Source:* Department of Economic Development (1988).

The research and publicity over industrial displacement on the Near North Side eventually helped begin to unmask some of the ideological claims being made by the real estate community to generate support for its goals and ambitions in the Clybourn Corridor. In particular, the familiar litany of the "highest and best use," which once held such weight in land-use conflicts of all kinds, had itself now become the subject of growing discussion and debate. Especially with the current focus of economic policy squarely on jobs instead of real estate development, property developers were hard-pressed to explain why their proposals were better for Chicago than preserving land for manufacturing, *even if they did lead to higher property values.* Furthermore, growing publicity over the role of zoning policy in determining land-use trends in contested areas of the Near North Side weakened developers' arguments that displaced manufacturers were victims of market forces alone. This change in the terms of discourse over industrial decline further legitimized LEED Council's organizing work and helped reduce the Sawyer administration's risks in supporting the PMD initiative.

By the summer of 1988, the debate over the PMD was rapidly approaching a climax. Once forty-third ward alderman Eisendrath introduced the ordinance into city council in late June, only two major hurdles remained: a community hearing to be held by the Department of Planning to explain the proposal and solicit comments, and a hearing by the Plan Commission to determine the industrial viability of the district and the need for PMD status. Both were scheduled for later that summer. At the close of the second hearing, the Plan Commission would issue its recommendations. Although final approval of the ordinance still rested with the city's fifty aldermen, a positive vote by the Plan Commission was not expected to be challenged in city council.

Ultimately, both hearings proved to be dominated heavily by PMD supporters. Of twenty-eight individuals testifying at the Department of Planning's hearing on the PMD in July, four were opposed to the PMD, while twenty-four supported the initiative. Those arguing against the ordinance included two Lincoln Park residents, a realtor, and one area manufacturer. Testifying in favor of the PMD were representatives from eight nearby industrial firms, two labor unions, and six community organizations, along with seven area residents and one industrial worker (Department of Planning 1988). The following month, after a lengthy session that included five hours of additional testimony, the Plan Commission voted 7–0 in favor of the PMD.

In October 1988, over two years after former forty-third ward alderman Martin Oberman's task force on industrial displacement originally proposed the idea, city council voted to approve the Plan Commission's recommendation to create the city's first Planned Manufacturing District in the Clybourn Corridor portion of the forty-third ward.[9] The basic features of the ordinance remained largely as originally conceived by the task force. The new district would consist of two parts: a forty-one acre core zone surrounded by a seventy-four acre buffer zone. Residential conversions would be prohibited in both portions of the district, but certain commercial and retail development would be allowed in the buffer zone at the discretion of the zoning board. The Plan Commission was given the authority to review the PMD periodically and recommend changes to, or repeal of, the ordinance should it be deemed ineffective in fulfilling its intended objectives.[10]

Passage of the Clybourn Corridor PMD ordinance represented, without a doubt, a key legislative milestone in Chicago. Never before had city officials acted so aggressively to protect central area manufacturers threatened by the pressures of nearby commercial and residential redevelopment. Yet both supporters and opponents of the measure alike were well aware that important questions still lay ahead. The threat of a lawsuit by Clybourn Corridor manufacturers opposed to the initiative had already been raised, and the city's tendency to vacillate between support for the industrial and real estate communities throughout the duration of the conflict raised questions about whether area manufacturers and property developers would accept the decision as final.

The debate over the PMD brought a number of other issues to the surface as well. Protecting manufacturers from real estate speculation was one thing, but PMDs alone would clearly not be enough to halt the decline of Chicago's manufacturing base, much less rejuvenate industry. In addition to preserving the integrity of the city's industrial districts, city government would also need to proactively support industrial development in the city—through planning, infrastructure improvements, financial assistance, and other such efforts. In short, the city would need to begin furnishing Chicago manufacturers with the same kinds of public support the downtown business community had enjoyed for the past half-century. The following chapter focuses on the aftermath of the Clybourn Corridor PMD debate, examining how elements of a citywide industrial policy have begun to take root in Chicago despite the return of the downtown business leadership to a central position within the city's governing coalition.

## Conclusion

The events in this chapter appear to depart in a number of ways from the expectations of most contemporary urban political economists. Most importantly, the alliance between land-based interests and city officials that urban theorists today view as a nearly inescapable component of present-day urban regimes failed to materialize around an economic development strategy for the intensification of land use on Chicago's Near North Side. Instead, officials from the Harold Washington and Eugene Sawyer administrations sided with neighborhood organizations and their allies around a policy initiative designed to preserve well-paying blue-collar jobs by maintaining Near North Side property values at below-market levels.

How were Washington and Sawyer administration officials able to resist the pull of the real estate community and its allies? Consider, first of all, the alliance between Near North Side community organizations and manufacturers, which provided the former with a set of economic resources and the latter with the organizational capacity to influence public policy. In essence, this coalition allowed city officials to circumvent the accumulation/legitimation divide within which urban political economists today tend to frame virtually all conflict between downtown and the neighborhoods. Relieved in this case of the necessity to balance legitimate neighborhood concerns with the need for economic growth, both Washington and Sawyer officials were more free than usual to make decisions consistent with the interests of their administrations' neighborhoods political base.

Significant as well is the role of public policy in this story. The growing transformation of the Clybourn Corridor from a manufacturing district to a residential, shopping, and entertainment area for downtown office workers was not the result of simple economic pressures, global or otherwise, that urban political economists typically single out as the driving force behind urban economic change. As this chapter illustrates, real estate speculators and developers took advantage of an easy-to-manipulate zoning ordinance to inflate property values in the Clybourn Corridor above the level that could support manufacturing. As commercial and residential incursion into the area increased, industry performance standards for noise, odors, and vibrations created an additional wedge for the real estate community by placing profitable manufacturers out of compliance with the city zoning ordinance. Ultimately, the zoning ordinance itself became the object of struggle in a dispute that would determine, politically, which of these two equally viable economic strategies would prevail.

To be sure, real estate developers and their allies represented formidable adversaries, continually testing the mettle of Washington and Sawyer administration officials. Yet the power of the development community rested less on objective economic conditions than on its ability to define growth in terms most beneficial to its own membership. This proved increasingly difficult once Washington and his jobs-based economic development agenda arrived on the scene. Despite the *Tribune*'s attempts to portray supporters of the PMD initiative as antigrowth and antidevelopment, it ultimately became clear that the real estate-based growth strategy of rising property values and property tax revenues was simply one of two contested economic development strategies in the Clybourn Corridor, the other being the preservation of the area's industrial base along with the well-paying manufacturing jobs it supported. Based on simple economic criteria alone, there was no rational basis for choosing commercial or residential redevelopment over manufacturing.[11] Like Printing House Row and the Chicago garment district years earlier, politics would play a leading role in determining the trajectory of redevelopment. In this case, however, the outcome would be shaped through a vision shared by a coalition of neighborhood organizations, manufacturers, workers, and their allies in city government instead of real estate developers, downtown business leaders, and sympathetic city officials.

# Chapter Six

# Toward a Citywide Industrial Policy

Despite widespread evidence supporting the argument by urban political economists that city officials today find themselves irresistibly drawn into alliances with land-based interests around downtown revitalization efforts, cases do emerge from time to time that fit this model either imperfectly or not at all. The Harold Washington and Eugene Sawyer administrations' support for the Clybourn Corridor Planned Manufacturing District initiative discussed in the previous chapter represents one such case, but there have been various others as well. In the late 1970s, for example, Cleveland's populist mayor Dennis Kucinich engaged in a series of head-to-head confrontations with the city's downtown business community, abolishing tax abatements for downtown construction projects and at one point returning a $41 million federal grant for a downtown rail system, calling it a "contemptuous substitute" for the real transit needs of Clevelanders (Swanstrom 1985, 8). In Hartford, progressive city council leader Nicholas Carbone tested the boundary between public and private sectors by helping the city gain part ownership of a number of downtown development projects, which officials then used to win commitments for minority hiring in the construction and operation of the developments (Clavel 1986).

Contemporary urban political economists readily acknowledge such cases but deny they represent departures from existing theory. If anything, the experiences of progressives such as Kucinich in Cleveland and Carbone in Hartford are said to confirm their views, because both regimes were ultimately toppled by progrowth coalitions dominated by downtown business elites. During Kucinich's first term in office, downtown bankers angry with the new mayor's confrontational negotiating style sent the City of Cleveland into default by refusing to refinance $14 million in short-term notes. Playing on fears that Kucinich was damaging the city's investment climate, probusiness candidate George Voinovich easily beat Kucinich in the next mayoral election. Likewise, Nicholas Carbone's unsuccessful bid for mayor of Hartford in

1979 was followed by the rapid dismantling of the neighborhood-oriented programs he had pushed through city council during previous years.

In Chicago, when Richard M. Daley emerged as the winner of a 1989 special election called to fill the late Mayor Washington's unexpired term, many observers anticipated a similar retrenchment. Daley's campaign had been heavily bankrolled by downtown attorneys, developers, and business leaders upset with their limited access to City Hall during the previous six years. In his campaign speeches and literature, Daley presented himself as a staunch advocate of economic growth committed to solidifying Chicago's status as a world-class city by building on its strengths as a corporate-financial center. He criticized the recently established Clybourn Corridor PMD and appeared to display little understanding of, or interest in, other types of neighborhood economic development and revitalization efforts.

However, while Daley officials have in fact eliminated or curtailed certain of Harold Washington's neighborhood-oriented policies and programs, such reversals have been fewer than anticipated, and in some instances the administration has even expanded upon programs introduced by Washington. Industrial policy is a case in point. Daley eventually reversed his campaign stance against planned manufacturing districts and, despite strong opposition from key members of his downtown business-dominated governing coalition, pushed successfully for the passage of two additional PMDs in the North River Industrial Corridor in 1991. Efforts by Daley officials to curb industrial displacement have been supplemented more recently with capital improvements, tax increment financing, and other policies and programs designed to help rejuvenate Chicago's industrial base.

By all appearances, the Richard M. Daley administration began as an effort to recreate the progrowth alliance of downtown business leaders and city officials that governed Chicago from 1955 to 1983. Indeed, downtown redevelopment efforts have played a central role in the Daley administration's overall economic development policy agenda. Yet as we saw in Chapter 4, the political arrangements that sustained Chicago's postwar progrowth regime fell increasingly into crisis by the late 1970s, paving the way for Harold Washington's election victory in 1983. As this chapter will show, efforts to reconstruct the old regime on new political terrain have been only partially successful. Meanwhile, proponents of a local-producer strategy for neighborhood redevelopment have continued to seize opportunities to move their agenda forward in important ways.

## The Richard M. Daley Administration: Between Machine and Reform

The April 1989 special election for mayor once again divided the city of Chicago along racial lines. The race shaped up as a three-way contest among acting Mayor Eugene Sawyer, Richard M. Daley, and Timothy Evans, an

African-American alderman who had served as the late Mayor Washington's floor leader in city council. Sawyer and Evans each sought to build support among Washington's former coalition of blacks, Latinos, and lakefront liberals, but neither candidate was able to generate any enthusiasm to speak of outside the black community. With Sawyer and Evans dividing the African-American vote, Daley coasted to victory with strong support in the city's white ethnic, Latino, and lakefront wards (Grimshaw 1992).

The election campaign proved to be a referendum of sorts on the Washington administration's balanced growth economic development agenda. The *Chicago Tribune* helped set the terms of debate with a seven-part series entitled "Chicago on Hold," published late in the summer of 1988 shortly before the campaign got underway. The series was a direct attack on community activists, progressive politicians, and former Washington administration officials working to resist gentrification and displacement pressures in inner-city neighborhoods. According to series author John McCarron, such individuals were little more than self-serving opportunists, drumming up political support by using downtown area redevelopment projects to play on the fears of neighborhood residents, workers, and business owners. McCarron also criticized the proposed PMD ordinance, ridiculing the notion that preserving Chicago's industrial base was either possible or desirable and arguing that growth in service-sector employment would offset the decline in factory jobs (McCarron 1988).

Candidate Daley presented himself as the alternative to what McCarron scornfully referred to as the "anti-development crusade," distancing himself from controversial programs and policies such as PMDs being advanced from within the neighborhoods. Daley's economic development platform was structured around the corporate-center strategy for downtown redevelopment. His campaign speeches reinforced this theme, generally containing only token references to traditional manufacturing while emphasizing the importance of the downtown area to the city's overall economic prosperity. Addressing the Chicago Kiwanas Club several weeks before the Democratic primary, Daley argued:

> We should strive to preserve and expand manufacturing. But we must also look to areas that promise greater job growth. We can't afford to focus on only one economic sector and ignore the growth industries of the 1990s. Chicago is one of the nation's three largest financial centers. Financial services provided 330,000 Chicago jobs in 1986—about ten percent of total metropolitan employment. These financial jobs are growing at twice the rate of other employment. . . . Chicago is home to world-class universities and cultural institutions. We have trained professionals, a vibrant downtown, and a leading convention center. The next mayor should use these qualities to attract service and financial industries. (Daley 1989)

Relying heavily on large donations from corporate officials and leading downtown business establishments, Daley amassed a record $7.1 million in campaign contributions (Gibson 1989a). By contrast, Eugene Sawyer managed to raise just $3 million, while Timothy Evans's severely underfunded campaign raised less than $500,000 (Goozner and Ziemba 1989; Gibson 1989b). In March 1989, the Evans campaign released a report contending that 30 percent of Daley's donations came from just one percent of his contributors, and that 40 percent came from lawyers, large law firms, and real estate developers (Hardy and Casuso 1989). Developer J. Paul Bietler, whose firm accounted for one of Daley's four donations of $100,000 or more, explained Daley's strong support in the real estate community as follows:

> We're tired of the anti-development posture that has been promulgated at City Hall in the last six years. The extent of the contributions to Daley's campaign by the real estate community, I think, is clearly making that message known. In Daley we see someone whom we believe is capable of seeing the bigger picture; someone who is capable of solving problems in a more logical way; someone who won't seek taxes [on development] without first establishing a dialogue with the real estate community. (Goozner and Ziemba 1989)

Daley's own politics have been characterized as a curious and often contradictory blend of machine and reform (Grimshaw 1992; Ferman 1991). His roots in the machine are deep and personal, yet during a six-year stint as Cook County state's attorney from 1983 to 1989, he made high-quality, professional appointments and resisted any temptation to reserve lower-level jobs for Democratic party loyalists (Grimshaw 1992, 212–213). In the 1989 mayoral campaign, he presented himself as a classic managerial reformer, pledging to put city government on a more businesslike footing by privatizing certain government services, making city workers more productive, and eliminating the city's $150 million budget deficit. In general, Daley has made good on these promises, yet his upbringing within the machine has made its mark on his administration as well.

For example, in his acceptance speech on April 4, 1989, Daley promised his administration would maintain the participatory governing style introduced by the late Mayor Washington, a clear attempt to distance himself from the centralized model of governing embraced by his father (Dold and Hardy 1989). However, within a short period of time, the administration's decision-making powers had been concentrated in the hands of an inner circle made up of three long-term Daley aides, none of whom held reform credentials. Many of the administration's top bureaucrats were left virtually powerless, unable to make even the smallest decisions without first receiving approval from the mayor's top echelon of advisors (Hornung 1990).

Daley's efforts to privatize certain government functions revealed similar tensions between machine and reform. During the first several years of his administration, one-time bastions of patronage, such as city-run janitorial and towing services, were farmed out to private contractors, helping Daley bring the city's budget deficit under control. At the same time, however, reports began to surface that many of the mayor's key political contributors were receiving lucrative city contracts for legal work and other services. One particularly generous law firm did $445,000 worth of business with the city during Daley's first year in office, nearly three times more business than any other firm (Gibson 1990). Critics soon began to charge that "pinstripe patronage" was filling the void left by the Shakman Decree's restrictions on political hiring and firing, breathing new life into a crippled machine.

In the economic development policy arena, Daley quickly undertook steps to establish himself as a builder in the same tradition as his father, emphasizing flashy downtown area development projects. Within months of his election in 1989, Daley convinced the Illinois state legislature to finance a $150 million renovation of Navy Pier, a rusting, underutilized municipal dock near the Loop that the city wanted to convert to an entertainment complex. During the first two years of his administration, Daley also helped engineer a $987 million expansion of the McCormick Place convention complex and was influential in the planning and construction of the $175 million United Center, a new basketball/hockey stadium on the Near West Side (Reardon 1992a). In addition, plans were announced for the construction of a third major airport in Chicago; a $2 billion, privately financed casino and entertainment complex; and a $775 million trolley system to transport tourists and office workers through Chicago's expanding downtown area (Reardon 1992a; Washburn 1993).

Yet despite his centralized governing style and preoccupation with grandiose development projects, Daley displayed flashes of sensitivity during the first years of his administration to the concerns of neighborhood residents, workers, and business owners located outside the Loop and affluent lakefront wards. A number of progressives received top-level appointments in the mayor's new cabinet, including David Mosena, a strong proponent of industrial retention within the Washington and Sawyer administrations, and Joseph James, former director of economic development and international trade for the city of Austin, Texas. Daley also sponsored a city ordinance requiring that 25 percent of all city contracts be awarded to minority-owned firms and established the Capital Improvements Advisory Committee in 1991 to provide a forum for public input into and oversight of the allocation of funds for citywide capital improvements projects (Kass 1990; Ferman and Grimshaw 1992, 122).

Overtures to the neighborhoods such as these were an indication of the degree of change that Chicago's political landscape had undergone during the previous several decades. As we saw in earlier chapters, Chicago politics during the machine era were marked by a separation between electoral politics and public policy, whereby patronage appointments and selective incentives were utilized to assemble winning electoral coalitions of neighborhood voters, while policy benefits were channeled into the hands of downtown landowners and other business elites. By the time Richard M. Daley was elected mayor in 1989, however, any attempt to recreate this set of arrangements would have certainly been futile. Not only were key machine resources like patronage and federal urban programs in short supply, but Harold Washington had also created a climate of high expectations within the city's low- and moderate-income neighborhoods by funding the organizing efforts of community-based organizations, providing them with access to key decision-making arenas, and helping to create a new sense of legitimacy for community-based political activity. As political scientist William Grimshaw has argued,

> "Son of Boss" may well be bent on reinstating a centralized and closed style of machine government; however, he is entangled in the web of reform spun by Washington. Blacks, women, lakefront liberals, Hispanics, and other dispossessed groups who had been empowered by Washington's reforms are disinclined to give up their gains. They want to maintain the access, decision-making influence, and material and symbolic benefits they acquired under reform government. (Grimshaw 1992, 208)

By all indications, Richard M. Daley's governing coalition is not unlike that of his father, dominated by real estate developers and other downtown business elites, lawyers and large law firms, and some party regulars (Ferman and Grimshaw 1992, 122). By and large, public policy under the new Daley administration has been consistent with the interests of this coalition, as Daley's penchant for large-scale, downtown redevelopment projects would appear to suggest. Yet due to the mobilization of low- and moderate-income neighborhoods and the absence of resources to help dampen neighborhood expectations, Daley has been compelled to expand the circle of public-policy beneficiaries in Chicago, selectively broadening his governing coalition to include some degree of representation for certain neighborhood groups and organizations.

The Richard M. Daley administration thus straddles a number of contradictions, occupying the middle ground between machine and reform, between centralization and decentralization, and between downtown and the neighborhoods. Despite his personal upbringing within the machine and his strong ties to the downtown business community, Daley himself has shown a willingness to embrace the policy concerns of neighborhood organizations and their allies on a selective basis, even when doing so places him at odds with prominent members of his governing coalition. These tensions and contradictions are evident in the Daley administration's approach to industrial policy.

## Industrial Land Use

During the time the Clybourn Corridor PMD proposal was being debated in the mid-to-late 1980s, land-use conflicts between manufacturers and commercial and residential property developers were beginning to emerge in other portions of the North River Industrial Corridor as well. As we saw in Chapter 5, developers of the River Lofts commercial/residential complex on Goose Island successfully lobbied the city for a zoning variance in 1987 despite strong opposition from Goose Island manufacturers. By 1988, land speculators betting that gentrification would ultimately sweep the island had purchased much of the available industrial property there, driving property values well above industrial rates and making expansion space for Goose Island manufacturers increasingly unaffordable (Goozner 1988b). Similar real estate pressures were also developing in the nearby Elston Corridor sub-area of the North River Industrial Corridor (see Map 4). By the time the Clybourn Corridor PMD was established in October 1988, planning was underway to create additional PMDs in each of these two areas.

The Local Employment and Economic Development (LEED) Council, the major organizational force behind the Clybourn Corridor PMD initiative, also led the effort to set aside Goose Island and the Elston Corridor as the city's next two PMDs. During 1988 and 1989, LEED Council staff members met with representatives from all companies in each area to explain the PMD concept and to build support for the initiatives. Once a core group of supporters had been identified and mobilized around the proposals, staff members worked with the companies to achieve a consensus regarding the PMD boundaries and specific land-use guidelines. As in the Clybourn Corridor, the support base among area manufacturers was eventually broadened with appeals to labor and nearby community organizations.

On Goose Island, the PMD planning process was dominated by the Chicago Milwaukee Corporation (CMC), a railroad company that owned a twenty-five acre unused railyard on the island, which made it Goose Island's largest landowner. In 1987, CMC had agreed to develop an industrial park on the property following guarantees provided by Washington administration officials for tax concessions and public infrastructure improvements. However, with land speculators driving the value of Goose Island property progressively higher during 1987 and 1988, CMC began to rethink its plans. In July 1988, the company voiced its opposition to the proposal for a PMD on Goose Island and announced that its plans for an industrial park there had been put on hold (Goozner 1988b). The following month, CMC President Edwin Jacobson insisted the company's Goose Island property would be developed for "the highest and best use that would be most beneficial for the company's shareholders" (Hornung 1988). According to CMC Vice President Wayne Delfino, "retail, residential, office or even a hotel—or any combination

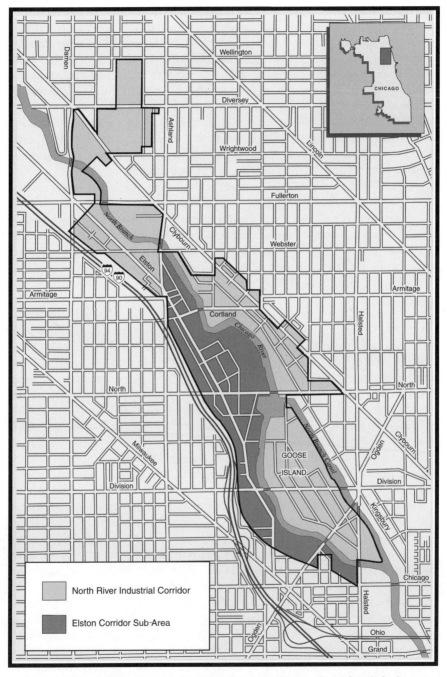

Map 4. North River Industrial Corridor with Elston Corridor Sub-Area

thereof—would all be better uses than industrial" (Fitzgerald 1988).

Despite the opposition of certain large landowners like CMC, a broad base of support around the Goose Island and Elston Corridor PMD proposals had emerged by the time Richard M. Daley succeeded Eugene Sawyer as mayor of Chicago in the spring of 1989. Daley's election victory, however, appeared to represent a major stumbling block for the coalition of PMD supporters. In his election campaign, Daley had expressed deep reservations about the value of PMDs in the North River Industrial Corridor, insisting that residential and commercial developments of the sort CMC wished to construct were more desirable uses than manufacturing for riverfront property. In a January 1989 interview with *Crain's Chicago Business,* Daley argued,

> Everybody talks about bringing manufacturing back. There aren't going to be any more soap factories on Clybourn Avenue. . . . This city is changing. You're not going to bring manufacturing back. . . . The [Chicago] river is too important. The river should not be a dumping ground for industries. The river is going to be for townhouses, homes, apartments, and offices. (*Crain's Chicago Business,* 30 January 1989)

To complicate matters further, neither of the two aldermen in whose wards the Goose Island and Elston Corridor PMDs were to be located were strong supporters of the initiatives. Both were machine aldermen reluctant to back legislation that promised to undermine their authority over land use. Furthermore, their half-hearted support for the process thus far had been prompted largely by pressure from the Washington and Sawyer administrations. With the election of a mayoral candidate on record as opposing more PMDs, it appeared that, if anything, pressure from the Mayor's Office would now be applied in the opposite direction. To virtually no one's surprise, forty-second ward alderman Burton Natarus withdrew his support for the Goose Island PMD several months after Daley was elected, arguing the proposal would "interfere with the natural marketplace" and reduce land values.[1] Lacking both mayoral and aldermanic support, the PMD proposals for Goose Island and the Elston Corridor faced an extremely uncertain future by the summer of 1989.

During the early stages of his administration, however, Daley withheld judgment on the proposal for additional PMDs in the North River Industrial Corridor. Instead, he asked the Departments of Planning and Economic Development to conduct a thorough analysis of the industrial viability of Goose Island and the Elston Corridor and make recommendations on the need for protective legislation. The selection of these two departments was significant. Both were headed by progressive administrators who had chosen to retain a number of Washington and Sawyer appointees to staff key positions within their respective agencies. As a result, each department contained a solid core of bureaucrats who were familiar with the PMD concept and committed to moving the process forward.

Not surprisingly, departmental staff built a strong case for the industrial viability of both Goose Island and the Elston Corridor, arguing that displacement pressures posed a serious threat to profitable manufacturers in each area. According to reports issued jointly by the Departments of Planning and Economic Development, both locations were ideal sites for manufacturing because of their proximity to downtown, convenient access to transportation of various kinds, industrial infrastructure, and diverse industrial bases (Department of Planning 1990a, 1990b). Industrial real estate markets were found to be strong, with demand for suitable industrial space well exceeding the limited supply in each area. Speculative pressures were blamed for inflating property values above industrial rates and holding industrial expansion in both locations to less than its full potential.

At roughly the same time, an additional study of Goose Island was carried out by a task force convened by LEED Council in response to Mayor Daley's initial lack of enthusiasm for the Goose Island PMD proposal. The study, which received technical assistance from the Departments of Planning and Economic Development, included an economic and revenue impact analysis of two different land-use scenarios for Goose Island: a commercial/residential scenario and an industrial scenario. Researchers projected that preserving Goose Island as an industrial district would contribute $337 million more to the Chicago area's Gross Regional Product by the year 2001 than a commercial/residential scenario, due largely to the comparatively higher economic multipliers associated with industrial development. In addition, although property tax revenues were projected to be higher under a commercial/residential scenario, when revenues from additional sources were taken into account, industry came out well ahead of commercial or residential alternatives (LEED Council 1990).

Mayor Daley's opposition to the two new PMD proposals continued to soften during the winter and spring of 1990. Then in June of that year he made a startling announcement: he had reconsidered his campaign position against planned manufacturing districts and was now prepared to support the planning process for the Goose Island and Elston Corridor PMDs.[2] Caving into pressure from the administration, the aldermen representing both areas soon agreed to back the initiatives as well. Later that month, despite strong editorial criticism from the *Tribune* and appeals from property developers urging him to rethink his decision, Daley personally introduced both ordinances into city council.[3] With the backing of the administration and both area aldermen, the ordinances easily survived a full city council vote later that fall.

Daley's decision to reverse his campaign stance against PMDs and to take a position opposed by many of his allies in the real estate community was prompted by a number of considerations. First, Daley's new planning commissioner, David Mosena, a supporter of the PMD proposals, had quickly gained the confidence and respect of the mayor, so much so that Daley went on to appoint him chief of staff after his reelection in 1991. Mosena's clout with the mayor allowed him effectively to end-run Daley's inner circle of advisors, none of whom appeared to share Mosena's enthusiasm for industrial protection (Hornung 1991). Once his staff had marshaled sufficient evidence in support of the new PMD initiatives, Mosena was able to present the information directly to the mayor, ensuring that his department's findings and recommendations would get a fair hearing from Daley himself. Mosena's personal lobbying effort on behalf of the PMDs is generally singled out as the key reason for Daley's change of heart on the issue (Goozner 1990).

Yet Mayor Daley also faced strong community pressure to continue the Washington and Sawyer administrations' policy of industrial retention. Unlike a number of other neighborhood-oriented initiatives introduced by Washington and Sawyer, the PMD proposals originated within the community, not the administration, and were thus more difficult to kill. Supporting the PMDs was a way for Daley to respond to the policy demands of a politically mobilized community without compromising his strong progrowth, prodevelopment policy agenda. The combination of key bureaucratic support, community pressure, and research demonstrating the value of North Side manufacturers to Chicago's economy all help explain the mayor's willingness to reconsider his position on PMDs.

## Industrial Land-Use Plans

In addition to its support for the Goose Island and Elston Corridor PMD initiatives, the Daley administration also released a series of industrial land-use plans for the North, South, and West Sides of Chicago between 1991 and 1994, the first such plans issued by the City of Chicago since 1970 (Department of Planning and Development 1991, 1992, 1994). Like PMDs, the new plans were intended to head off conflicts between manufacturers and commercial or residential property developers by clearly identifying areas of the city the administration was committed to retaining for industrial use. Unlike PMDs, however, they contained no legal mechanisms to adjudicate such disputes. With the publication of the third and final plan of the series in 1994, Department of Planning and Development staff had identified twenty-two separate industrial corridors on the North, South, and West Sides of the city, representing a total of 13,761 acres of land.

Although published by the Daley administration, the new industrial land-use plans were the culmination of a planning process that began during the Washington administration. Acting on the recommendations of a task force on industrial and commercial land use established by Mayor Washington in 1986, the Eugene Sawyer administration's Department of Planning began an inventory of industrial land several years later on Chicago's North Side, the area of the city where land-use conflicts between manufacturers and real estate developers had become most pronounced (City of Chicago 1987, 12). A broad segment of the North Side community—including industrial development organizations, real estate brokers, bankers, and industry representatives—participated in the planning process. With the assistance of these groups and individuals, city planners mapped out the boundaries of four North Side industrial corridors, releasing their findings in a draft report published in January 1989 (Department of Planning 1989). In most cases, the plan called for "complete protection of all M-zoned land" within a particular industrial corridor. Besides identifying the boundaries of individual corridors, the plan included specific recommendations for infrastructure improvements, marketing assistance, and other business services for area manufacturing firms.

The Daley administration's industrial land-use plans were an extension of this planning process, with a number of key differences. First, the base of community participation in the planning process was far narrower than before, limited to the four or five industrial development organizations active in each of the three study areas. Second, the new plans focused exclusively on land use and infrastructure improvements; provisions for marketing and other business assistance present in the Sawyer administration's earlier plan were dropped. Finally, the recommendation for complete protection of manufacturing-zoned land that had figured prominently in the Sawyer administration's plan was replaced by a weaker proposal recommending that rezoning requests inside the twenty-two designated industrial corridors be subject to a more stringent review process than petitions for zoning changes elsewhere.

Although the latter provision was never implemented, the Daley administration has shown some commitment to maintaining the industrial integrity of the corridors. In the summer of 1995, for example, developer Ron Shipka approached the city with plans to build a six-hundred-unit residential development on a recently vacated twenty-acre industrial site within the North River Industrial Corridor, several blocks north of the Clybourn Corridor PMD. Zoned for heavy manufacturing at the time, the site could be developed for residential use only if city officials would agree to Shipka's request for a zoning variance. Sold as industrial property, the parcel was worth roughly $4 million. With a zoning change, Shipka was willing to pay $17 million (Driscoll 1996).

Shipka's plans quickly drew criticism from nearby manufacturers, who anticipated a barrage of complaints and possible legal action from residents of the new development upset with the noise and odors produced by neighboring industrial firms. The most prominent critic was the Vienna Sausage Manufacturing Company, which employed 480 workers in a 100,000-square-foot food processing plant directly across the Chicago River from the proposed development. Vienna insisted that an approval of Shipka's rezoning request would ultimately force the company to relocate. According to Vienna Chairman James Bodman, "Our first choice is to stay in Chicago. But we smoke wood for our sausage, we clean grease out of the water and, on hot days, it smells here. Add our diesel trucks and noisy rooftop refrigeration systems, and it will be only a matter of time before nearby residents drive us out" (Murphy 1996).

Ward alderman Terry Gabinski was initially in favor of rezoning the site. However, Daley officials were unwilling to support the proposal without first testing the market for industrial buyers. With the assistance of LEED Council, Department of Planning and Development staff began marketing the property to North Side manufacturers in need of expansion space. When a number of buyers surfaced, Daley came out firmly against the rezoning request, arguing that individuals who had spent several hundred thousand dollars for a condominium would soon pressure the city to close down nearby factories.[4] Gabinski, a close ally of the mayor in city council, soon relented, and by spring of 1996 the proposal was considered dead.

Despite cases such as this one, the weak provisions governing rezoning requests in the city's new industrial land-use plans have left the administration relatively free to accommodate the interests of commercial and residential property developers, when it so chooses. In 1994, for instance, developers in the nearby Addison Industrial Corridor approached area alderman Richard Mell with a plan to build 330 townhouses on an eleven-acre, manufacturing-zoned site occupied until recently by a shipbuilding company. The property was worth roughly $5 per square foot as industrial space, but the owners were asking nearly three times that price in anticipation of a zoning change allowing residential redevelopment of the site (Reardon 1995).

Mell, a prominent machine alderman whose name had briefly surfaced as a possible choice for acting mayor following Harold Washington's death in 1987, wanted the development approved, arguing the property would otherwise lie vacant. However, opposition to the project soon began to materialize. *Crain's Chicago Business* published a number of editorials in 1995 and 1996 urging Mell to withhold support for the rezoning request. Several neighborhood organizations active in the area, including the North Business and Industrial Council and the Lake View Citizens' Council, also became strong vocal critics of the proposal. Finally, a number of neighboring industrial firms, including an electronic games manufacturer employing one thousand workers, insisted that complaints from residents of the proposed new development would ultimately force nearby industries to relocate (Snyder 1995).

Although planning officials initially asked Mell to withhold his endorsement of the proposal pending the outcome of an effort by the city to market the property to an industrial user, both the administration and Alderman Mell continued to leave the door open to a zoning change. A 1996 proposal that would have divided the site between two manufacturing firms eventually collapsed when the property owners refused to lower their asking price for the land to an industrial rate. The following year a compromise plan was announced: four acres of the site would be retained for industrial use, while seven additional acres would be rezoned and developed as a residential complex of townhomes and condominiums. Such high-profile rezonings within the city's officially designated industrial corridors have been relatively infrequent, but they have damaged the city's policy on industrial land use by sending mixed signals to industries and property developers, undermining the stability necessary for both groups to undertake long-range plans.

## Resources for Industrial Development

The Daley administration's industrial land-use planning efforts, while significant, represented only one piece of a comprehensive industrial policy for the city of Chicago. By the 1990s, many of the city's industrial corridors showed the effects of long-standing neglect. Decades of street resurfacings had made viaducts in many industrial areas impassable to large trucks, forcing drivers to take time-consuming circuitous routes in order to reach local industries. Potholes eighteen inches deep or more were a common sight on many industrial streets. In addition to public infrastructure concerns, many firms required assistance with job training, marketing, achieving compliance with environmental regulations, and securing conveniently located expansion space within the city.

During the early 1990s, the Daley administration began to take a more aggressive stance toward industrial retention, supplementing its efforts to protect the integrity of the city's industrial districts with a number of programs and policies designed to support industrial development in Chicago more actively than in the past. The change in policy was prompted by a number of considerations. First, the administration's attempts to safeguard manufacturing-zoned property through PMDs and industrial land-use plans continued to draw heavy criticism from real estate developers, who pointed to abandoned industrial buildings and undeveloped property in places like Goose Island as evidence the policy was not working. In a somewhat ironic twist, the real estate community's growing demands that the city reverse its policy on industrial land use pushed officials to begin taking the necessary steps to produce tangible results in the PMDs and other officially recognized industrial corridors.

In addition, Mayor Daley experienced a major embarrassment in the summer of 1992 when city officials were unable to locate a suitable new site for the catalog operation of Spiegel, Inc., which had outgrown its existing quarters on Chicago's Southwest Side. Spiegel, its 2,200-employee payroll making it the largest employer in Mayor Daley's own neighborhood of Bridgeport, announced in late September that it had selected a suburb of

Columbus, Ohio, as the location for its new warehousing and distribution center. Spiegel's departure, coming at a time when the city was in the midst of negotiations over a planned third Chicago airport and a $2 billion casino and entertainment complex, highlighted the mayor's preoccupation with flashy, headline-grabbing megaprojects, and the failure of his administration to develop a comprehensive set of policies to retain well-paying manufacturing jobs for Chicago residents.

To top it all off, Daley's megaprojects were themselves beginning to encounter considerable hostility in the Illinois state legislature, which proved to be far less forthcoming with funding and approval for the mayor's pet projects than for those of his father several decades earlier. In 1991, Daley successfully pushed a proposal for a $987 million expansion of the McCormick Place convention center through the legislature, but only after plans for a $398 million domed stadium had been dropped from the project (Reardon and Pearson 1991). Plans for a new Chicago airport and casino and entertainment complex did not fare as well. By the end of 1992, both projects had collapsed due to the unwillingness of downstate and suburban lawmakers to support the construction of high-profile developments that appeared to hold few benefits for their noncity constituents.

Legislative roadblocks like these were rare during the peak years of the Richard J. Daley machine, when state assembly approval of large development projects for Chicago oftentimes required little more than a telephone call from the mayor. During the 1950s and 1960s, much of the population, industry, and wealth of the state of Illinois was concentrated in Chicago, giving Mayor Daley and the Cook County Democratic machine considerable clout in the Illinois state legislature. According to political scientist Milton Rakove, Daley worked out a quid pro quo arrangement with downstate Republican legislators under which they agreed to give him what he wanted for Chicago as long as he agreed not to interfere with their control over state government patronage and other perquisites of office (Rakove 1975, 209).

The power relationships that undergirded this set of arrangements have since changed considerably, due chiefly to the effects of suburbanization. Between 1952 and 1992, Chicago's share of the Illinois vote dropped from 41 percent to 22 percent, and a growing proportion of the state's wealth and productive capacity is now concentrated in portions of the metropolitan area outside the city of Chicago (Judd and Swanstrom 1994, 304). As a result, Chicago has far less power than it once did in the state capitol. The former alliance between Chicago Democratic machine politicians and downstate Republican legislators has given way to a new alliance between suburban and downstate lawmakers increasingly hesitant to provide funds or approval for what many of their constituents view as pork-barrel projects for Chicago politicians. Still stinging from the legislative defeats of his airport and casino proposals in late 1992, Daley announced in January 1993 that his new economic development priorities would consist of relatively unglamorous objectives such as maintaining infrastructure, improving city services, and retaining business in the city (Reardon 1993).

## The Model Industrial Corridors Initiative

One of the Daley administration's early efforts to expand its industrial policy beyond simple land-use controls was a program established in 1994 called the Model Industrial Corridors Initiative. By the summer of 1993, the administration was nearing completion of its industrial land-use plans for the North, South, and West Sides of the city and was now ready to take a more proactive stance toward retaining manufacturing jobs in the twenty-two industrial corridors identified in the plans. In a strong demonstration of his newfound sympathies for Chicago manufacturers, Daley authorized the hiring of LEED Council executive director Donna Ducharme as the city's top industrial development officer in July 1993, placing her in charge of program development within the newly designated industrial corridors.

Soon after her appointment in the Department of Planning and Development, Ducharme convened a task force to help define the ideal features of a viable, inner-city industrial corridor and to develop a program to help individual corridors better achieve these characteristics. The task force—a diverse group including manufacturers, real estate brokers, developers, representatives from industrial development organizations, and city planning staff—agreed on a set of five basic objectives: industrial corridors should be safe, accessible and functional, competitive and marketable, well-managed, and attractive. The Model Industrial Corridors Initiative was established to meet these objectives by funding industrial development organizations participating in the city's Local Industrial Retention Initiative (LIRI) program to write strategic plans for their service areas addressing these five goals. Each group was also promised anywhere from $1 million to $1.5 million to seed the implementation of their plans. By 1997, funding proposals submitted by twelve LIRI organizations from the North, South, and West Sides of Chicago had been approved by the city.

One of the first organizations funded under the new program was Greater Southwest Development Corporation, a Southwest Side industrial development organization whose service area consists of a nine-hundred-acre industrial corridor anchored by a number of large food-products manufacturers, including Tootsie Roll, Nabisco, and Kool-Aid. Greater Southwest's strategic plan, issued in March 1995, is representative of the types of plans that organizations participating in the Model Industrial Corridors Initiative have produced. Its primary focus is land use and infrastructure. Among other things, the plan identifies locations where the need for street repairs, viaduct upgrades, and other physical improvements is most urgent. It also contains a survey of vacant land parcels in the corridor with the best prospects for industrial redevelopment, along with proposals for marketing the property (Greater Southwest Development Corporation 1995).

In addition to the above recommendations, the plan contains proposals for increasing intracorridor networking relationships among area firms and for improving the skills of the local workforce. In a survey of corridor firms carried out as part of the Model Corridors planning process, nearly 50 percent of companies expressed an interest in common warehousing and cooperative purchasing of raw materials or finished goods. Opportunities for the area's larger manufacturers to use the services of local rather than outside suppliers are identified as well. In addition, firm owners singled out the need for job training as a top priority. Under the plan, employers would work with nearby educational institutions to develop new programs designed to meet the specific training needs of local employers. Both these efforts, job training and the fostering of intracorridor networking relationships, would be overseen by a steering committee made up of local business and community representatives.

Under Ducharme's leadership, the Model Industrial Corridors Initiative was developed as a decentralized planning process. By providing LIRI organizations with the resources to write and implement their own strategic plans, the administration has helped create a strong organizational presence in the neighborhoods that is committed to seeing the process through to completion. LIRI organizations participating in the program work closely with area manufacturers to prepare their strategic plans; as a result, the manufacturers are themselves generally strong supporters of the process, willing to devote time and resources to ensure that the plans are fully implemented. Aside from improving the program's chances of success, the decentralized planning process has helped the administration broaden its base of support in the neighborhoods by offering policy benefits to LIRI organizations and their members and allies.

## Capital Improvements for Industrial Infrastructure

A certain number of the industrial infrastructure projects identified as priorities in the strategic plans written by industrial development organizations participating in the Model Industrial Corridors Initiative can be financed by the seed money that the city provides for the implementation of each plan. However, the considerable costs of such projects as bridge and viaduct upgrades mean that additional funding sources are oftentimes necessary. The City of Chicago allocates funds for industrial infrastructure through its capital budget. As we have seen in previous chapters, city officials have historically concentrated capital improvements dollars disproportionately in the Loop and nearby areas. The Richard M. Daley administration's infrastructure priorities are not inconsistent with this pattern, but in recent years the share of the city's capital improvements funds targeted to industrial areas has increased.

In large part, this increase has come about through the efforts of a city-wide coalition of seventy-five neighborhood organizations called the Neighborhood Capital Budget Group (NCBG), which was founded in 1987 to provide Chicago citizens with a greater voice in the capital budgeting process. The City of Chicago's procedure for planning and funding capital projects centers around the Capital Improvements Program, a comprehensive list of citywide capital improvements scheduled to be implemented within five years. Until recently, the general public was excluded from the capital budgeting process. Under pressure from NCBG, however, the Daley administration established the Capital Improvements Advisory Committee in 1991, which provides formal channels for public input into the drafting of the city's Capital Improvements Programs.

While democratizing the planning process somewhat, community participation in the formulation of the Capital Improvements Program does not ensure that Chicago neighborhoods will actually receive a growing share of capital improvements funds. This is because the Capital Improvements Program is only a plan; it cannot be fully implemented until revenue sources have been identified for each project. Typically, projects listed in the first year of the plan have received funding commitments from the city and are likely to be completed within a reasonable time period. The status of projects further down the line in the third, fourth, and fifth years of the plan is far less certain. Many are never completed at all. In a 1982 study, the Metropolitan Housing and Planning Council determined the city had implemented no more than 70 percent of its planned capital improvements projects during the previous decade (Nagel 1982).

In February 1992, NCBG published a study of the Daley administration's 1992–1996 Capital Improvements Program which revealed that $350 million in neighborhood infrastructure improvements listed in the plan had no identifiable funding sources (Reardon 1992b). Included in this amount were over half the industrial infrastructure projects recommended in the administration's recently published industrial land-use plan for the city's West Side. The study, which received significant media coverage, estimated the administration could leverage an additional $880 million in private investment funds by fully financing the city's 1992–1996 Capital Improvements Program. NCBG urged the administration to sell revenue bonds to cover the $350 million shortfall.

The timing of the study was fortuitous. Less than two months later, the Chicago River burst through a hole in the city's century-old system of underground freight tunnels, flooding scores of downtown buildings and bringing business in the Loop to a virtual standstill for several days. The flood highlighted the poor condition of much of the city's aging infrastructure and put additional pressure on the Daley administration to secure the revenues necessary to finance long-overdue repairs. In May 1992, Mayor Daley announced plans to sell $160 million in General Obligation Bonds for infrastructure improvements, over 90 percent of which were to be located in neighborhood residential and industrial areas (Davis 1992). Since then, the administration has issued bonds for neighborhood infrastructure on an annual basis.

The bond offerings, largely the result of pressure by NCBG, have reduced the disparity between neighborhood industrial infrastructure projects identified in the city's Capital Improvements Program and those that are actually completed. Table 11 evaluates the degree to which street and viaduct improvements identified in four Capital Improvements Programs issued by the Daley administration were implemented by the city. The administration's performance from 1990 to 1992 was abysmal. Of a total of $37 million promised, only $8 million were actually invested. Bond issues for neighborhood infrastructure from 1992 onward helped narrow this gap considerably. During 1993 and 1994, the city funded nearly 70 percent of industrial street and viaduct improvements listed in the Capital Improvements Programs, a less than stellar performance but clearly an improvement.

The Daley administration's record on industrial infrastructure compares favorably with that of the Washington and Sawyer administrations. Table 12 shows the dollar amounts budgeted by the Washington/Sawyer and Daley administrations for industrial infrastructure improvements within the seven industrial corridors identified in the city's North Side industrial land-use plan issued in 1992.[5] During the six-year period from 1983 to 1988, the Washington and Sawyer administrations committed just over $22 million for industrial infrastructure within the North Side industrial corridors, while the Daley administration spent roughly $28.5 million during the five-year period

**Table 11.** Promised versus Actual Investments in
Industrial Streets and Viaducts, 1990–1994

| Year | Amount Promised | Amount Invested |
|------|-----------------|-----------------|
| 1990–1991 | $18,638 | $2,689 |
| 1992 | $18,376 | $5,329 |
| 1993 | $19,041 | $19,228 |
| 1994 | $43,103 | $22,919 |
| **Total** | **$99,158** | **$50,165** |

*Source:* Neighborhood Capital Budget Group (1995).   *Note:* Dollar amounts are in thousands. Calculations are based on the 1990–1994 through 1994–1998 Capital Improvements Programs for the city of Chicago.

between 1990 and 1994. From 1990 to 1994, the Daley administration completed infrastructure investments worth a total of $80 million in the city's twenty-two officially recognized industrial corridors, while securing funding for an additional $90 million worth of improvements (Department of Planning and Development 1996).

**Table 12.** Capital Improvements Expenditures in the
North Side Industrial Corridors, 1983–1994

| Improvement<br>Project | 1983–1988<br>Washington/Sawyer | 1990–1994<br>Daley |
|---|---|---|
| Street | $10,525 | $12,465 |
| Intersection/Signalization | $528 | $125 |
| Bridge | $ — | $9,400 |
| Viaduct | $11,204 | $6,636 |
| **Total** | **$22,257** | **$28,626** |

*Sources:* Department of Planning (1989); Department of Planning and Development (1996). *Note:* Dollar amounts are in thousands. Table includes projects completed and projects funded for construction.

Effective community pressure has caused the Daley administration to reprioritize its capital budgeting process in order to increase funding for industrial infrastructure. Yet the city's capital budget remains, above all, highly skewed in favor of the downtown area. An analysis of the city's Capital Improvements Programs covering the years 1990 through 1999 reveals that the downtown area is slated to receive an annual average of $19.4 million in economic development infrastructure funds during the 1990s. Meanwhile, forty-two of the city's other forty-nine wards will receive a yearly average of just $1.5 million or less in development funds (Neighborhood Capital Budget Group 1996, 14). This gap is beginning to narrow somewhat, but there can be no doubt that the Daley administration's capital improvements priorities continue to reflect the strong position that downtown business interests occupy in the city's present governing coalition.

## Tax Increment Financing

In recent years, the City of Chicago has come to rely increasingly on a relatively new policy innovation called tax increment financing (TIF) to provide public improvements and other economic development incentives for Chicago industries. Tax increment financing authorizes the creation of special districts where taxes paid on any increase in land values are set aside for rede-velopment projects within the district boundaries. The key requirement for the establishment of a TIF district is the finding that, absent significant public investment, property values within the targeted area are likely to remain at or near existing levels for the foreseeable future. Once a district has been created, the assessed value of the land is frozen, and all incremental tax revenues from this point forward are placed in a TIF fund to be used for redevelopment pur-poses. Eligible redevelopment activities include land acquisition, site prepara-tion, building rehabilitation, public capital improvements, and job training and other related educational programs. State legislation requires that all Illi-nois TIF districts be dissolved after a maximum of twenty-three years.

By 1997, Chicago had seventeen industrial TIF districts covering well over 3,000 acres of land. According to data compiled by the Department of Plan-ning and Development, industrial TIF districts in Chicago had, by that point, created roughly 2,660 new jobs and retained approximately 6,750 others, of-tentimes by financing costly predevelopment work such as environmental re-mediation of brownfield sites (Department of Planning and Development 1998, 7). On Goose Island, for example, a recently established TIF district played a key role in securing commitments from several major investors, lead-ing to the construction of a 120,000-square-foot Federal Express distribution center and a 375,000-square-foot window-manufacturing facility. Both com-panies were persuaded to build there when the city agreed to use TIF funds for environmental cleanup and job-training purposes (Fingeret 1998).

Although tax increment financing has been used successfully as an indus-trial development tool in Chicago, the program is not without its detractors. In particular, critics charge that the Daley administration has used the policy too liberally, establishing TIF districts in areas like the central business district where, it is argued, private investment dollars would have been forthcoming without such aggressive city intervention. In such cases, tax increment financ-ing may divert revenue from local taxing authorities, taking funds that would otherwise go to the school board, Park District, and other units of local gov-ernment and utilizing them for economic development purposes alone (Washburn and Martin 1998).

## Evaluating Industrial Policy in Chicago

It is still far too early to say with any degree of certainty whether planned manufacturing districts, tax increment financing, the Model Industrial Corri-dors Initiative, and other programs and policies introduced by the Washing-ton, Sawyer, and Daley administrations to protect and support industrial de-velopment in Chicago have been successful. Major investments on the part of manufacturing firms require long-range planning. Expansion plans made by companies within the city's three PMDs in the years following passage of the initiatives in some cases have yet to be fully implemented. Current data on job and firm retention and growth within the PMDs may thus not be reliable indicators of future trends. Programs like tax increment financing and the Model Industrial Corridors Initiative are even more difficult to evaluate, since many industrial TIF districts are less than two years old and few LIRI organizations participating in the city's Model Industrial Corridors Initiative have moved beyond the planning phase of the program.

Despite these limitations, it may still be possible to make some preliminary judgments on the effectiveness of Chicago's newly emerging industrial policy. One way of gauging the extent to which the three PMDs and the city's new industrial land-use plans are likely to curb the displacement of manufacturers within Chicago industrial districts is to examine recent trends in property values within the PMDs and officially recognized industrial corridors. If the real estate community is convinced that the city is serious about preserving these areas for industrial development alone, we would expect to see a decline in real estate speculation and a stabilization of land values in such locations. Faced with the likelihood that rezoning requests there would be denied, speculators would have little incentive to bid up the price of industrial land to commercial or residential rates. As property values level off, nearby expansion space should become increasingly affordable to area manufacturers, while property tax increases associated with rising land values should become less pronounced and burdensome to industrial firms.

Tables 13, 14, and 15 illustrate trends in land values from 1975 to 1994 for three locations: the Clybourn Corridor PMD; the Goose Island PMD; and the Ravenswood Corridor, a North Side industrial corridor in which loft conversions to residential use began to occur during the late 1980s. Property values within the Goose Island PMD and the Ravenswood Industrial Corridor rose substantially during the 1980s but leveled off after 1990. In the Clybourn Corridor, land values stabilized only within the core zone of the PMD, while values in the PMD buffer zone more than kept pace with the price of commercially zoned property nearby. This comes as no particular surprise, since industrial and commercial development are *both* permitted uses within the PMD buffer zone.[6] If the Clybourn buffer zone is excluded from consideration, however, all three areas exhibited considerable price stability from 1990 to 1994, following sizeable increases during the 1980s. This, coupled with the fact that property values in the vicinity of each area continued to increase measurably during the early 1990s, is a strong indication that land speculators and property developers are taking the city's new industrial retention policies seriously.

Of course, the ultimate test of any city's industrial policy is its effect on job and firm retention and growth. Again, it is still much too soon to make definitive judgements, but early data are of interest. Table 16 shows job and firm retention rates in the three PMDs and four of the city's officially recognized industrial corridors between 1988 and 1992.[7] During this time, the city of Chicago lost a total of 534 manufacturing firms and 33,700 manufacturing jobs, declines of 12 and 15 percent, respectively. As Table 16 indicates, the performance of industrial firms within the city's PMDs was considerably better than this. In the three PMDs combined, the number of industrial firms rose by 3 percent, while manufacturing employment experienced a 7 percent decline. By once again eliminating the Clybourn Corridor buffer zone from the picture, the 7 percent decline in manufacturing jobs becomes a 4 percent increase. With the possible exception of the Ravenswood Corridor, the four industrial corridors listed in Table 16 also showed considerably greater stability than the city of Chicago as a whole.

These preliminary findings suggest that Chicago's industrial policy is already having an impact. Considering that much of the private investment activity that recent policies and programs like planned manufacturing districts

**Table 13.** Land Values in and near Core Zone
of Clybourn Corridor PMD, 1975–1994

| Location | 1975 | 1980 | 1985 | 1990 | 1994 |
|---|---|---|---|---|---|
| PMD Core Zone | $2.00 | $2.50 | $3.00 | $6–12.00* | $6–12.00* |
| PMD Buffer Zone | $2.50 | $2.50 | $4.00 | $40.00 | $50.00 |
| Corner of North and Clybourn *(Opposite SE Corner of PMD)* | $2.00 | $2.50 | $15.00 | $30.00 | $40.00 |

*Sources:* Olcott (1975, 1980, 1985, 1990, 1994).   *Note:* Amounts for PMD core and buffer zones represent maximum land values.   *Includes areas within southern portion of PMD buffer zone.

**Table 14.** Land Values in and near Goose Island PMD, 1975–1994

| Location | 1975 | 1980 | 1985 | 1990 | 1994 |
|---|---|---|---|---|---|
| Goose Island PMD | $1.75 | $2.00 | $2.00 | $9.00 | $12.00 |
| Corner of Halsted and Blackhawk *(two blocks east of PMD)* | $2.00 | $2.00 | $2.50 | $12.00 | $15.00 |

*Sources:* Olcott (1975, 1980, 1985, 1990, 1994).   *Note:* Amounts represent dollars per square foot. Amounts for Goose Island PMD are maximum land values.

and tax increment financing seem likely to generate has not yet been fully realized, the modest job and firm growth within the city's three PMDs is cause
for optimism. Still, if Chicago is to compete successfully with suburban industrial parks and other noncity locations, administration officials will need to
concentrate further resources and planning on industrial areas of the city.
Programs such as the Model Industrial Corridors Initiative, while promising,
are highly underfunded. As with land use, efforts to reprioritize capital improvements, public financing, and other economic development incentives to

**Table 15.** Land Values in and near Ravenswood Industrial Corridor,
1975–1994

| Location | 1975 | 1980 | 1985 | 1990 | 1994 |
|---|---|---|---|---|---|
| Ravenswood Industrial Corridor | $2.25 | $2.50 | $3.00 | $6.00 | $6.00 |
| Corner of Ashland and Wilson *(two blocks east of corridor)* | $4.00 | $3.75 | $4.50 | $9.00 | $11.00 |

*Sources:* Olcott (1975, 1980, 1985, 1990, 1994).   *Note:* Amounts represent dollars per square foot.
Amounts for Ravenswood Industrial Corridor are maximum land values for M-zoned property.

**Table 16.** Changes in Industrial Firms and Employment
in PMDs and Industrial Corridors, 1988 and 1992

| Location | 1988 Firms | 1988 Jobs | 1992 Firms | 1992 Jobs | Percent Change Firms | Percent Change Jobs |
|---|---|---|---|---|---|---|
| Pilsen Corridor | 75 | 1,484 | 72 | 1,582 | -4 | 7 |
| North River Corridor | 122 | 6,565 | 110 | 6,871 | -10 | 5 |
| Addison Corridor | 46 | 2,372 | 51 | 2,325 | 11 | -2 |
| Ravenswood Corridor | 101 | 2,688 | 99 | 1,991 | -2 | -26 |
| PMDs | 154 | 5,221 | 159 | 4,832 | 3 | -7 |
| PMDs minus Clybourn Buffer Zone | 112 | 4,111 | 119 | 4,261 | 6 | 4 |
| City of Chicago | 4,377 | 220,600 | 3,843 | 186,900 | -12 | -15 |

*Sources:* LEED Council (1996); U.S. Bureau of the Census (1987, 1992).
*Note:* Jobs represent manufacturing employment.

reduce disparities between downtown and the neighborhoods will continue
to pit neighborhood residents, workers, and manufacturers against powerful
land-based interests concerned chiefly with generating public support for redevelopment projects in the downtown area. Organizational pressure from
the neighborhoods will no doubt continue to play a crucial role in determining the city's response.

## Conclusion

By all appearances, Richard M. Daley's victory in Chicago's 1989 mayoral
contest represented the final nail in the coffin of the Harold Washington reform movement. Daley's campaign speeches emphasizing the importance of a
vibrant downtown commercial core to Chicago's economy and his strong financial support within the downtown business community left few doubts
about where his economic development priorities would lie. Surely, efforts
undertaken by Harold Washington to broaden the base of participation in
city government, to reallocate resources in favor of low- and moderate-income neighborhoods, and to resurrect Chicago's declining manufacturing
sector would quickly become a thing of the past. While few anticipated a return of the machine in its classic form, most expected Daley's leadership style
and policy choices at least to approximate those of his father.

Such an agenda may well have been utmost in the mind of the younger
Daley as well. However, Richard M. Daley has found himself on much different political terrain than his father was decades earlier. Patronage jobs, city
contracts, and other material incentives that propelled the elder Daley to six
election victories between 1955 and 1976 even as he concentrated policy
benefits in the hands of a select group of downtown business leaders became
increasingly scarce by the late 1970s. Meanwhile, community-based organizations previously excluded from decision-making arenas became legitimate
and well-respected participants in policy discussions and debates under the
Harold Washington administration, in some cases forming alliances with
neighborhood manufacturers around economic policies and programs holding direct rewards for community residents and workers. These organizations
and their coalition partners were not anxious to relinquish their gains following the death of Harold Washington in 1987 and Eugene Sawyer's loss to
Richard M. Daley several years later. Responding to new political realities,
Daley has selectively broadened his governing coalition to include certain
representatives from Chicago's working-class and industrial neighborhoods.

Neighborhood manufacturers seeking protection and support from city
government have fared particularly well under the Daley administration. Due
in no small part to the publicity surrounding the Clybourn Corridor PMD
debate during the mid-to-late 1980s, policies designed to protect inner-city
manufacturing districts from encroachment by commercial or residential de-

velopment now enjoy broad-based support within Chicago's working-class neighborhoods. Following the example set by Washington and Sawyer, Daley has used city government support for neighborhood manufacturers as a means of bridging the accumulation/legitimation divide that frequently jeopardizes the long-term success of redistributive programs and policies in contemporary cities. By supporting PMDs, neighborhood infrastructure programs, and the like, Daley has expanded his base of support in the neighborhoods without compromising his administration's strong progrowth, prodevelopment economic-policy stance. In doing so, he has clearly ruffled some feathers in certain segments of the real estate community, but his otherwise strong support for downtown development has left his standing within much of the downtown business community largely untarnished.

Seen through the lens of urban political economy, the administration of Richard M. Daley resembles that of his father in key respects. Downtown redevelopment has once again become the centerpiece of economic development policy. The alliance between business leaders and city officials has been reestablished, and the divide between governing and electoral coalitions has, to some degree, been recreated. In reality, however, Chicago's current governing arrangements are less a return to the old regime than a partially successful attempt to reconstruct the old regime under new political and economic conditions. Business leaders today must share the stage with new actors, ideas, and economic development strategies that fit uneasily into the public/private, accumulation/legitimation divides of contemporary urban theory. The corporate-center strategy may once again be the economic development strategy of choice, but Chicago also has the makings of a citywide industrial policy. Assuming that neighborhood coalition-building around industrial retention and redevelopment remains as effective as it has been in the recent past, Chicago's newly emerging industrial policy is likely to gather momentum, even within an administration whose economic development priorities appear to lie elsewhere.

# Conclusion

The redevelopment of postwar Chicago was shaped, in significant part, through politics. Soon after World War II, proponents of a corporate-center strategy for downtown commercial and residential redevelopment won the necessary political backing to impose their vision of a postindustrial city on the central area of Chicago. In time, however, their plans were challenged and ultimately compromised by another set of interests committed to preserving the manufacturing jobs base of the near-downtown area. Proponents of a local-producer strategy for neighborhood redevelopment formed an alliance with the Harold Washington administration, helping to effect a regime change in which local economic development priorities, in addition to the distribution of economic rewards, were rearranged to benefit new segments of the urban community. More recently, manufacturers and their allies have successfully extended their local-producer strategy, pressuring the Richard M. Daley administration to assemble additional components of a citywide industrial policy.

## Rethinking Urban Political Economy

The political contest between advocates of the corporate-center and local-producer strategies in Chicago has gone largely unnoticed by contemporary urban scholars because existing theory teaches that urban political conflict, where economic development questions are concerned, centers on redistributive and regulatory matters—not the trajectory of economic growth itself. Within the urban political economy paradigm, the key struggles are those waged by low- and moderate-income neighborhood residents seeking a greater share of the benefits of economic growth, along with protection from displacement caused by major land-use changes. When urban political economists speak of the "business community" and its role in city politics, what they are really talking about is a particular *segment* of the business community, chiefly those land-based interests that form the nucleus of urban growth machines. Business establishments located outside the central business district count for relatively little in contemporary urban theory, as do coalition-building efforts between such enterprises and community-based organizations.

It is worth considering for a moment why this is so. Urban political economy, as we saw in Chapter 1, begins with a series of propositions about the government-economy relationship and the behavior of present-day capitalist firms. Chief among these assumptions is the division of labor between state and market, which relegates policymaking to popularly elected officials and economic decision-making to holders of private investment capital. According to political scientist Stephen Elkin, social well-being depends to a great extent on market transactions because major social decisions are made through the activities of private business firms afforded considerable discretion (Elkin 1987a, 130). Given the limited powers of city government, investment must be induced rather than commanded, creating a privileged position for business in city politics. Decisions by private investors acting in the marketplace create problems, such as deindustrialization and urban economic restructuring, which city officials must wrestle with. While officials may exercise some degree of choice in responding to such developments, the marketplace ultimately sets the parameters for political intervention. As Alan DiGaetano argues,

> [T]he relationship between the economy and the local state is not a direct one, but is mediated by city governing coalitions. That is, while the economic context sets the boundaries for what is possible in urban development politics, a city's governing coalition interprets what can and should be done within that context. (DiGaetano 1989, 279)

Urban political economists argue that the balance of power between city officials and private investors in the post–World War II era has shifted noticeably in favor of the latter, due chiefly to the effects of a second key feature of the urban political economy: the rising mobility of capital. The transportation and communications revolution has made investors increasingly footloose, capable of moving plants and equipment to distant locations on relatively short notice. Capital mobility has set up a bidding war among cities for private investment, forcing city officials to offer an array of incentives to capitalist firms in order to sustain adequate levels of investment activity. Although place-based assets—such as the agglomeration economies often found in central business districts—remain indispensable to certain investors, they are not a constraint on mobility. Since the value of all such assets is said to be reflected in land prices, investors can always sell their holdings and move elsewhere without being penalized by the market.

Finally, urban theorists generally maintain that mobile investors make location decisions based on a narrow economic logic. Specifically, firm owners and managers estimate the future costs of doing business in various places, locating new facilities where they are anticipated to generate the highest profits for the enterprise. This logic of decision-making, combined with capital mobility, accounts for the current trend of industrial decentralization and concentration of corporate and financial activity downtown. Manufacturers seek low-cost land and labor in suburban, rural, and Third World settings, while high-level corporate and financial institutions take advantage of myriad business support services that the central business districts of large cities offer.

. . .

These three propositions—the division of labor between state and market, the mobility of capital, and the instrumental rationality of capitalist firm behavior—lead, in turn, to a number of conclusions about urban politics that are central to the urban political economy paradigm.

*An alliance exists between city officials and landed interests.* Public officials, held accountable along with private investors for the city's economic performance, must forge a working relationship with the business community. While the specifics of this relationship may vary over time and space, it is almost certain to involve a close alliance between city officials and major landowners, both of whom share an interest in promoting high-intensity land uses. According to Stephen Elkin, this alliance has been sealed in the postwar era by the mobility of capital.

> Among other things, local politicians are drawn into alliance with those whose interests are tied to preserving the value of local land uses because both are deeply concerned to hold and attract mobile capital. Those who hold fixed capital in land need to attract high-intensity use to maintain and enhance its value. And local politicians wish to have the political benefits that a vibrant local economy will send their way. (Elkin 1994, 136)

*Economic development is synonymous with real estate development and rising land values.* For urban political economists, economic growth means fostering higher and better uses for property by attracting mobile investors. To use the terminology employed by Logan and Molotch (1987), the goal of development is to enhance the exchange value of land. The benefits of growth—including jobs and other material rewards, rising property-tax revenues, and favorable publicity for city officials—all follow from this objective.

*Development politics divide along a growth/antigrowth axis.* Economic growth, despite its advantages, is not without controversy. Efforts to boost exchange values of land through rearranging and intensifying land use may disrupt residential use values by driving up rents or otherwise causing displacement. Moreover, because the market has generated a pattern of investment activity that increasingly concentrates wealth downtown, redistributive policies are necessary if economic disparities between downtown and the neighborhoods are to be reduced. Officials from some cities have sought to address such concerns by taxing downtown growth and using the proceeds for neighborhood development or by establishing quotas for minority participation in city-sponsored redevelopment projects. However, claims that such efforts damage the local business climate and scare away mobile investors have made public officials extremely cautious about pursuing policies and programs like these.

The above propositions and the conclusions to which they seem to lead may indeed successfully capture certain rough characteristics of the urban political economy. Still, the portrait that emerges is a relatively featureless one, largely devoid of the kinds of actors, alliances, conflicts, and political opportunities that the story told in this book focuses upon. Urban theorists today frequently lament the dominance of growth machines in city politics and the plight of low- and moderate-income city neighborhoods, yet they are often at a loss to identify possibilities for change. By reexamining the central propositions of the urban political economy paradigm in view of the evidence presented in this study, we can begin to see why. Simply put, urban political economy defines opportunities for genuine political agency in exceptionally narrow terms, far more so than the evidence here seems to support.

Consider, first of all, the division of labor between state and market. Urban political economists interpret the corporate-center strategy for downtown redevelopment embarked upon by cities like Chicago, Baltimore, and New York following World War II as a response to urban economic restructuring. According to the prevailing viewpoint, structural economic change left policymakers with a limited range of options. They could downplay matters of economic development and focus attention instead on service provision to neighborhood constituents. However, given a commitment to economic growth, officials were drawn inevitably toward a development strategy that required major land-use changes in the downtown area. The market, in other words, set the parameters for political response.

Yet what precisely are the market forces in the story of downtown redevelopment in Chicago? Clearly, private investors made decisions that had certain consequences, but efforts to untangle their activities from those of city officials committed to a particular program of redevelopment are problematic. For example, rising land values in Chicago's central area were an important cause of industrial decline there, but land speculators were guided in their actions by land-use plans furnished by city officials and a pattern of public capital investments and other incentives designed to foster commercial and residential development in this part of the city. Had the city's priorities been otherwise, there is no reason to assume that land prices would have escalated to the extent they did. The notion that structural economic change mandated a particular course of action by city officials becomes even less plausible when we consider the origins of the Daley administration's downtown redevelopment program in the late 1950s, well before officials could have discerned any long-term trend of industrial decentralization.

The corporate-center strategy in Chicago was the product of an alliance between landed interests and city officials, not a political response to structural economic change. Actors from the public and private sectors worked hand-in-hand to produce land-use changes that would reshape both the physical appearance of the city and its underlying economic structure. There were, of course, good reasons for public officials to enter into such an alliance. The growth coalition of land-based interests was well-organized, politically astute, and controlled substantial economic resources. In addition, major land-use projects provided politicians with visibility and a steady stream of material benefits that could be used to build and maintain public support. The point, however, is that the business-government alliance was not an intervening variable responding to structural economic change but an autonomous force responsible for basic economic outcomes.

Consider, as well, the other central propositions of the urban political economy paradigm: capital mobility and the instrumental rationality of firm decision-making. To be sure, technological innovations relaxed locational constraints on certain types of business establishments in the postwar era, encouraging many industrial firms in particular to seek low-cost land and labor outside city limits. However, the pattern of industrial decentralization was uneven across industries and industry segments. Large, vertically integrated firms utilizing mass-production techniques to capture scale economies fled willingly in many cases, while smaller, vertically *dis*integrated firms utilizing flexibly specialized production methods to achieve economies of scope left only when redevelopment pressures presented them with few alternatives.

In Chicago, segments of key central area industries like printing and apparel were deeply dependent upon the economies of place provided by near-downtown locations. Part of this advantage came through agglomeration economies—the reduction of individual firm costs that result from the location of a variety of business services nearby. Since agglomeration economies are realized through simple exchange relations between and among firms, they are reflected in land values. That is, landowners are free to trade such assets in the marketplace because other firms can presumably realize the same benefit from the land.

Yet there were more than simple agglomeration economies at work in Chicago's central area industrial districts. As we saw in Chapter 3, interfirm relations in the printing and apparel industries were permeated by noncapitalist values like trust and cooperation, which led in turn to information-sharing, job referrals, and other reciprocal arrangements among firms. Place-based assets like these were fostered through spatial proximity, yet, unlike agglomeration economies, they were the product of *individual social relationships*, which made them unavailable for purchase and sale in the marketplace. As such, their value was not incorporated into the price of land. When central area industrial land prices did finally rise significantly, it was due to an entirely different phenomenon: real estate speculation by commercial and residential property developers. Ultimately, government intervention designed to curb property value increases was selectively applied, not to inhibit economic growth but to preserve a particular form of capitalist production dependent upon rooted relations of place.

. . .

Having examined the key assumptions of the urban political economy framework in view of the evidence provided in this study, we are now in a position to set forth an alternative set of conclusions about the urban political economy that takes into account the possibilities for meaningful political agency identified in the story told here.

*The nature of the business-government alliance is historically specific.* Given the importance placed by voters on healthy rates of economic growth and the dependence of city tax revenues on private investment activity, politicians who ignore the concerns of business are unlikely to enjoy lengthy and prosperous political careers. However, the alliance between city officials and landed interests that so preoccupies urban political economists is only one of multiple possible scenarios for business-government cooperation. Since higher land values may be detrimental to certain types of capitalist production, such as geographically rooted forms of industrial capital, city officials may take steps to curb real estate speculation or otherwise act in ways contrary to the interests of the real estate community without compromising their commitment to economic growth. The nature of the business-government alliance is thus politically contingent, not structurally determined.

*The definition of economic development is politically contested.* Recall that urban political economists define economic growth as the intensification of land use. Efforts to rearrange and intensify land use increase the exchange value of land, generating profits for developers and enhancing the city's property-tax base. Yet, as we have just seen, capitalist firms depend on place-based assets that are not always reflected in the price of land. Indeed, the development of property for higher and better uses may well be a hindrance to certain types of capitalist growth, should land speculation break up viable producer networks. By interpreting growth as a measure of the exchange value of land alone, urban political economy has taken sides with landed interests in an ideological conflict over how economic development is to be defined.

Chicago's planned manufacturing district initiatives came about, in no small part, through a successful struggle to sever the identification of economic growth with real estate development alone. Proponents of PMDs voiced a theme first articulated during the Harold Washington mayoral campaign—that job creation, not real estate development, should be the ultimate goal of economic development policy. Once the definition of growth became the object of ongoing political struggle, developers' claims that their proposals represented the highest and best uses for city land rang increasingly hollow, particularly since redevelopment often meant replacing high-paying manufacturing jobs with low-level service-sector positions. When research focusing on contested areas of the city such as Goose Island projected that, despite lower property values, the returns to the city would be higher for manufacturing than for residential or commercial scenarios, even formerly skeptical city officials became increasingly forceful proponents of industrial retention.

*Development politics include conflict over different growth strategies.* Although political cleavages between downtown and the neighborhoods remain a central fixture of urban development politics, this divide does not always involve struggles between neighborhood residents and business elites over the costs and benefits of growth. Contrary to dualities often posed in the urban political economy literature, city officials are not necessarily forced into balancing acts between accumulation and legitimation, or between the exchange values and use values of land held dear by land-based interests and neighborhood residents, respectively. Rather, because neighborhoods are themselves repositories of key productive assets, conflict may involve competition for the political resources necessary to implement growth strategies being advanced by different groups. Should alliances develop among neighborhood manufacturers, workers, and community-based organizations, as they did in Chicago, city officials may be supportive of *both* neighborhood interests and viable forms of economic growth.

. . .

The alternative urban political economy outlined in the last few pages has important implications for urban regime formation. Scholars utilizing the relatively new paradigm of urban regime theory have built on the assumptions of urban political economy to identify the various types of urban governance structures that are viable in liberal democratic societies such as ours (see, for example, Stone 1987b, 1993; Stone, Orr, and Imbroscio 1991; Elkin 1985). Unsurprisingly, the typologies set forth fall within a relatively narrow range. City officials, their choices limited by capital mobility, fiscal pressures, and other structural constraints, find themselves drawn by necessity into alliances with downtown business elites around redevelopment efforts that hold few benefits for low- and moderate-income neighborhoods. Progressive regimes representing neighborhood interests are unsustainable in all but a few situations, since the need to focus resources on economic growth overwhelms all other considerations.

If the argument of this book is correct, however, and the structural factors at work in city politics are less pervasive than they are generally imagined to be, then the possibilities for regime formation are likewise more open-ended than scholars generally hold. Governing coalitions committed to fostering economic development need not rule at the expense of neighborhoods. Rather, alliances among locally rooted producers, workers, and community-based organizations could serve as the cornerstone for urban regimes committed to building on place-based productive assets that exist in city neighborhoods. Instead of balancing the interests of downtown business elites in economic growth against those of low- and moderate-income city residents in consumption, such a regime would tap the potential of neighborhoods to become centers of flexibly specialized, locally rooted production. The extent to which Chicago's local-producer strategy for neighborhood redevelopment has carried over into the Richard M. Daley administration, despite the administration's close ties with downtown business, is powerful evidence of the feasibility of urban regimes built around such alliances.

## Chicago Exceptionalism?

Although this study focuses on the historical experiences of one city, I have suggested that the story told here contains lessons that extend well beyond Chicago. Such an argument is convincing, however, only to the extent that similar political and economic development choices and conflicts have emerged in other cities as well. If the political culture or economic conditions of postwar Chicago are in important respects unique or exceptional, there are limits to the value of this case for more comprehensive theory building.

The presence of viable networks of small- and medium-sized producers in other postwar central cities is, in fact, well documented. In cities such as New York, Boston, San Francisco, and Los Angeles, industries from sectors like printing, apparel, food processing, medical supplies, and electronics have clustered in well-defined districts, oftentimes subcontracting with neighboring firms and taking advantage of nearby business services (see, for example, Hall 1959; Rapkin 1963, 91–114; Kenyon 1964; Scott 1988; Fernandez Kelly 1989; King 1987; Angwin 1996). As in Chicago, key industry segments have shown considerable resilience in the face of industry restructuring, meeting the competition of lower-cost producers outside city limits with high-quality, specialized products and rapid turnaround times. In many cases industries have been forced to contend with commercial and residential redevelopment pressures as well. Documented case studies of industrial displacement include

New York City, Baltimore, San Francisco, New Orleans, Philadelphia, Boston, Syracuse, and Portland, in addition to Chicago (Center for Urban Economic Development 1985; King 1988a; Zukin 1982; City of New York 1981).

A number of cities besides Chicago have also implemented policies designed to protect centrally located industrial districts from competing land uses. In New York City, for example, real estate pressures developing during the 1970s began to threaten the integrity of Manhattan's garment district, where commercial zoning allowed the conversion of industrial loft buildings to office space "as of right" (Zukin 1982; City of New York 1981). Responding to pressure from industry groups, apparel-related labor unions, and community representatives, the city planning commission established new zoning restrictions for the garment district in April 1987. Under the new regulations, developers are allowed to convert industrial space to office use only if they guarantee that an equal amount of space will be preserved for manufacturing (King 1988a; Kennedy 1988). The measure protects over three million square feet of manufacturing space within the district.

In Boston, growing demand for downtown office space began to threaten centrally industrial districts like Fort Point Channel and the Newmarket area during the mid-1980s (Malone 1987; King 1988a). At that time, the city zoning ordinance allowed property zoned for manufacturing to be reused for commercial purposes without a zoning change or any other formal review process. As in Chicago, rents and property values in the near-downtown area experienced strong upward pressures during the 1980s, threatening profitable manufacturers from sectors requiring central locations, such as printing and publishing. In response, the Boston Redevelopment Authority and the Economic Development and Industrial Corporation developed a proposal to establish light manufacturing districts where the conversion of manufacturing space to nonindustrial uses would be tightly regulated. Under the proposal, approved by the Boston Zoning Commission in December 1988, developers may convert no more than 40 percent of an industrial building within an officially recognized manufacturing district to office space (King 1988c). Permitted industrial uses in the twelve new districts established since 1988 include printing and publishing, computer and related industries, medical research and development, and a number of other light industries.

Finally, city officials in Portland, Oregon, have established sixteen industrial sanctuaries throughout the city since 1981, each designed to discourage gentrification or conversion and to promote future industrial development (King 1988a). Within such areas, most office and retail development is either forbidden or carefully regulated, while residential uses are limited to caretakers' living quarters and artists' living and work space. In addition, Portland planning officials have used infrastructure improvements, low-interest loans for manufacturers, and tax increment financing to promote industrial development within the sanctuaries. From 1981 to 1988, manufacturing jobs within the sanctuaries increased by 30 percent even though citywide blue-collar employment experienced a 10 percent decline (King 1988a).

On the surface, these policies appear to resemble the planned manufacturing districts established on Chicago's Near North Side during the late 1980s and early 1990s, which protected the integrity of North Side manufacturing districts by calling a halt to the issuing of zoning variances for nonmanufacturing uses. Yet there is an important difference. In New York City, Boston, and Portland, policies designed to protect manufacturers were developed within the city bureaucracy for the benefit of manufacturers and their allies. In each case, city officials perceived a need for protective legislation and acted accordingly. Chicago's planned manufacturing districts, by contrast, originated within the neighborhoods themselves. A coalition of neighborhood organizations, manufacturers, and labor unions developed the legislation with little formal participation by the city and then pressured often reluctant officials to act. Only after a strong, independent political base had been organized in favor of the districts did government officials agree to endorse the proposals.

To understand why manufacturers and community organizations rather than bureaucrats were the driving force behind protective legislation for manufacturing in Chicago, it is necessary to consider for a moment the impact of the Democratic machine on community politics in postwar Chicago. Recall that machine politicians maintained support through the provision of particularistic benefits like political patronage and material incentives and rewards, a practice that made them unlikely champions of divisive legislation such as planned manufacturing districts aimed at addressing the collective aspirations of neighborhood constituents. In cities like New York and Boston, political machines were undermined by the steady erosion of their Irish and German immigrant electoral bases before and after World War II, a trend that paved the way for new progressive and reform regimes in which neighborhood activists sometimes gained a foothold (DiGaetano 1991). Chicago, by contrast, was a different story. Responding to similar demographic changes, Richard J. Daley reinvigorated the Chicago machine by reaching out to non-Irish white ethnics and African Americans (Rakove 1975). A massive infusion of federal funds during the 1960s and 1970s helped Daley and his successors, Michael Bilandic and Jane Byrne, keep the machine alive until Harold Washington's election in 1983, long after machine governments elsewhere had gone into decline.

Neighborhood politics in Chicago thus developed by necessity on fiercely independent political footing. During the 1960s and 1970s, when neighborhood groups elsewhere began to forge partnerships with progressive city officials, community organizations in Chicago found access to formal political channels largely closed off to them by an intransigent machine. Chicago neighborhoods decimated by economic crisis and deindustrialization were forced to take matters into their own hands. Only through protest, community-based planning, and extensive coalition-building could they expect to gain the attention of largely indifferent machine politicians. Chicago's planned manufac-turing districts developed within this rich tradition of community organizing and community-based planning, fostered by the long-standing presence of a highly unresponsive political machine.

Does the resilience of the machine make Chicago an exceptional case? In some respects, perhaps, but the likely success of policies that challenge growth machines ultimately turns on the basis of community support that undergirds them, not on whether they originate inside or outside city hall. Chicago's planned manufacturing district initiatives were able to withstand the death of Mayor Washington and the initial skepticism of Richard M. Da-ley because of the diverse coalition of supporters that organizations like the Local Economic and Employment Development (LEED) Council had painstakingly assembled on behalf of the proposals. By contrast, Boston's plan to create light manufacturing districts nearly collapsed in its infancy when progressive city officials from the Raymond Flynn administration tried to move the plan forward before a strong, independent political base had been mobilized around the proposal (King 1988b). The legacy of the ma-chine helped produce a strong, community-based challenge to the corporate-center strategy in Chicago. Whether similar challenges elsewhere enjoy the necessary level of community support to survive the opposition of property developers and their allies over the long term remains to be seen.

## The Shape of Things to Come

Like many American cities today, Chicago stands at a crossroads. The corporate-center strategy has produced a dazzling array of impressive new de-velopments in the downtown area. With the completion of the $987 million McCormick Place expansion in January 1997, Chicago became home to the largest exhibition and meeting facility in North America. A spectacular new museum and entertainment complex on Navy Pier has proved to be a major tourist draw. Yet the spillover from new developments such as these has led to few visible improvements in the city's low- and moderate-income neighbor-hoods. New jobs are being created in the tourist and convention trades, but the majority of them are low-paying and unskilled. Meanwhile, suburban commuters and residents of wealthier lakefront wards hold most of the better-paying, knowledge-intensive positions opening up within the downtown ser-vice sector. Urban redevelopment in Chicago has become a "tale of two cities." Pockets of prosperity and renewal are surrounded by depressed areas largely untouched by the revitalization occurring in other parts of the city (Levine 1989, 25).

As in other cities, Chicago's downtown renaissance has been spearheaded by a progrowth coalition of land-based interests and other business elites. Although occupying a central position within the governing coalition of current mayor Richard M. Daley, Chicago's growth machine has nonetheless struggled in recent years. The emergence of a broad-based, politically sophisticated neighborhood movement prevents business elites today from unilaterally dictating the terms of redevelopment as they once did. In addition, with population shifts increasingly tilting the balance of power in the Illinois state legislature in favor of suburban and rural areas, state lawmakers have grown reluctant to approve large-scale development projects in Chicago that promise few benefits for the rest of the state. Since 1985, plans for a 1992 world's fair in Chicago, a third Chicago airport, a casino and entertainment complex, and a downtown light rail system have all collapsed due to community opposition, unsupportive state legislators, or some combination of both.

Recent setbacks to the corporate-center strategy, together with pressure from within the neighborhoods, are creating space for a new dialogue over Chicago's economic future. "Balanced growth" has entered the vocabulary of many Chicagoans. Interest in the preservation of Chicago's manufacturing base has been substantially reawakened, and the contribution of Chicago manufacturers to the city's overall economy is more widely appreciated now than perhaps at any time since the 1960s. Even Mayor Daley, initially no friend of industry, has become a convert, supporting planned manufacturing districts and other policies to retain industrial firms in the city. Proponents of a local-producer strategy for neighborhood revitalization continue to make inroads into the Daley administration's downtown business-dominated governing coalition, carrying with them possibilities for the formation of alternative regimes.

Even so, the movement from planned manufacturing districts to the consolidation of a new regime in which neighborhood manufacturers would replace downtown corporations, financial institutions, and real estate developers as the key beneficiaries of economic development policy represents a substantial leap. Attempts to form such a local-producer regime face significant hurdles. To begin with, global economic pressures continue to chip away at the city's manufacturing base. Recent tax giveaways necessary to retain large Chicago manufacturers like Nabisco and Tootsie Roll underscore the mobility of certain types of producers and the ease with which they are able to play cities off against one another to win the most generous package of benefits (see Strahler 1996). Unless firms like these can be more deeply integrated into the local economy, through the fostering of local supplier relationships, for example, the costs to the city of retaining them may well exceed the benefits they provide.

A local-producer regime faces other serious obstacles as well. The activities of neighborhood-based industrial development organizations have increased the organizational capacity of Chicago manufacturers, creating a structure for programs like the Model Industrial Corridors Initiative to develop within. Yet the emerging associational ties among neighborhood producers are still no match for those of the downtown business elite, whose well-oiled network of civic cooperation offers opportunities for the execution of highly visible, complex economic development projects involving substantial economic resources. The bottom line is that, under a local-producer regime, city officials would be forced to work harder to bring together the resources necessary to complete large numbers of relatively low-profile economic development projects, most of which would likely receive little attention or publicity outside of the neighborhoods in which they were located.

Finally, despite effective community organizing and coalition-building during the past few decades, troublesome divisions continue to separate the natural popular constituencies of a local-producer regime. Industrial development organizations have done an effective job of organizing local manufacturers, while resident-based community organizations are well-established in many lower-income and working-class communities. Yet all too often industrial- and resident-based groups from identical community areas work in isolation from one another. Furthermore, when coalition-building does take place, as it did in connection with planned manufacturing district initiatives on the Near North Side, labor is oftentimes only a weak link in the alliance. With unionization rates currently hovering at 20 percent of the labor force or less, many industrial workers lack the necessary forum to develop and articulate collective demands, making outreach efforts involving labor difficult and time-consuming. Last, but by no means least, racial and ethnic cleavages continue to impede coalition-building across working-class neighborhoods. For many working-class whites, in particular, resentment of downtown business leaders is well surpassed by racial animosity toward black workers living nearby. City trenches are perhaps less pronounced and impenetrable than in years past, but they continue to divide Chicago neighborhoods.

Chicago's present governing coalition is, in many respects, an unstable one, balancing a weakened growth machine against politically mobilized communities frustrated by the failure of downtown redevelopment to uplift their neighborhoods. While a return to the exclusive business-government partnership fostered by the late Richard J. Daley is not out of the question, several alternative scenarios are conceivable as well. Under the first of these, a less arrogant, more conciliatory growth machine might emerge in reenergized fashion. Members of this coalition might be willing to compromise their plans in order to win financial backing from downstate legislators and, at the very least, pay lip service to the redistributive demands of neighborhood organizations. More likely than not, the gulf between downtown and the neighborhoods would continue to widen under such a scenario, the trickle of benefits from downtown growth creating few new opportunities for the redevelopment of low- and moderate-income neighborhoods. By necessity, economic development policy would remain highly centralized. Business elites would continue to dominate important policy and planning decisions, although input from neighborhood groups might be solicited on a somewhat more regular basis.

There is another possibility. Chicago producers, workers, and community residents might begin to build more directly on the economies of place achievable through the wise and efficient use of local resources. Drawing on the legitimate manufacturing expertise that exists in the city's working-class and industrial neighborhoods, Chicago communities could better shield themselves from the effects of global economic restructuring by developing flexible, innovative networks of production. The alliance between neighborhood producers, workers, and community residents could, in turn, serve as the constituency for a new regime supported by an alternative set of economic resources to those held by the downtown growth machine.

The seeds of such a regime are clearly visible in the activities of industrial development organizations and in programs and policies such as planned manufacturing districts and the recent Model Industrial Corridors Initiative. Weaving experiments such as these into more broad-based political and economic alliances will require both strong political leadership and a greater awareness among neighborhood producers, workers, and community residents of the powers they can achieve when relations of mutual trust and respect supplant those of indifference and hostility. It is a path strewn with countless obstacles, unlikely to reward its supporters with highly visible signs of progress, but one that nonetheless offers considerable promise for the revitalization of Chicago neighborhoods left in the shadows of downtown redevelopment.

# Notes

## 1: The Politics of Urban Economic Development

1. Economies of scope occur when one firm is able to produce a variety of products more efficiently than separate firms could. Economies of scale refer to productivity gains, or decreases in average production costs, that result from increasing the scale of production.

2. For a parallel argument, see Swanstrom (1993).

## 2: Downtown Redevelopment and the Chicago Political Machine

1. For purposes of this study, the central area is bounded by Lake Michigan to the east, North Avenue to the north, Ashland Avenue to the west, and Cermak Road to the south.

2. Business establishments represented in the CCAC included Sears, Roebuck and Co.; First Federal Savings and Loan; Carson Pirie Scott; Commonwealth Edison Co.; Peoples Gas Co.; First National Bank of Chicago; Hart Schaffner & Marx; Standard Oil Co.; Skidmore, Owings & Merrill; Hilton Hotels Corp.; Illinois Central Industries; Chicago Title and Trust Co.; Harris Trust and Savings Bank; CNA Financial Corp.; Continental Illinois National Bank; Inland Steel Co.; Scribner & Co.; Marshall Field & Co.; Northern Trust Co.; and Real Estate Research Corporation.

3. After his election, Daley announced his intention to resign as chair of the Cook County Democratic Central Committee, but it was a promise he failed to keep. He eventually claimed the party refused to accept his resignation (Biles 1995, 55).

4. The CCAC is listed first among private sector groups consulted by the city in preparation of the 1958 Development Plan.

5. The downtown emphasis of the RERC plan is not surprising, considering that RERC attorney James C. Downs, Jr. was president of the CCAC during the time the plan was prepared.

6. The key actors in the Chicago 21 Corporation were Thomas Ayers (chairman and president, Commonwealth Edison), John H. Perkins (president, Continental Illinois National Bank), Raymond C. Wieboldt, Jr. (president, Dearborn Park Corporation), Ferd Kramer (Draper and Kramer), Donald Erikson (senior partner, Arthur Andersen and Co.), Warren G. Skoning (vice-president, Sears, Roebuck and Co.), and Philip Klutznick (chairman, Urban Investment and Development Company).

7. In a study of the City of Chicago's capital budgets issued during the 1970s and 1980s, Greer (1986) found a strong correlation between the spatial distribution of public and private investment dollars.

8. Of 744 total acres slated for clearance by the Commission, 646 fell within a two-mile radius of the Loop (Department of City Planning 1959, 120–121).

9. The 1977–1981 Capital Improvements Program was published during the Michael Bilandic administration but largely prepared in the last years of the Daley administration (Greer 1986, 34).

10. For purposes of this study, the northwest corridor extends from North Avenue to Irving Park Road along the Kennedy Expressway (1.5 miles on either side) for a total of nine square miles. The southwest corridor extends westward from

Halsted Street to the city limits along the Stevenson Expressway (1.5 miles on either side) for a total of fifteen square miles. The central area is roughly eleven square miles, including 1.5 square miles occupied by the Loop.

11. For example, the reconstruction of bridges over the Chicago River to improve transportation between the Loop and the near-downtown area became a key public investment priority during this period.

12. HUD's definition of economic distress made the entire city of Chicago eligible for UDAG funds.

13. Firms receiving IRBs averaged 172 employees in size (Clemons, Giloth, and Tostado 1985, 2).

14. See "Council Votes Far Reaching Zoning Laws," *Chicago Tribune*, 30 May 1957, sec. 1, p. 8.

15. The 1942 Comprehensive Amendment allowed nonconforming industrial concerns to continue operating for the duration of the useful lives of the buildings in which they were housed, generally seventy-five to one hundred years (see Municipal Code of Chicago, Chapter 194A).

16. Amortization schedules for elimination of nonconforming uses were based on the assessed value and type of construction of the building housing the offending use. Buildings assessed at $5,000 or less were given two to four years to be brought into conformance. More valuable structures had anywhere from ten to forty years to comply, depending on whether they were made of brick, concrete, or wood.

17. Noise generated by manufacturing facilities on the boundaries of residential or business districts was not to exceed 79 decibels. Any use creating intense earth-shaking vibrations had to be set back at least 250 feet from the boundaries of residential, business, or commercial districts (Committee on Buildings and Zoning 1955b, 98a).

18. Because of rapid technological advances in building construction, periodic revisions are essential if a municipal building code is to incorporate modern construction standards on a consistent basis.

19. The composition of the committee reflected Daley's belief that public disputes were most efficiently resolved by limiting debates to the most powerful interests concerned. When asked why no community organizations were represented on the advisory committee, a Daley administration staff member responded, "We don't feel that is conducive to a rational analysis of the situation" (Jones 1985, 30).

20. The Rehabilitation Code became Chapter 78.1 of the Municipal Code of Chicago.

21. See Gary Washburn, "'Restrictive' Codes Thwart a Loft Revival," *Chicago Tribune*, 18 January 1981, sec. N14, p. 1.

## 3: Rethinking Industrial Decline

1. The discussion in this section draws heavily on Ranney and Wiewel (1987, 1988) and Wiewel, Ranney, and Putnam (1990).

2. See Wiewel, Ranney, and Putnam (1990, 373) and Ranney and Wiewel (1987, 65) for a helpful technical explanation of both letterpress and offset printing.

3. The printing production process encompasses three primary phases: (1) prepress, which includes layout, typesetting, and other activities necessary to prepare an im-

age for printing; (2) press, where the ink is actually applied to paper; and (3) binding.

4. See Chapter 2. Not so incidentally, 1982 was also the year in which loft conversion activity in Printing House Row reached its peak (Pruska-Carroll 1987, 37).

5. The other forty-seven firms presumably either failed to survive displacement from their original Printing House Row locations or went out of business for other reasons.

6. The Chicago Apparel Center is a large exhibition center and buying facility for apparel manufacturers and designers, one of four regional marts in the country. It contains 850 showrooms, includes a hotel, and employs approximately 3,000 people.

### 4: Community Economic Development and the Crisis of Machine Politics

1. See, for example, "Downtown Growth Helps Taxpayers," *Chicago Tribune,* 30 October 1986, sec. 1, p. 22.

2. See Finks (1984) and Horowitt (1989) for comprehensive discussions of Alinsky's organizing career.

3. The Alinsky model of neighborhood organizing is detailed in Alinsky's two organizing manifestos. See Alinsky (1969, 1971).

4. "Block-busting" was a practice through which real estate agents reaped windfall profits by inducing panic selling among white homeowners in neighborhoods experiencing racial transition. Homes were typically resold to African-American families at inflated prices.

5. LEED Council's organizing efforts around the issue of industrial displacement are described at length in Chapter 5.

6. See *Shakman v. the Democratic Organization of Cook County et al.,* no. 69 C 2145 (U.S. District Court for the Northern District of Illinois, Eastern Division).

7. See also "Her Honor Flirts with Business," *Business Week,* 10 December 1979, pp. 61–66.

8. In 1990, the federal government was forced to assume payments on the $158 million mortgage when the project's developers defaulted on the loan. See J. Linn Allen, "Blazing a Trail West," *Chicago Tribune,* 7 July 1996, sec. S, p. 1.

9. See, for example, "Chicago's Budget and Its Bond Rating," *Crain's Chicago Business,* 20 October 1986, p. 12.

10. See DeLeon (1992) for a similar argument based on the Art Agnos administration in San Francisco.

11. A final version of the CWED Policy Statement was never published, although several additional drafts of the document were issued in late 1982 and early 1983.

12. CWED participants on the economic development issues team included Robert Mier, John Kretzmann, and Donna Ducharme.

### 5: The Battle for the Near North Side

1. See Chapter 2.

2. According to one account, Oberman's refusal to engage in backroom deals made him the butt of jokes among machine aldermen (Rivlin 1992, 118).

3. See, for example, William E. Schmidt, "Chicago Plan Aims to Curb Factory

Loss," *New York Times,* 10 December 1987, sec. 1, p. 1; and Merrill Goozner, "City Out to Forge Compromise in Industrial-Residential Clash," *Crain's Chicago Business,* 3 November 1986, p. 1.

4. See "Pro-PMD? That was then, this is now," *Crain's Chicago Business,* 22 August 1988, p. 10.

5. See, for example, Merrill Goozner, "Clybourn Zoning Fight Breaks All the Rules," *Chicago Tribune,* 27 July 1988, sec. 1, p. 1.

6. For example, CANDO developed the Securing Older Buildings Project to identify ways to continue using older industrial buildings for manufacturing purposes.

7. Plan Commission approval is required for zoning changes on land parcels two acres or larger in size and for all parcels along the Chicago River. From 1983 to 1987, Washington's Plan Commission supported 139 requests for rezonings of industrial property and opposed only one (Mier 1987b).

8. See "Chicago's Sham Industrial Policy," *Chicago Tribune,* 20 July 1987, sec. 1, p. 8.

9. In early 1988, the name of the ordinance was changed from Protected Manufacturing District to Planned Manufacturing District.

10. See Municipal Code of Chicago, Chapter 194D.

11. In fact, the studies of the Clybourn Corridor by the Department of Economic Development, the Mayor's Office of Employment and Training, and Creticos and Masotti cited earlier in the chapter suggest that, if anything, retaining the corridor as an industrial district was the more lucrative development strategy of the two.

### 6: Toward a Citywide Industrial Policy

1. See "Let Goose Island Have Its Golden Eggs," *Chicago Tribune,* 8 June 1989, sec. 1, p. 24.

2. See Ray Hanania, "Daley Unveils Plan To Protect Two Areas," *Chicago Sun-Times,* 14 June 1990, p. 63.

3. See "Don't Stop the Clock on Goose Island," *Chicago Tribune,* 18 June 1990, sec. 1, p. 10.

4. See "Daley Sides Frankly with Sausage Plant," *Chicago Tribune,* 2 March 1996, sec. 1, p. 5.

5. Comparable data for industrial corridors located on the city's South and West Sides are not currently available.

6. The Clybourn Corridor PMD is the only one of the city's three PMDs divided into core and buffer zones.

7. The North River, Addison, Ravenswood, and Pilsen Industrial Corridors are the only industrial corridors for which data are presently available.

# Bibliography

Abbott, Carl. 1987. *The new urban America: Growth and politics in Sunbelt cities.* Chapel Hill: University of North Carolina Press.

Abravanel, Martin D., and Paul K. Mancini. 1980. Attitudinal and demographic constraints. In *Urban revitalization,* ed. Donald B. Rosenthal. Beverly Hills: Sage.

Ad Hoc Working Committee for Residential Rehabilitation. 1978. Progress report of findings to date regarding residential rehabilitation and the Chicago Building Code. Chicago: Ad Hoc Working Committee for Residential Rehabilitation.

Alinsky, Saul D. 1969. *Reveille for radicals.* New York: Vintage Books.

———. 1971. *Rules for radicals: A practical primer for realistic radicals.* New York: Vintage Books.

Angwin, Julia. 1996. Price wars unraveling local clothing makers. *San Francisco Chronicle,* 20 March, 1(C).

Auerbach, Jesse. 1980a. Cooperation stabilizes community. *The Neighborhood Works,* 12 September, 1.

———. 1980b. Development without displacement. *The Neighborhood Works,* 8 February, 1.

Babcock, Richard F. 1972. The new Chicago Zoning Ordinance. In *Urban land use policy: The central city,* ed. Richard B. Andrews. New York: The Free Press.

Babcock, Richard F., and Wendy U. Larsen. 1990. Industrial-strength zoning. In *Special districts: The ultimate in neighborhood zoning,* ed. Richard Babcock. Cambridge: Lincoln Institute of Land Policy.

Bachrach, Peter, and Morton S. Baratz. 1962. Two faces of power. *American Political Science Review* 56: 947–952.

Banfield, Edward C. 1961. *Political influence.* Glencoe, IL: Free Press.

Barry, Patrick. 1986. Downtown growth threatens industry. *The Neighborhood Works* 9 (March): 1, 14–15.

Bartelt, David W. 1989. Renewing center city Philadelphia: Whose city? Which public's interests? In *Unequal partnerships: The political economy of urban redevelopment in postwar America,* ed. Gregory D. Squires. New Brunswick, NJ: Rutgers University Press.

Barton-Aschman Associates. 1970. *Commercial land-use policies and locational principles.* Chicago: Barton-Aschman Associates.

Beauregard, Robert A. 1984. Structure, agency, and urban redevelopment. In *Cities in transformation,* ed. Michael Peter Smith. Beverly Hills: Sage.

———, ed. 1989. *Economic restructuring and political response.* London: Sage.

Bennett, Larry. 1989. Postwar redevelopment in Chicago: The declining politics of party and the rise of neighborhood politics. In *Unequal partnerships: The political economy of urban redevelopment in postwar America,* ed. Gregory D. Squires. New Brunswick, NJ: Rutgers University Press.

Bennett, Larry, Kathleen McCourt, Philip W. Nyden, and Gregory D. Squires. 1988. Chicago's North Loop Redevelopment Project: A growth machine on hold. In *Business elites and urban development,* ed. Scott Cummings. Albany: State University of New York Press.

Bennett, Larry, Gregory D. Squires, Kathleen McCourt, and Philip Nyden. 1987.

Challenging Chicago's growth machine: A preliminary report on the Washington administration. *International Journal of Urban and Regional Research* 11: 351–362.

Berk, Gerald, and Todd Swanstrom. 1994. Expanding the agenda of regime theory: Republican cities in the age of industry. Paper delivered at the 1994 annual convention of the American Political Science Association (31 August–4 September), New York, NY.

———. 1995. The power of place: Capital (im)mobility, pluralism, and regime theory. Paper delivered at the 1995 annual convention of the Urban Affairs Association, (3–6 May), Portland, OR.

Berry, Brian, Irving Cutler, Edwin Draine, Y. Kiang, Thomas Tocalis, and Pierre de Vise. 1976. *Chicago: Transformations of an urban system.* Cambridge: Ballinger.

Best, Michael H. 1989. Sector strategies and industrial policy: The furniture industry and the Greater London Enterprise Board. In *Reversing industrial decline?* ed. Paul Hirst and Jonathan Zeitlin. Oxford: Berg.

Betancur, John J., Deborah E. Bennett, and Patricia A. Wright. 1991. Effective strategies for community economic development. In *Challenging uneven development: An urban agenda for the 1990s,* ed. Philip W. Nyden and Wim Wiewel. New Brunswick: Rutgers University Press.

Biles, Roger. 1995. *Richard J. Daley: Politics, race, and the governing of Chicago.* DeKalb: Northern Illinois University Press.

Blair, John P., Rudy H. Fichtenbaum, and James A. Swaney. 1984. The market for jobs: Locational decisions and the competition for economic development. *Urban Affairs Quarterly* 20: 64–77.

Bluestone, Barry, and Bennett Harrison. 1982. *The deindustrialization of America.* New York: Basic Books.

Body-Gendrot, Sophie N. 1987. Grass-roots mobilization in the Thirteenth Arrondissement of Paris: A cross-national view. In *The politics of urban development,* ed. Clarence Stone and Heywood Sanders. Lawrence: University Press of Kansas.

Boyte, Harry C. 1980. *The backyard revolution.* Philadelphia: Temple University Press.

Brusco, Sebastiano. 1982. The Emilian model: Productive decentralization and social integration. *Cambridge Journal of Economics* 6: 167–184.

Buccitelli, Michael. 1995. Interview by author, 19 January, Chicago.

Cafferty, Pastora San Juan, and William C. McCready. 1982. The Chicago public-private partnership experience: A heritage of involvement. In *Public-private partnerships in American cities,* ed. R. Scott Fosler and Renee A. Berger. Lexington, MA: Lexington Books.

Calavita, Nico. 1992. Growth machines and ballot box planning: The San Diego case. *Journal of Urban Affairs* 14: 1–24.

Capraro, James, Andrew Ditton, and Robert Giloth. 1985. *Neighborhood economic development: Working together for Chicago's future.* Chicago: Department of Economic Development.

Carroll, Margaret. 1980. Saving old buildings: Stumbling blocks go with the territory. *Chicago Tribune,* 15 March, 13(N1).

Carsel, Wilfred. 1940. *A history of the Chicago Ladies' Garment Workers' Union.* Chicago: Normandie House.

Castells, Manuel. 1985. High technology, economic restructuring, and the urban-regional process in the United States. In *High technology, space and society,* ed. Manuel Castells. London: Sage.

Center for Urban Economic Development. 1983. *Strategies for target area industrial development.* Chicago: Center for Urban Economic Development, University of Illinois at Chicago.

————. 1985. *Industrial displacement in major American cities and related policy options.* Chicago: Center for Urban Economic Development, University of Illinois at Chicago.

————. 1987. Printing employment in Chicago: Trends and prospects. Chicago: Center for Urban Economic Development, University of Illinois at Chicago.

————. 1988. *Printing in Chicago: The final report of the printing industry task force.* Chicago: Center for Urban Economic Development, University of Illinois at Chicago.

Center for Urban Studies. 1966. *Mid-Chicago economic development study.* Vol. 2. Chicago: Mayor's Committee for Economic and Cultural Development.

Chicago Association of Neighborhood Development Organizations. 1994. *CANDO 1994 annual report.* Chicago: CANDO.

Chicago Central Area Committee. 1973. *Chicago 21: A plan for the central area communities.* Chicago: Chicago Central Area Committee.

Chicago Plan Commission. 1952. *Chicago industrial study summary report.* Chicago: Chicago Plan Commission.

Ciccone, F. Richard. 1979. Byrne beat Bilandic: Black vote, CTA woes, snow cited. *Chicago Tribune,* 1 March, 1(1).

Cicin-Sain, Biliana. 1980. The costs and benefits of neighborhood revitalization. In *Urban revitalization,* ed. Donald B. Rosenthal. Beverly Hills: Sage.

City of Chicago. 1981. *Five year capital improvements program, 1981–1985.* Chicago: City of Chicago.

————. 1984. *"Chicago works together": 1984 Chicago development plan.* Chicago: City of Chicago.

————. 1987. *Report of the Mayor's Task Force on Neighborhood Land Use: Industrial and commercial land use.* Chicago: City of Chicago.

City of New York. 1981. *Lofts: Balancing the equities.* New York: City Planning Commission.

Clavel, Pierre. 1986. *The progressive city.* New Brunswick, NJ: Rutgers University Press.

Clavel, Pierre, and Wim Wiewel, eds. 1991. *Harold Washington and the neighborhoods.* New Brunswick, NJ: Rutgers University Press.

Clemons, Gwendolyn, Robert Giloth, and Ricardo Tostado. 1985. *Monitoring Chicago's industrial revenue bond performance: 1977–1984.* Chicago: Department of Economic Development.

Cohen, Robert B. 1979. The internationalization of capital and U.S. cities. Ph.D. dissertation, New School for Social Research.

Commercial Club of Chicago. 1984. *Make no little plans: Jobs for metropolitan Chicago.* Chicago: Commercial Club of Chicago.

Commission on Chicago Historical and Architectural Landmarks. 1983. *Printing House Row district: Preliminary summary of information.* Chicago: Commission on Chicago Historical and Architectural Landmarks.

Committee on Buildings and Zoning. 1955a. *A report on the proposed comprehensive amendment to the Chicago Zoning Ordinance.* Chicago: City Council Committee on Buildings and Zoning.

Committee on Buildings and Zoning. 1955b. *Proposed comprehensive amendment to the Chicago Zoning Ordinance*. Chicago: City Council Committee on Buildings and Zoning.

Community Workshop on Economic Development. 1982. Draft platform of the Community Workshop on Economic Development. Chicago: CWED.

———. 1987. *Digging in: Community-grown business ventures*. Chicago: CWED.

Corplan Associates. 1964. *Technological change: Its impact on industry in metropolitan Chicago, printing and publishing industries*. Chicago: Illinois Institute of Technology Research Institute.

Costigan, Joseph. 1996. Interview by author, 20 February, Chicago.

Crenson, Matthew A. 1971. *The un-politics of air pollution: A study of non-decision-making in the cities*. Baltimore: Johns Hopkins University Press.

Creticos, Peter A., and Louis H. Masotti. 1988. The economic effect of Chicago industrial businesses: An examination of Clybourn Avenue manufacturers. Chicago: Creticos and Associates.

Cummings, Scott, ed. 1988. *Business elites and urban development: Case studies and critical perspectives*. Albany: State University of New York Press.

Dahl, Robert A. 1961. *Who governs?* New Haven: Yale University Press.

Daley, Richard M. 1989. City government and Chicago's economic future. Speech to members of the Chicago Kiwanis Club, 14 February.

Davis, Robert. 1992. Daley plans bond sale to fix infrastructure. *Chicago Tribune*, 22 May, 3(2C).

DeLeon, Richard E. 1992. The urban antiregime: Progressive politics in San Francisco. *Urban Affairs Quarterly* 27: 555–579.

De Meirleir, Marcel J. 1950. Manufacturing occupance in the west central area of Chicago. Ph.D. dissertation, University of Chicago.

Department of City Planning. 1958. *Development plan for the central area of Chicago*. Chicago: Department of City Planning.

———. 1959. *Five year capital improvements program 1959–1963*. Chicago: Department of City Planning.

———. 1960. *Locational patterns of major manufacturing industries in the city of Chicago*. Chicago: Department of City Planning.

———. 1961. *Industrial movements and expansion, 1947–1957*. Chicago: Department of City Planning.

———. 1964. *Basic policies for the comprehensive plan of Chicago*. Chicago: Department of City Planning.

Department of Development and Planning. 1967. *The comprehensive plan of Chicago, conditions and trends: Population, economy, land*. Chicago: Department of Development and Planning.

Department of Economic Development. 1987. *Cooperation for survival and growth: New designs for apparel manufacturing in Chicago*. Chicago: Department of Economic Development.

———. 1988. Clybourn Corridor Planned Manufacturing District. Chicago: Department of Economic Development.

Department of Planning. 1978. *1977–1981 capital improvements program*. Chicago: Department of Planning.

———. 1982. *Chicago 1992 comprehensive plan*. Chicago: Department of Planning.

———. 1988. *Report of proceedings of a public hearing re: Planned Manufacturing District (PMD) application, Clybourn Corridor, 43rd Ward.* Department of Planning, 27 July.

———. 1989. *Corridors of industrial opportunity: A plan for industry on Chicago's North Side (draft).* Chicago: Department of Planning.

———. 1990a. Staff report to the Chicago Plan Commission: Goose Island Planned Manufacturing District. Chicago: Department of Planning.

———. 1990b. Staff report to the Chicago Plan Commission: Elston Corridor Planned Manufacturing District. Chicago: Department of Planning.

Department of Planning and Development. 1991. *Corridors of industrial opportunity: A plan for industry in Chicago's West Side.* Chicago: Department of Planning and Development.

———. 1992. *Corridors of industrial opportunity: A plan for industry in Chicago's North Side.* Chicago: Department of Planning and Development.

———. 1994. *Corridors of industrial opportunity: A plan for industry in Chicago's South Side.* Chicago: Department of Planning and Development.

———. 1996. *Industrial corridor capital investment 1995: A guide to industrial improvement projects.* Chicago: Department of Planning and Development.

———. 1998. *Proposed industrial redevelopment project areas: Tax increment financing program.* Chicago: Department of Planning and Development.

DiGaetano, Alan. 1989. Urban political regime formation: A study in contrast. *Journal of Urban Affairs* 11: 261–281.

———. 1991. Urban political reform: Did it kill the machine? *Journal of Urban History* 18: 37–67.

Dold, R. Bruce, and Thomas Hardy. 1989. Chicago elects second Mayor Daley. *Chicago Tribune,* 5 April, 1(1).

Domhoff, G. William. 1983. *Who rules America now?* New York: Simon and Schuster.

Dreier, Peter, and Bruce Ehrlich. 1991. Downtown development and urban reform: The politics of Boston's linkage policy. *Urban Affairs Quarterly* 26: 354–375.

Driscoll, Paul A. 1996. Wieners or losers: Chicago sausage maker says either it or big residential proposal must go. *Chicago Tribune,* 3 March, 3(16).

Ducharme, Donna. 1991. Planned Manufacturing Districts: How a community initiative became city policy. In *Harold Washington and the neighborhoods,* ed. Pierre Clavel and Wim Wiewel. New Brunswick: Rutgers University Press.

———. 1995. Interview by author, 26 January, Chicago.

Ducharme, Donna, Robert Giloth, and Lynn McCormick. 1986. *Business loss or balanced growth: Industrial displacement in Chicago.* Chicago: Department of Economic Development.

Elkin, Stephen. 1985. Twentieth century urban regimes. *Journal of Urban Affairs* 7: 11–28.

———. 1987a. *City and regime in the American republic.* Chicago: University of Chicago Press.

———. 1987b. State and market in city politics: Or, the "real" Dallas. In *The politics of urban development,* ed. Clarence Stone and Heywood Sanders. Lawrence: University Press of Kansas.

———. 1994. Business-state relations in the commercial republic. *Journal of Political Philosophy* 2: 115–139.

Emmons, David. 1977. *Dearborn Park/South Loop New Town: A project in the Chicago 21 plan.* Chicago: Citizens Information Service of Illinois.

Enstad, Robert. 1980. Even without shops, Dearborn Park project is drawing "pioneers." *Chicago Tribune,* 14 August, 1(N6).

Erie, Steven P. 1988. *Rainbow's end.* Berkeley: University of California Press.

Fainstein, Susan S. 1990. Economics, politics, and development policy: The convergence of New York and London. In *Beyond the city limits,* ed. John R. Logan and Todd Swanstrom. Philadelphia: Temple University Press.

Fainstein, Susan S., and Norman I. Fainstein. 1983. Regime strategies, communal resistance, and economic forces. In *Restructuring the city,* ed. Susan Fainstein, Norman Fainstein, Richard Hill, Dennis Judd, and Michael Smith. New York: Longman.

———. 1989. Technology, the new international division of labor, and location: Continuities and disjunctures. In *Economic restructuring and political response,* ed. Robert A. Beauregard. London: Sage.

Fainstein, Susan S., Norman I. Fainstein, and P. Jefferson Armistead. 1983. San Francisco: Urban transformation and the local state. In *Restructuring the city,* ed. Susan Fainstein, Norman Fainstein, Richard Hill, Dennis Judd, and Michael Smith. New York: Longman.

Fainstein, Susan S., Ian Gordon, and Michael Harloe, eds. 1992. *Divided cities: New York and London in the contemporary world.* Cambridge: Blackwell.

Feagin, Joe R. 1983. *The urban real estate game.* Englewood Cliffs, NJ: Spectrum.

Ferman, Barbara. 1991. Chicago: Power, race, and reform. In *Big city politics in transition,* ed. H. V. Savitch and John Clayton Thomas. London: Sage.

Ferman, Barbara, and William J. Grimshaw. 1992. The politics of housing policy. In *Politics of policy innovation in metropolitan Chicago,* ed. Kenneth Wong and Terry Nicholas Clark. Greenwich, CT: JAI Press.

Fernandez Kelly, Patricia. 1989. International development and industrial restructuring: The case of garment and electronics industries in Southern California. In *Instability and change in the world economy,* ed. Arthur MacEwan and William K. Tabb. New York: Monthly Review Press.

Fingeret, Lisa. 1998. Chicago approves 1,500-acre TIF chunk. *Real Estate Journal,* 16 February, 1.

Finks, P. David. 1984. *The radical vision of Saul Alinsky.* New York: Paulist Press.

Fish, John Hall. 1973. *Black power/white control: The struggle of the Woodlawn Organization in Chicago.* Princeton: Princeton University Press.

Fitzgerald, Michael. 1988. Developer opposes Goose Island PMD. *Inside Lincoln Park,* 3 August.

Folz, David H., Linda Gaddis, William Lyons, and John M. Scheb. 1993. Saturn comes to Tennessee: Citizen perceptions of project impacts. *Social Science Quarterly* 74: 793–803.

Fremon, David K. 1988. Chicago politics ward by ward. Bloomington: Indiana University Press.

Frieden, Bernard J., and Lynne B. Sagalyn. 1989. *Downtown, Inc.: How America rebuilds cities.* Cambridge: MIT Press.

Froebel, Folker, Jurgen Heinrichs, and Otto Kreye. 1977. The tendency towards a new international division of labor. *Review* 1: 73–88.

Fuller, Dorothy. 1996. Interview by author, 2 February, Chicago.

Gapp, Paul. 1973. Power elite drafts city master plan. *Chicago Tribune,* 21 May, 1(1).

Gardiner, John A., and Theodore R. Lyman. 1978. *Decisions for sale: Corruption and reform in land-use and building regulation.* New York: Praeger.

Gaventa, John. 1980. *Power and powerlessness: Quiescence and rebellion in an Appalachian valley.* Urbana: University of Illinois Press.

Gibson, Ray. 1989a. Daley campaign reaps $7.1 million, sets fund-raising record. *Chicago Tribune,* 4 July, 2(2C).

———. 1989b. Evans borrows as contributions lag. *Chicago Tribune,* 21 March, 1(2).

———. 1990. Daley backers reap lucrative rewards via city contracts. *Chicago Tribune,* 29 July, 1(2C).

Gills, Doug. 1991. Chicago politics and community development: A social movement perspective. In *Harold Washington and the neighborhoods,* ed. Pierre Clavel and Wim Wiewel. New Brunswick: Rutgers University Press.

Giloth, Robert, and John Betancur. 1988. Where downtown meets neighborhood: Industrial displacement in Chicago, 1978–1987. *Journal of the American Planning Association* 54: 279–290.

Giloth, Robert, and Marlinda Menashe. 1981. Rehab the brewery for more jobs? *The Neighborhood Works,* 8 May, 1.

Giloth, Robert, and Robert Mier. 1989. Spatial change and social justice: Alternative economic development in Chicago. In *Economic restructuring and political response,* ed. Robert A. Beauregard. London: Sage.

Glickman, Norman J. 1987. Cities and the international division of labor. In *The capitalist city: Global restructuring and community politics,* ed. Michael Smith and Joe Feagin. Oxford: Basil Blackwell.

Goff, Lisa. 1987. Clybourn mall builder to woo city with linkage. *Crain's Chicago Business,* 28 September, 2.

———. 1988. Finkl's story: Why industry needs protection. *Crain's Chicago Business,* 8 August, 1.

Gonwa, Margaret. 1996. Interview by author, 17 May, Chicago.

Goodman, Robert. 1979. *The last entrepreneurs: America's regional war for jobs and dollars.* New York: Simon and Schuster.

Goozner, Merrill. 1986. City out to forge compromise in industrial-residential clash. *Crain's Chicago Business,* 3 November, 1.

———. 1988a. Clybourn zoning fight breaks all the rules. *Chicago Tribune,* 27 July, 1(1).

———. 1988b. Industry may give up fight for Goose Island. *Chicago Tribune,* 20 July, 3(3).

———. 1990. Collision course: City planners, largest landholder differ on what to do with Goose Island property. *Chicago Tribune,* 26 September, 1(8).

Goozner, Merrill, and Stanley Ziemba. 1989. Big gifts to Daley reflect city's divisions. *Chicago Tribune,* 26 February, 3(7).

Gordon, David M. 1978. Capitalist development and the history of American cities. In *Marxism and the metropolis,* ed. William K. Tabb and Larry Sawers. New York: Oxford University Press.

Gottdiener, Mark. 1987. *The decline of urban politics: Political theory and the crisis of the local state.* London: Sage.

Govas, Ken. 1995. Interview by author, 18 January, Chicago.

Granovetter, Mark. 1985. Economic action and social structure: The problem of embeddedness. *American Journal of Sociology* 91: 481–510.

Greater Southwest Development Corporation. 1995. Strategic plan for the Greater Southwest Model Industrial Corridor. Chicago: Greater Southwest Development Corporation.

Green, Brian M., and Yda Schreuder. 1991. Growth, zoning, and neighborhood organizations: Land use conflict in Wilmington, Delaware. *Journal of Urban Affairs* 13: 97–110.

Greer, James L. 1983. The politics of declining growth: Planning, economic transformation, and the structuring of urban futures in American cities. Ph.D. dissertation, University of Chicago.

———. 1986. *Capital investment in Chicago: Fragmented processes, unequal outcomes.* Chicago: Center of Urban Research and Policy Studies, University of Chicago.

Grimshaw, William J. 1992. *Bitter fruit: Black politics and the Chicago machine, 1931–1991.* Chicago: University of Chicago Press.

Gruber, William. 1979. Business, finance execs see little vote impact. *Chicago Tribune,* 1 March, 6(6).

Gustafson, W. Eric. 1959. Printing and publishing. In *Made in New York: Case studies in metropolitan manufacturing,* ed. Max Hall. Cambridge: Harvard University Press.

Hall, Max. 1959. *Made in New York: Case studies in metropolitan manufacturing.* Cambridge: Harvard University Press.

Hardy, Thomas, and Jorge Casuso. 1989. Evans assails Daley's contributions. *Chicago Tribune,* 17 March, 3(2C).

Harloe, Michael, Peter Marcuse, and Neil Smith. 1992. Housing for people, housing for profits. In *Divided cities: New York and London in the contemporary world,* ed. Susan S. Fainstein, Ian Gordon, and Michael Harloe. Cambridge: Blackwell.

Harrison, Bennett. 1992. Industrial districts: Old wine in new bottles? *Regional Studies* 26: 469–483.

Hartman, Chester W. 1974. *Yerba Buena: Land grab and community resistance in San Francisco.* San Francisco: Glide.

Harvey, David. 1978. The urban process under capitalism: A framework for analysis. *International Journal of Urban and Regional Research* 2: 101–131.

———. 1986. *The urbanization of capital.* Baltimore: Johns Hopkins University Press.

Helfgott, Roy B. 1959. Women's and children's apparel. In *Made in New York: Case studies in metropolitan manufacturing,* ed. Max Hall. Cambridge: Harvard University Press.

Hill, Richard C. 1978. Fiscal collapse and political struggle in decaying central cities in the United States. In *Marxism and the metropolis,* ed. William K. Tabb and Larry Sawers. New York: Oxford University Press.

———. 1983. Crisis in the motor city: The politics of economic development in Detroit. In *Restructuring the city,* ed. Susan Fainstein, Norman Fainstein, Richard Hill, Dennis Judd, and Michael Smith. New York: Longman.

Hirst, Paul, and Jonathan Zeitlin, eds. 1989. *Reversing industrial decline? Industrial structure and policy in Britain and her competitors.* Oxford: Berg.

Hoffman, Kurt. 1985. Clothing, chips and competitive advantage: The impact of microelectronics on trade and production in the garment industry. *World Development* 13: 371–392.

Hollander, Elizabeth. 1987. Memorandum to George Munoz, 14 May.

———. 1988. Memorandum to Eugene Sawyer, 7 April.

Holli, Melvin G. 1995. Jane M. Byrne: To think the unthinkable and do the undoable. In *The mayors: The Chicago political tradition,* ed. Paul M. Green and Melvin G. Holli. Carbondale: Southern Illinois University Press.

Hoover, Edgar, and Raymond Vernon. 1959. *Anatomy of a metropolis.* Cambridge: Harvard University Press.

Hornung, Mark. 1988. CMC unit trying to duck Goose Island deal? *Crain's Chicago Business,* 8 August, 2.

———. 1990. Daley inner circle: Pols, kin, fat cats. *Crain's Chicago Business,* 23 April, 4.

———. 1991. He wants government to work: Why pragmatic Mosena was Daley's pick to run city staff. *Crain's Chicago Business,* 10 June, 3.

Horowitt, Sanford. 1989. *Let them call me rebel: Saul Alinsky, his life and legacy.* New York: Knopf.

Illinois Department of Employment Security. 1972. *Where workers work in the Chicago standard metropolitan statistical area.* Springfield: State of Illinois.

———. 1979. *Where workers work in the Chicago standard metropolitan statistical area.* Springfield: State of Illinois.

———. 1983. *Where workers work in the Chicago standard metropolitan statistical area.* Springfield: State of Illinois.

———. 1984. *Where workers work in the Chicago standard metropolitan statistical area.* Springfield: State of Illinois.

———. 1985. *Where workers work in the Chicago standard metropolitan statistical area.* Springfield: State of Illinois.

Illinois Institute of Technology. 1963. *City of Chicago industrial renewal study.* Chicago: Illinois Institute of Technology.

Imbroscio, David L. 1995. An alternative approach to urban economic development: Exploring the dimensions and prospects of a "self-reliance" strategy. *Urban Affairs Review* 30: 840–867.

Influential Contacts, Ltd. 1981. *Contacts influential: Commerce and industry directory.* Chicago: Influential Contacts, Ltd.

Inside Contacts. 1993. *Inside contacts USA: Marketing information directory.* Chicago: Inside Contacts.

———. 1995. *Inside contacts USA: Marketing information directory.* Chicago: Inside Contacts.

Jones, Bryan D. 1985. *Governing buildings and building government: A new perspective on the old party.* University, AL: University of Alabama Press.

Jones, Bryan D., and Lynn W. Bachelor. 1984. Local policy discretion and the corporate surplus. In *Urban economic development,* ed. Richard D. Bingham and John P. Blair. London: Sage.

Joravsky, Ben. 1982. Organizers look beyond Alinsky for power. *The Neighborhood Works* 5 (May): 10–12.

———. 1988. No entry, gentry: New rules for the Clybourn Corridor. *Chicago Reader,* 2 September.

———. 1990. Alinsky's legacy. In *After Alinsky: Community organizing in Illinois*, ed. Peg Knoepfle. Springfield, IL: Illinois Issues.

Judd, Dennis R. 1983. From cowtown to Sunbelt city: Boosterism and economic growth in Denver. In *Restructuring the city*, ed. Susan Fainstein, Norman Fainstein, Richard Hill, Dennis Judd, and Michael Smith. New York: Longman.

Judd, Dennis R., and Todd Swanstrom. 1994. *City politics: Private power and public policy.* New York: Harper Collins.

Kain, John F. 1968. The distribution and movement of jobs and industry. In *The metropolitan enigma*, ed. James Q. Wilson. Cambridge: Harvard University Press.

Kantor, Paul. 1987. The dependent city: The changing political economy of urban economic development in the United States. *Urban Affairs Quarterly* 22: 493–520.

Karapin, Roger. 1994. Community organizations and low-income citizen participation in the U.S.: Strategies, organization, and power since the 1960s. Paper delivered at the 1994 annual convention of the American Political Science Association (31 August–4 September), New York, NY.

Kass, John. 1990. Minorities get a cut of city business. *Chicago Tribune*, 1 August, 1(2C).

Katznelson, Ira. 1981. *City trenches: Urban politics and the patterning of class in the United States.* New York: Pantheon.

Kennedy, Shawn G. 1988. Side streets getting fashion showrooms. *New York Times*, 8 May, 7(X).

Kenyon, James B. 1964. The industrial structure of the New York Garment Center. In *Focus on geographic activity: A collection of original studies*, ed. Richard S. Thoman and Donald J. Patten. New York: McGraw-Hill.

King, John. 1987. BRA director's proposed rule changes have developers up in arms. *Boston Globe*, 13 December, 37(A).

———. 1988a. Protecting industry from yuppies and other invaders. *Planning* 54: 4–8.

———. 1988b. Boston zone change for light industry hits opposition. *Boston Globe*, 22 April, 66.

———. 1988c. New plan for light manufacturing offered. *Boston Globe*, 5 November, 41.

Kleppner, Paul. 1985. *Chicago divided: The making of a black mayor.* DeKalb, IL: Northern Illinois University Press.

Kretzmann, John. 1996. Interview by author, 29 May, Chicago.

Kristensen, Peer Hull. 1992. Industrial districts in West Jutland, Denmark. In *Industrial districts and local economic regeneration*, ed. Frank Pyke and Werner Sengenberger. Geneva: International Institute for Labour Studies.

Lebow, Joan. 1985. SA's plea to Koch: Help keep us on SA. *Women's Wear Daily*, 16 May.

LEED Council. 1990. Keeping jobs for Chicago's future: A development impact assessment of Goose Island. Chicago: LEED Council.

———. 1996. Draft report on Chicago Planned Manufacturing Districts. Chicago: LEED Council.

Lemonides, James. 1984. Stoking the smokestacks. *The Neighborhood Works* 7 (March): 1, 11–17.

———. 1995. Interview by author, 17 January, Chicago.

Levine, Marc V. 1989. The politics of partnership: Urban redevelopment since 1945.

In *Unequal partnerships: The political economy of urban redevelopment in postwar America*, ed. Gregory D. Squires. New Brunswick, NJ: Rutgers University Press.

Liametz, Carl. 1996. Interview by author, 20 February, Chicago.

Lindblom, Charles E. 1977. *Politics and markets.* New York: Basic Books.

Logan, John R., and Harvey L. Molotch. 1987. *Urban fortunes: The political economy of place.* Berkeley: University of California Press.

Logan, John R., and Todd Swanstrom. 1990. Urban restructuring: A critical view. In *Beyond the city limits: Urban policy and economic restructuring in comparative perspective*, ed. John R. Logan and Todd Swanstrom. Philadelphia: Temple University Press.

Longhini, Greg. 1987. Memorandum to David Mosena, 10 November.

Longworth, R. C. 1981. Chicago: City on the brink. *Chicago Tribune,* 13 May, 1(1).

Lorenz, Edward H. 1988. Neither friends nor strangers: Informal networks of subcontracting in French industry. In *Trust: Making and breaking co-operative relations*, ed. D. Gambetta. Oxford: Basil Blackwell.

————. 1989. The search for flexibility: Subcontracting networks in British and French engineering. In *Reversing industrial decline?* ed. Paul Hirst and Jonathan Zeitlin. Oxford: Berg.

Ludgin, Mary. 1989. *Downtown development: Chicago, 1987–1990.* Chicago: Department of Planning.

Ludgin, Mary, and Louis H. Masotti. 1985. *Downtown development: Chicago, 1979–1984.* Chicago: Center for Urban Affairs and Policy Research, Northwestern University.

————. 1986. *Downtown development: Chicago, 1985–1986,* Chicago: Center for Urban Affairs and Policy Research, Northwestern University.

Lugar, Michael I. 1984. Federal tax incentives as industrial and urban policy. In *Sunbelt/snowbelt: Urban development and regional restructuring,* ed. William K. Tabb and Larry Sawyers. New York: Oxford University Press.

Lukes, Steven. 1974. *Power: A radical view.* London: MacMillan.

Maar, James. 1996. Interview by author, 7 February, Chicago.

Magee, Mabel A. 1930. *Trends in location of the women's clothing industry.* Chicago: University of Chicago Press.

Malone, M. 1987. Fort Point Channel rezoning plan offered. *Boston Globe,* 2 December, 30.

Manufacturers News, Inc. 1951. *Illinois manufacturers directory.* Chicago: Manufacturers News.

————. 1960. *Illinois manufacturers directory.* Chicago: Manufacturers News.

————. 1970. *Illinois manufacturers directory.* Chicago: Manufacturers News.

Markusen, Ann. 1985. *Steel and southeast Chicago: Reasons and opportunities for industrial renewal.* Evanston: Center for Urban Affairs and Policy Research, Northwestern University.

Martin, Cathie J. 1991. *Shifting the burden: The struggle over growth and corporate taxation.* Chicago: University of Chicago Press.

Massey, Doreen. 1987. The shape of things to come. In *International capitalism and industrial restructuring,* ed. Richard Peet. Boston: Allen and Unwin.

Mayor's Committee for Economic and Cultural Development. 1966. *Mid-Chicago economic development study.* Vol. 1. Chicago: Mayor's Committee for Economic and Cultural Development.

Mayor's Council of Manpower and Economic Advisors. 1974. *Chicago's economy.* Chicago: Mayor's Council of Manpower and Economic Advisors.

————. 1977. *Chicago's economy on the move.* Chicago: Mayor's Council of Manpower and Economic Advisors.

McCarron, John. 1988. Chicago on hold· Politics of poverty. *Chicago Tribune,* 28 August, 1(1).

McClellan, Keith. 1966. A history of Chicago's industrial development. In *Mid-Chicago economic development study.* Vol. 3, ed. Center for Urban Studies, University of Chicago. Chicago: Center for Urban Studies, University of Chicago.

McClory, Robert. 1986. *The fall of the fair.* Chicago: Chicago 1992 Committee.

McCormick, Lynn. 1994. The rise and fall of collaborative labor relations in Chicago's small-firm metalworking network. Paper delivered at the 1994 annual convention of the Industrial Relations Research Association, (3–5 January), Boston, MA.

McDonald, John F. 1984. *Employment location and industrial land use in metropolitan Chicago.* Champaign: Stipes.

McKnight, John, and John Kretzmann. 1984. Community organizing in the 80s: Toward a post-Alinsky agenda. *Social Policy* 14 (winter): 15–17.

Meltzer, Jack. 1963. *Zoning for residential development in the central area.* Chicago: Jack Meltzer Associates.

Metropolitan Housing and Planning Council. 1980. Chicago Building Code and residential rehabilitation: A working paper. Chicago: Metropolitan Housing and Planning Council.

Metzger, John T., and Marc A. Weiss. 1988. *The role of private lending in neighborhood development: The Chicago experience.* Evanston: Center for Urban Affairs and Policy Research, Northwestern University.

Midwest Center for Labor Research. 1989. The deindustrialization of Chicago. Chicago: Midwest Center for Labor Research.

Mier, Robert. 1986. Memorandum to Al Miller, 18 July.

————. 1987a. Memorandum to Jane Ramsey, 10 August.

————. 1987b. Memorandum to Ernest Barefield, 2 October.

Mier, Robert, and Kari J. Moe. 1991. Decentralized development: From theory to practice. In *Harold Washington and the neighborhoods,* ed. Pierre Clavel and Wim Wiewel. New Brunswick: Rutgers University Press.

Mier, Robert, and Wim Wiewel. 1983. Business activities of not for profit organizations: Surviving the New Federalism? Chicago: Center for Urban Economic Development, University of Illinois at Chicago.

Micr, Robert, Wim Wiewel, and Lauri Alpern. 1992. Decentralization of policy making under Mayor Harold Washington. In *Politics of policy innovation in metropolitan Chicago,* ed. Kenneth Wong and Terry Nicholas Clark. Greenwich, CT: JAI Press.

Mollenkopf, John H. 1981. Community and accumulation. In *Urbanization and urban planning in capitalist society,* ed. Michael Dear and Allen J. Scott. London: Methuen.

————. 1983. *The contested city.* Princeton: Princeton University Press.

Molotch, Harvey. 1976. The city as a growth machine: Toward a political economy of place. *American Journal of Sociology* 82: 309–332.

Molotch, Harvey, and John Logan. 1984. Tensions in the growth machine: Overcoming resistance to value-free development. *Social Problems* 31: 483–499.

Mosena, David R. 1987a. Memorandum to Robert Mier and Elizabeth Hollander, 11 September.

———. 1987b. Memorandum to Elizabeth Hollander, 29 September.

Moses, Leon, and Harold F. Williamson. 1967. The location of economic activity in cities. *American Economic Review* 57: 211–222.

Mott, Andrew. 1984. Mixing organizing with development. *The Neighborhood Works* 7 (January): 1, 24–27.

Murphy, H. Lee. 1996. New plan for Cotter and Co. site intensifies fight with industry. *Crain's Chicago Business*, 5 February, 1.

Nagel, Laura O. 1982. *Portfolio for the future: Chicago's long range infrastructure planning needs.* Chicago: Metropolitan Housing and Planning Council.

Neighborhood Capital Budget Group. 1995. *A matter of delivery: A report on the City of Chicago's industrial street and viaduct improvement programs, 1990 through 1999.* Chicago: Neighborhood Capital Budget Group.

———. 1996. *Moving beyond the basics: Building Chicago for the next century.* Chicago: Neighborhood Capital Budget Group.

Nickel, Denise R. 1995. The progressive city? Urban redevelopment in Minneapolis. *Urban Affairs Review* 30: 355–377.

Noyelle, Thierry J., and Thomas M. Stanback, Jr. 1983. *The economic transformation of American cities.* Totowa, NJ: Rowman and Allanheld.

O'Connor, James. 1973. *The fiscal crisis of the state.* New York: St. Martin's Press.

O'Connor, Len. 1975. *Clout: Mayor Daley and his city.* Chicago: Henry Regnery Co.

Olcott, George C. 1950. *Olcott's land values blue book of Chicago.* Chicago: George C. Olcott and Co.

———. 1960. *Olcott's land values blue book of Chicago.* Chicago: George C. Olcott and Co.

———. 1965. *Olcott's land values blue book of Chicago.* Chicago: George C. Olcott and Co.

———. 1970. *Olcott's land values blue book of Chicago.* Chicago: George C. Olcott and Co.

———. 1975. *Olcott's land values blue book of Chicago.* Chicago: George C. Olcott and Co.

———. 1980. *Olcott's land values blue book of Chicago.* Chicago: George C. Olcott and Co.

———. 1985. *Olcott's land values blue book of Chicago.* Chicago: George C. Olcott and Co.

———. 1988. *Olcott's land values blue book of Chicago.* Chicago: George C. Olcott and Co.

———. 1990. *Olcott's land values blue book of Chicago.* Chicago: George C. Olcott and Co.

———. 1994. *Olcott's land values blue book of Chicago.* Chicago: George C. Olcott and Co.

Orr, Marion E., and Gerry Stoker. 1994. Urban regimes and leadership in Detroit. *Urban Affairs Quarterly* 30: 48–73.

Pavlos, Elliott Arthur. 1975. Chicago's Crosstown: A case study in urban expressways.

In *The manipulated city*, ed. Stephen Gale and Eric C. Moore. Chicago: Maaro-ufa Press.

Peet, Richard. 1987. Industrial restructuring and the crisis of international capitalism. In *International capitalism and industrial restructuring*, ed Richard Peet. Boston: Allen and Unwin.

Perlman, Janice E. 1976. Grassrooting the system. *Social Policy* 7 (Sept./Oct.): 4–20.

Peterson, Paul E. 1981. *City limits*. Chicago: University of Chicago Press.

Philip Zeitlin Associates. 1982. *Chicago Zoning Ordinance review*. Chicago: Philip Zeitlin Associates.

Piore, Michael, and Charles Sabel. 1984. *The second industrial divide: Possibilities for prosperity*. New York: Basic Books.

Polsby, Nelson W. 1963. *Community power and political theory*. New Haven: Yale University Press.

Pruska-Carroll, Marika. 1987. The Printers Row: A case of industrial displacement. Masters Project, University of Illinois at Chicago.

Pyke, Frank, Giacomo Becattini, and Werner Sengenberger, eds. 1990. *Industrial districts and inter-firm cooperation in Italy*. Geneva: International Institute for Labour Studies.

Pyke, Frank, and Werner Sengenberger, eds. 1992. *Industrial districts and local economic regeneration*. Geneva: International Institute for Labour Studies.

Rakove, Milton L. 1975. *Don't make no waves, don't back no losers*. Bloomington: Indiana University Press.

———. 1982. Jane Byrne and the new Chicago politics. In *After Daley: Chicago politics in transition*, ed. Samuel K. Gove and Louis Masotti. Chicago: University of Illinois Press.

Ranney, David C., and Wim Wiewel. 1987. *The graphic communications industry in the Chicago metropolitan area*. Chicago: Center for Urban Economic Development.

———. 1988. *Technological change and industrial restructuring: The graphic communications industry*. Chicago: Center for Urban Economic Development.

Rapkin, Chester. 1963. *The South Houston industrial area: A study of the economic significance of firms, the physical quality of buildings, and the real estate market in an old loft section of Lower Manhattan*. New York: Department of City Planning.

Rast, Joel S. 1993. The social output of the post-Fordist firm: Lessons from the automobile industry. Unpublished manuscript.

Real Estate Research Corporation. 1970. *Industrial functions in the Chicago central communities*. Chicago: Real Estate Research Corporation.

Reardon, Kenneth M. 1990. Local economic development in Chicago 1983–1987. Ph.D. dissertation, Cornell University.

Reardon, Patrick T. 1992a. Just like dad, Daley building a legacy. *Chicago Tribune*, 29 March, 1(2C).

———. 1992b. Infrastructure work could pump $880 million into city, study says. *Chicago Tribune*, 25 February, 4(2C).

———. 1993. Daley had big plans, but now just big problems. *Chicago Tribune*, 10 January, 1(2C).

———. 1995. Mayor worries about keeping factories afloat. *Chicago Tribune*, 28 August, 1(1).

———. 1996. Mell may keep site industrial. *Chicago Tribune,* 17 April, 3(2).

Reardon, Patrick T., and Rick Pearson. 1991. McCormick goes McLean: No dome in new plan. *Chicago Tribune,* 22 May, 1(1).

Rich, Michael J. 1993. *Federal policymaking and the poor.* Princeton: Princeton University Press.

Rivlin, Gary. 1992. *Fire on the prairie: Chicago's Harold Washington and the politics of race.* New York: Henry Holt and Co.

Robinson, Carla J. 1985. Analysis of the Chicago apparel and fashion industry. Chicago: Department of Economic Development.

Robinson, Tony. 1995. Gentrification and grassroots resistance in San Francisco's Tenderloin. *Urban Affairs Review* 30: 483–513.

Rosen, George. 1980. *Decision-making Chicago style: The genesis of a University of Illinois campus.* Urbana: University of Illinois Press.

Rosenthal, Donald B., ed. 1980. *Urban revitalization.* Beverly Hills: Sage.

Sabel, Charles F. 1989. Flexible specialization and the re-emergence of regional economies. In *Reversing industrial decline?* ed. Paul Hirst and Jonathan Zeitlin. Oxford: Berg.

Sandro, Phillip H. 1988. Job impact analysis program economic impact statement. Chicago: Mayor's Office of Employment and Training.

Saxenian, AnnaLee. 1994. *Regional advantage: Culture and competition in Silicon Valley and Route 128.* Cambridge: Harvard University Press.

Schattschneider, E. E. 1960. *The semisovereign people.* New York: Holt, Rinehart and Winston.

Scherrer, Christoph. 1991. Seeking a way out of Fordism: The US steel and auto industries. *Capital and Class* 44: 93–120.

Schmidt, William E. 1987. Chicago plan aims to curb factory loss. *New York Times,* 10 December, 1(1).

Schneider, Mark. 1992. Undermining the growth machine: The missing link between local economic development and fiscal payoffs. *Journal of Politics* 54: 214–230.

Scott, Allen J. 1988. *Metropolis: From the division of labor to urban form.* Berkeley: University of California Press.

Sengenberger, Werner, and Frank Pyke. 1992. Industrial districts and local economic regeneration: Research and policy issues. In *Industrial districts and local economic regeneration,* ed. Frank Pyke and Werner Sengenberger. Geneva: International Institute for Labour Studies.

Shea, Vickie. 1996. Interview by author, 25 May, Chicago.

Shearer, Derek. 1973. CAP: New breeze in the Windy City. *Ramparts* 12 (October): 12–16.

Shefter, Martin. 1985. *Political crisis/fiscal crisis: The collapse and revival of New York City.* New York: Basic Books.

Shlay, Anne B., and Robert P. Giloth. 1987. The social organization of a land-based elite: The case of the failed Chicago 1992 World's Fair. *Journal of Urban Affairs* 9: 305–324.

Slonka, Tom. 1981. Housing subsidies put to work. *The Neighborhood Works,* 9 January, 1.

Smith, Neil. 1982. Gentrification and uneven development. *Economic Geography* 58: 139–155.

Snyder, David. 1995. Dick Mell, alderman vs. Dick Mell, industrialist. *Crain's Chicago Business,* 3 April, 10.

Squires, Gregory D., ed. 1989. *Unequal partnerships: The political economy of urban redevelopment in postwar America.* New Brunswick, NJ: Rutgers University Press.

Squires, Gregory D., Larry Bennett, Kathleen McCourt, and Philip Nyden. 1987. *Chicago: Race, class, and the response to urban decline.* Philadelphia: Temple University Press.

Stanback, Thomas M., and Thierry J. Noyelle. 1982. *Cities in transition: Changing job structures in Atlanta, Denver, Buffalo, Phoenix, Columbus (Ohio), Nashville, Charlotte.* Totowa, NJ: Allanheld, Osmun and Co.

Stone, Clarence N. 1976. *Economic growth and neighborhood discontent.* Chapel Hill: University of North Carolina Press.

———. 1980. Systemic power in community decisionmaking: A restatement of stratification theory. *American Political Science Review* 74: 978–990.

———. 1987a. The study of the politics of urban development. In *The politics of urban development,* ed. Clarence Stone and Heywood Sanders. Lawrence: University Press of Kansas.

———. 1987b. Summing up: Urban regimes, development policy, and political arrangements. In *The politics of urban development,* ed. Clarence Stone and Heywood Sanders. Lawrence: University Press of Kansas.

———. 1989. *Regime politics: Governing Atlanta, 1946–1988.* Lawrence: University Press of Kansas.

———. 1993. Urban regimes and the capacity to govern: A political economy approach. *Journal of Urban Affairs* 15: 1–28.

Stone, Clarence N., Marion E. Orr, and David Imbroscio. 1991. The reshaping of urban leadership in U.S. cities: A regime analysis in urban life and transition. In *Urban life in transition,* ed. Mark Gottdiener and Chris G. Pickvance. Newberry Park, CA: Sage.

Stone, Clarence N., and Heywood Sanders. 1987. *The politics of urban development.* Lawrence: University Press of Kansas.

Stone, Donald. 1974. *Industrial location in metropolitan areas.* New York: Praeger.

Strahler, Steven R. 1995. "Can't" has become the cant in Daley's city that worked. *Crain's Chicago Business,* 12 June, 3.

———. 1996. How sweet the subsidy. *Crain's Chicago Business,* 6 May, 15.

Strong, James. 1989. Two outsiders picked for Daley cabinet. *Chicago Tribune,* 9 May, 1(3).

Sturdy, Frank. 1949. Old buildings topple in path of expressway. *Chicago Daily Tribune,* 30 November, 4(1).

Suttles, Gerald D. 1990. *The man-made city: The land-use confidence game in Chicago.* Chicago: University of Chicago Press.

Swanstrom, Todd. 1985. *The crisis of growth politics: Cleveland, Kucinich, and the challenge of urban populism.* Philadelphia: Temple University Press.

———. 1988. Urban populism, uneven development, and the space for reform. In *Business elites and urban development: Case studies and critical perspectives,* ed. Scott Cummings. Albany: State University of New York Press.

———. 1993. Beyond economism: Urban political economy and the postmodern challenge. *Journal of Urban Affairs* 15: 55–78.

Tobier, Emanual, and Mark A. Willis. 1981. The commercial printing industry: Is it still made in New York? In *New York City's changing economic base*, ed. Benjamin J. Klebaner. New York: Pica Press.

Tolliday, Steven, and Jonathan Zeitlin, eds. 1987. *The automobile industry and its workers: Between Fordism and flexibility*. New York: St. Martin's Press.

Tulloss, Janice K. 1995. Citizen participation in Boston's development policy: The political economy of participation. *Urban Affairs Review* 30: 514–537.

Turner, Robyne S. 1992. Growth politics and downtown development: The economic imperatives in Sunbelt cities. *Urban Affairs Quarterly* 28: 3–21.

U.S. Bureau of the Census. 1976. *Census of manufactures, 1972*. Washington, D.C.: U.S. Government Printing Office.

———. 1987. *Census of manufactures, 1987*. Washington, D.C.: U.S. Government Printing Office.

———. 1992. *Census of manufactures, 1992*. Washington, D.C.: U.S. Government Printing Office.

Vernon, Raymond. 1959. *The changing economic function of the central city*. New York: Committee for Economic Development.

Vindasius, Julia. 1988. Industry-led community development: A report on the targeted development project. Unpublished manuscript.

Vogel, Ronald K., and Bert E. Swanson. 1989. The growth machine versus the anti-growth coalition: The battle for our communities. *Urban Affairs Quarterly* 25: 63–85.

Warner, Kee, and Harvey Molotch. 1995. Power to build: How development persists despite local controls. *Urban Affairs Review* 30: 378–406.

Washburn, Gary. 1981. "Restrictive" codes thwart a loft revival. *Chicago Tribune*, 18 January, 1(N14).

———. 1993. Loop trolley estimate hits $775 million. *Chicago Tribune*, 29 July, 11(2C).

Washburn, Gary, and Andrew Martin. 1998. City OKs Pilsen redevelopment plan, *Chicago Tribune*, 11 June, 1(2).

Weiss, Marc A., and John T. Metzgar. 1989. Planning for Chicago: The changing politics of metropolitan growth and neighborhood development. In *Atop the urban hierarchy*, ed. Robert A. Beauregard. Totowa, NJ: Rowman and Littlefield.

Whitt, J. Allen. 1982. *Urban elites and mass transportation: The dialectics of power*. Princeton: Princeton University Press.

Wiewel, Wim. 1990. Economic development in Chicago: The growth machine meets the neighborhood movement. *Local Economy* 4: 307–316.

Wiewel, Wim, David Ranney, and George W. Putnam. 1990. Technological change in the graphic communications industry: Implications for economic development planning. *Economic Development Quarterly* 4: 371–382.

Wiewel, Wim, and Nicholas C. Reiser. 1989. The limits of progressive municipal economic development: Job creation in Chicago, 1983–1987. *Community Development Journal* 24: 111–119.

Winters Publishing Co. 1942. *Chicago central business and office building directory, 1942–1943*. Chicago: Winters Publishing Co.

Wong, Kenneth K. 1988. Economic constraint and political choice in urban policymaking. *American Journal of Political Science* 32: 1–18.

Wright, Patricia A. 1987. *The impact of federal and state Urban Development Action Grants on Chicago, 1979–1986*. Chicago: Center for Urban Economic Development, University of Illinois.

———. 1992. *Choices ahead: CDCs and real estate production in Chicago*. Chicago: Nathalie P. Vorhees Center for Neighborhood and Community Improvement.

Zeitlin, Jonathan. 1992. Industrial districts and local economic regeneration: Overview and comment. In *Industrial districts and local economic regeneration*, ed. Frank Pyke and Werner Sengenberger. Geneva: International Institute for Labour Studies.

Zeitlin, Jonathan, and Peter Totterdill. 1989. Markets, technology, and local intervention: The case of clothing. In *Reversing industrial decline?* ed. Paul Hirst and Jonathan Zeitlin. Oxford: Berg.

Ziemba, Stanley. 1976. "Village" development downtown under study. *Chicago Tribune*, 4 February, 3(1).

Zukin, Sharon. 1982. *Loft living: Culture and capital in urban change*. Baltimore: John Hopkins University Press.

# Index